Aristotle's "Not to Fear" Proof

for the

Necessary Eternality of the Universe

Aristotle's "Not to Fear" Proof

for the

Necessary Eternality of the Universe

Gregory L. Scott

ExistencePS Press
New York, NY

ExistencePS Press

Aristotle's "Not to Fear" Proof
for the Necessary Eternality of the Universe

First Edition

Paperback

Copyright © 2019

Gregory L Scott

All rights reserved.

New York, NY
United States of America

ISBN-13: 978-0-9997049-6-7

Library of Congress Control Number (LCCN):

2018912170

This book is dedicated to

Sarah Broadie

Contents

Acknowledgments.......................... xi

Introduction 1

PART 1 5

TEXTUAL SUPPORT FOR THE PROOF 7

"Not to Fear" Proof and Preliminary Remarks .. 9

The "Not to Fear" Proof 14

1) Motion has always existed................ 21

2) The physical universe has existed for infinite time because motion requires enmattered things.... 23

    Aristotle, Philoponus, and Sorabji............ 33

    Philoponus's Five Arguments 36

3) In infinite time, any (sort of genuine) possibility is actualized (the Principle of Genuine Sortal Plenitude). 67

    Different Versions of the Principle............ 77

    Aristotle's Senses of "Possibility" 81

    Mere Conceptual Versus Genuine Possibility ... 92

    Final Thoughts on Possibility................ 100

    Reactions to Hintikka's View 106

    Broadie on the Principle of Plenitude 124

    "Kind of Possibility" in *On Interpretation* 9...... 142

Why Artifacts like Cloaks are within Scope	155
4) Therefore, every sort of genuine possibility has already been actualized.	167
5) The universe (still) exists.	170
6) Thus, there has never been the sort of genuine possibility that would cause the universe to not exist.	171
7) The universe could not simply disappear into nothing.	172
8) Nor could the universe come from nothing.	174
9) Regarding (sorts of genuine) possibilities occurring, temporal infinity is the same as eternity.	175
10) Therefore, "the sun and the stars and the whole heaven are *ever active*, and there is no fear that they may sometime stand still, as the natural philosophers fear they may"	179
(11) What is necessary is "that which cannot be otherwise," and since what is *ever active* (that is, eternal) cannot be otherwise, what is *ever active* is necessary	180
12) Hence, eternal motion of the universe exists *necessarily*, which entails that the universe is not contingent, obviating the Unmoved Mover of Pure Actuality.	181
Leibniz on the Principle of Plenitude.	183
Barnes on Hintikka and the Principle	186

Contents

PART 2 193

Introduction to Part 2 195

Aristotle and Eternal Accidents 197

Why Did Aristotle Champion the Principle? 201

Ramifications for *De Caelo*, the Unmoved Mover of Lambda, and *Physics* 223

    Summary and the Platonic Influence 242

Doctrinal Reasons the "Not to Fear" Proof Was Not Seen. 247

    How Other 20th-century Scholars Missed the Inconsistency of Theta 8 and Lambda 250

    Recent Treatments of Theta 8 257

Historical Reasons the Proof was not Seen 279

    Theophrastus and Later Ancient Thinkers 300

    Conclusion. 315

Bibliography. 319

Index. 327

Index Locorum. 359

Acknowledgments

Part of the Not to Fear Proof was first given at The Society for Ancient Greek Philosophy (SAGP)/The Society for the Study of Islamic Philosophy and Science (SSIPS) Conference, 1994, SUNY Binghamton, NY. Related material pertaining to one of the premises, the Principle of Plenitude, or rather to a variation of its standard formulation, was given to The 17th Ancient Philosophy Workshop at The University of Texas at Austin, also in 1994. I am grateful to all who attended the sessions, and especially to those who offered replies and encouragement afterwards. Given the interest at the time, especially in Texas, I am sorry that it has taken me so long to supplement the brief presentations with the book-length arguments, but, as a famous musician once said, sometimes life gets in the way of plans.

Some overlapping topics were presented in "Aristotle, Big Bangs and Creationism," at the Philosophy Department, Kutztown University (PA), 1998, and I am grateful to Allan Bäck, John Lizza, and Phillip Ferreira for feedback. Another part of the book was presented more recently at the Society for Ancient Greek Philosophy (SAGP), Fordham University, 2014.

Much gratitude goes to Alexander Mourelatos, who not only introduced me to the Harry Ransom Center but aided me when I was a Visiting Research Scholar at the University of Texas, Austin, June 2017, allowing me to quicken the pace of the examination of the most recent related scholarship.

Finally, I owe at least a token of gratitude to Brad Inwood for his advice and to Lloyd Gerson and Richard Patterson for their feedback, given that I agree and disagree with their own work on various topics.

URL for Errata and Updates:

http://www.epspress.com/NotToFearUpdates.html

Aristotle's "Not to Fear" Proof

for the

Necessary Eternity of the Universe

Introduction

The Unmoved Mover of Aristotle's *Metaphysics* Lambda—his "God" of Pure Actuality that cannot go out of existence—has triggered immense bafflement, debate, and commentaries over the centuries. Werner Jaeger claimed that the doctrine was youthful and Aristotle repudiated it as he matured, which satisfies empirical minds who hold Aristotle to be one of the greatest scientists of all times as well as one of the greatest metaphysicians. Others argue that one can find evidence that Lambda (also called Book XII) was the product of Aristotle's last years. Some modern thinkers are still convinced, or at least worried, by the argument underlying the motivation for the Unmoved Mover. By being eternal *with no potential (and thus no potential to not exist)*, the Mover provides the ground for a *contingent* universe that even if eternal is contingently eternal and *could* therefore go out of existence. Fortunately, it does not, but the fortune is only guaranteed by the Mover. The core of the argument is given by Aristotle in *Metaphysics* XII 6:

> Since there were three kinds of substance, two of them natural and one unmovable, regarding the latter we must assert **that it is necessary that there should be an eternal unmovable substance**. For substances are the first of existing things, and if they are all destructible, all things are destructible... [Moreover] if there is something which is capable of moving things or acting on them, but is not actually doing so, there will not be movement; for that which has a capacity need not exercise it... [Thus] even if it [a mover] acts, this will not be enough, if its substance is potentiality; for there will not be *eternal* movement; **for that which is potentially [such as anything with matter] may possibly not be. There must, then, be such a principle, whose very substance is actuality**. Further, then, **these substances

must be without matter; for they must be eternal, at least if anything else is eternal. Therefore they must be actuality.[1]

In speaking of the related arguments, the French atheist philosopher André Comte-Sponville notes the difficulty of the ideas and writes:

> Of the three classical "proofs" of God's existence, this is the only one I find powerful, the only one that occasionally makes me vacillate or hesitate. Why? Because contingency is an abyss in which reason loses its bearings... [However, as Comte-Sponville adds:] Why should contingency not have the last word—or the final silence? Because it would be absurd? So what? Why shouldn't the truth be absurd?"[2]

Antony Flew, the recently deceased and well-known British philosopher, who was an atheist until late in life and who then co-wrote a book entitled *There is a God: How the World's Most Notorious Atheist Changed His Mind* (2007), explained why he had a reverse apostasy. As Flew says in part (seemingly in reply to Christian apologists, who William Grimes reports had greeted Flew's book as "a welcome counterblast to recent anti-religious best sellers like *God is Not Great* by Christopher Hitchens, *The God Delusion* by Richard Dawkins and *Letter to a Christian Nation* by Sam Harris"[3]):

> ...the God in whose existence I have belatedly come to believe...[is] *most emphatically not* the eternally rewarding

---

[1] *Metaphysics* XII 6, 1071b3ff, transl. by W.D. Ross in *The Complete Works of Aristotle*, vol. 2, ed. Jonathan Barnes (Princeton: Princeton University Press) 1984; his italics, but my boldfacing. All other translations of the *Metaphysics* are from this work, unless otherwise stated.

[2] André Comte-Sponville, *The Little Book of Atheist Spirituality* (New York: Penguin Books) 2006; transl. by Nancy Huston, 2007, p. 82. Even though I will reject the statement about absurdity, I heartily recommend the rest of the book.

[3] William Grimes, "Antony Flew, Philosopher and Ex-Atheist, Dies at 87," *New York Times*, p. B10, 4/17/10. Available online (10/20/16): http://www.nytimes.com/2010/04/17/arts/17flew.html?_r=0

Introduction

and eternally torturing God of either Christianity or Islam but the God of Aristotle that he would have defined—had Aristotle actually produced a definition of his (and my) God—as the first initiating *and sustaining cause* of the universe.[4]

If I am right in the arguments of this book, contingency will be very understandable and, *contra* Comte-Sponville, neither absurd nor any cause for reason to lose its bearings. Moreover, Jaeger will be vindicated at least in one respect. Not only has Aristotle relinquished the Unmoved Mover but he provides a better argument for the *necessary* eternality of the universe, including eternal motion, an argument that he accepts in the latest, and maybe even in the middle, stages of his life. Consequently, I stay away as much as possible from the dilemmas of Pure Actuality and only touch on the topic as needed.[5] If, as I argue, Aristotle renounced the Unmoved Mover, no need arises to add to the libraries of books on this topic.

Aristotle had other "unmoved movers" or "prime movers," which I keep in lower case, because they are not meant to be Pure Actuality and they have matter. An example is a man *qua* unmoved (or prime) mover whose arm is holding a stick, which itself moves some object, like a stone. Aristotle considers the man himself the prime mover in this case. Another example is the eternal outer heavens that by their motion cause the lower cosmos, the earth and the natural bodies within the earth to move forever (these prime movers cannot be the Unmoved Mover of Lambda 6 because Aristotle says there that the latter is without matter whereas obviously the outer heavens are visible and enmattered). I should emphasize immediately that even if I am right, and if Aristotle relinquished the Unmoved Mover in favor of

---

4   Grimes, *op. cit.*, p. B10; my italics.

5   For those new to this topic, one basic problem is how Pure Actuality can interact with anything in the physical universe, and vice-versa, when that Actuality has no matter, no potentiality, no boundary, no energy and no physical property of any kind whatsoever.

better doctrines like the Not to Fear Proof, the issue, for example, of how and why the prime movers of the heavens interact with the lower heaven for him may still be open for debate. Recent work by Monte Ransome Johnson has helped clarify some of the issues pertaining to topics such as whether Aristotle accepted one *cosmos* or multiple *cosmoi*,[6] and perhaps the arguments for the Not to Fear Proof will allow future, related research to proceed more effectively, but that is a topic for another time.

Although specialists in Aristotelian metaphysics are the primary audience of this work, I expect that some other classicists and those focussing on the history of theology also might be interested and I have tried to write accordingly. Thus, the Greek is translated and the basics of the various positions are explained for the non-specialists. No expertise in formal logic, especially involving the modals "necessary," "impossible," "possible," and "contingent," is required.

---

[6] Monte Ransome Johnson, "Aristotle on *Cosmos* and *Cosmoi*," forthcoming in *Cosmos in the Ancient World*, ed. P.S. Horky (Cambridge: Cambridge University Press) 2019; 74-107.

PART 1

Aristotle's "Not to Fear" Proof

TEXTUAL SUPPORT FOR THE PROOF

Aristotle's "Not to Fear" Proof

The "Not to Fear" Proof and Preliminary Remarks

Xenophanes:
One God, greatest among gods and men, not at all like to mortals *in body nor in thought*. (B23)

All of him sees, all thinks, all hears. (B24)

Rather, *without any toil* he makes all things shake and quiver *by the thought of his mind*. (B25)

He remains ever in the same place, moving not at all, nor is it appropriate for him to flit now here, now there. (B26)[1]

Aristotle:
Nor does eternal movement, if there be such, *exist potentially*; and, if there is an eternal mover, it is not potentially in motion (*except in respect of 'whence' and 'whither'; there is nothing to prevent its having matter for this*). **Therefore, the sun and the stars and the whole visible heaven are ever active, and there is no fear that they may sometime stand still, as the natural philosophers fear they may.**[2] (*Dio aei energei hēlios kai astra kai holos ho ouranos, kai ou phoberon mē pote stē, ho phobountai hoi peri phuseōs.*[3])

Philo:
Aristotle was surely speaking piously and devoutly when he objected that the world is ungenerated and imperishable, and **convicted of grave ungodliness those who maintained the opposite and thought that *the great visible god, which contains in truth sun and moon and the remaining pantheon of planets and fixed stars*, is no different from an artefact**; he used to say *in mockery* (we are told) that in the past *he had feared* for his house lest it be destroyed by violent winds or by fierce storms or by time or by lack of proper maintenance, but that now *a greater fear hung over him*, from those who by an argument were destroying the whole world.[4]

---

1   Transl. and edited by Daniel W. Graham, *The Texts of Early Greek Philosophy*, Part 1 (Cambridge: Cambridge University Press) 2010, p. 111; my italics in all four passages.

2   *Metaphysics* IX 8, 1050b19-24; my italics and bolding. Transl. by W.D. Ross, in in *The Complete Works of Aristotle*, ed. Barnes, *op. cit.*

3   Aristotle. *Aristotle's Metaphysics*, ed. W.D. Ross (Oxford: Clarendon Press) 1924.

4   Philo, *de aeternitate mundi* III 10-11; Fragment 18 (from Rose's 3rd

The Precise Claims of the "Not to Fear" Proof

In *Metaphysics* IX 8, also called Theta 8, after almost a chapter-long discussion of substance, actuality and potentiality, Aristotle gives a brief argument—part of a "proof" in the informal sense of the word even though not all premises are presented in that chapter—which concludes with one of the statements above, namely, that there is no fear that the sun, stars and whole visible heaven will ever stop. In other words, since the whole universe, The All (*to pan*), is comprised for him of those entities (which sometimes explicitly and other times implicitly include the earth and anything contained therein),[5] the Northern Greek from Stagira thereby indicates that the whole universe is always in motion. As explained in detail below, given his identification in relevant contexts of "always" with "necessary," this entails that the universe is eternal *necessarily*. This brief argument, which becomes the Not to Fear Proof in its fullest form from other statements in various Aristotelian texts, has garnered no attention historically relative to other arguments pertaining to the Unmoved Mover or to *De Caelo* (*On the Heavens*). However, the Unmoved Mover of Pure Actuality itself is supposed to guarantee that an infinite but *contingent* universe does not go out of existence. We have a serious inconsistency, then, because in Theta 8 the universe is *not* contingent but rather necessary.

In two of the most recent scholarly Anglo-American treatments of

---

edition of the *Fragmenta*, Teubner, 1886) as found in *The Complete Works of Aristotle*, ed. Barnes, *op. cit.*, p. 2393; my italics and bolding. I am grateful to D.S. Hutchinson for drawing my attention to not only this passage but the related work of M.R. Johnson, who discusses this passage for different, but related, reasons than the ones implied by my theses in this book (Johnson, *op. cit.*, 2019, pp. 85-6).

5   Cf. *De Caelo* I 9, where Aristotle gives the three meanings of "heaven": the substance of the extreme circumference of the whole; the sun, moon and some of the stars; and the entire universe with all the bodies, from the extreme circumference down to the earth.

The "Not to Fear" Proof and Preliminary Remarks

Book Theta, which will be examined in Part 2 of this book, one author, Jonathan Beere, does not even acknowledge in his very close reading and commentary the conclusion in Theta 8 that the sun and stars will never stop and calls the sentence immediately before it "cryptic."[6] He can in no way, then, see the inconsistency between Aristotle claiming that the universe is necessarily eternal in Theta 8 and that in Lambda it is contingently eternal. The second author, Stephen Makin, does astutely acknowledge the conclusion of the brief argument in Theta and recognizes well the import of the "not to fear" argument insofar as he discusses the ramifications of the sun eternally moving "without potentiality."[7] However, even though he also recognizes that in this same argument for Aristotle "what exists always *exists necessarily*," and even though all of this obviously entails that the physical universe is necessary, Makin for whatever reason in no way discusses the tension that is set up with the doctrine of Lambda. I examine these two authors much more in Part 2 but for the moment suffice it to say that, alternatively, the brief argument in Theta 8 has been seemingly considered by commentators to be merely a variation of the argument for the Unmoved Mover, despite the absence of Pure Actuality in its premises and despite of the inconsistencies between the two cases. I also discuss, then, these other commentators in Part 2 in the sections on why the Not to Fear Proof has not been recognized before.

In addition, I present a very recent case of a renowned British specialist, Myles Burnyeat, interpreting Theta 8 to be about God as a synonym for the Unmoved Mover, with fire and earth "imitating" God, as if such a phenomenon were even remotely possible when "God" has no potentiality and also when in Lambda "God" is supposed to think. That is, Aristotle, in describing the Unmoved Mover, paradoxically

---

6　　Jonathan Beere, *Doing and Being: An Interpretation of Aristotle's* Metaphysics *Theta* (Oxford: Oxford University Press) 2009, pp. 317-9.

7　　Stephen Makin, *Aristotle Metaphysics Book Theta, translated with an Introduction and Commentary* (Oxford: Clarendon Press) 2006, pp. 215-6.

calls it *Nous* or Mind, following and praising Anaxagoras in the *Physics*. At least one dilemma results from the Northern Greek describing something that in no way can be describable, because it has no matter, physicality, or boundaries of any sort whatsoever. Leaving aside this dilemma for the moment, we will see in Part 2 that, unlike Anaxagoras, who had *Nous* move the primordial soup in order to generate order in the universe, Aristotle only allows *Nous* to (selfishly) think of (itself) thinking. Aristotle's Unmoved Mover *never* pays attention to the physical universe or to anything in it, like human beings.

Two problems result for Burnyeat. The Unmoved Mover *qua* "God" is as far from the modern anthropomorphic notion of "God" as one can get given how the Mover never focusses on the universe whatsoever. Indeed, It does not even know the universe exists! The second problem is independent of the interaction with the physical universe and, as just touched upon, pertains simply to the nature of *Nous* itself. How can something that has absolutely no physicality whatsoever *think* (if we can call it a something rather than a mere mental construct that Aristotle postulated), when for Aristotle thinking always requires some type of brain or nervous system, as the greatest biologist of all time (according to Darwin) knew? In Part 2, when examining the history to see why no one previously grasped the Not the Fear Proof, we will see that this claim of Lambda about the nature of the Unmoved Mover thinking greatly bothered Cicero. I will also cover in Part 2 why the Not to Fear Proof is more powerful than the arguments for the ingenerability and indestructibility of the heavens in *De Caelo*, which some have thought is where Aristotle provides the best reasons for the eternality of the universe without the Unmoved Mover.

In short, I wish in this book to demonstrate that Aristotle championed the Not to Fear Proof in its entirety, as reproduced in a moment, and not just the part given in Theta 8. By the end, we will have ample evidence that the Proof accomplishes everything that he needs to ground the *necessary* eternal motion of the universe with no dependency

The "Not to Fear" Proof and Preliminary Remarks

whatsoever on the Unmoved Mover, a much more fitting scenario for an empiricist. It is beyond the scope of this book to decide whether the proof could withstand objections from a modern perspective, and, in any event, such an attempt would be vacuous, given that Aristotle did not have our advances, insights or prejudices. Here I only wish to unravel his thought, or at least show what is manifestly in his texts, for, although unlikely, it is possible he simply did not realize how his insights could be easily tied together to give the version I offer. It is also possible that, despite the argument in Theta 8, in his most mature years he continued to hold other, less empirical versions of a proof for the eternality of The All, ones that are identical or similar to the one relying on the Unmoved Mover.[8] However, my interpretation counters this possibility because it explains the heretofore puzzling silence of Aristotle's successors in the Lyceum, Theophrastus and Strato, regarding the Unmoved Mover. This topic is addressed at the very end of Part 2.

Let us start with my version of the Not to Fear Proof and the support in the Aristotelian corpus for each and every statement. Aristotelian infinity, including infinite time, will be explored in depth while examining Statement 2 and possibility while examining Statement 3.

---

8   Friedrich Solmsen championed the view that the Unmoved Mover of Lambda was created very late in Aristotle's life and says: "Unlike the Platonic world soul which is defined as always moving, Aristotle's prime mover is eternally unmoved" (*Aristotle's System of the Physical World: A Comparison with his Predecessors,* Cornell Studies in Classical Philology, Vol. XXXIII, Ithaca: Cornell University Press, 1960, p. 229).

The Not to Fear Proof

1) Motion—and time (as the measure of motion)—have always existed.
2) The physical universe has existed for infinite time because motion requires enmattered things.
3) In infinite time, any (sort of genuine) possibility is actualized (I call this The Principle of Plenitude, following historical usage, or more precisely because of the addition of "sort" and "genuine," the Principle of Genuine Sortal Plenitude, where "sortal" simply means sorts, kinds, classes, or types of things or of events).
4) Therefore, every sort of genuine possibility has already been actualized,—that is, "there is no (sort of) thing (really and completely) new under the sun," as the adage goes.
5) The universe (still) exists.
6) Thus, there has never been the sort of genuine possibility that would cause the universe to not exist.
7) The universe could not simply disappear into pure nothingness.
8) Nor could the universe come from pure nothingness.
9) Regarding (sorts of genuine) possibilities occurring, temporal infinity is the same as eternity.
10) Therefore, "the sun and the stars and the whole visible heaven are *ever active*, and there is no fear that they may sometime stand still, as the natural philosophers fear they may."
11) What is necessary is "that which cannot be otherwise," and since what is *ever active* (that is, eternal) cannot be otherwise, what is *ever active* is necessary.
12) Hence, motion of the universe exists eternally *and necessarily*, which entails that the universe is not contingent, obviating the Unmoved Mover of Pure Actuality.

Even though I proceed in this Part 1 with Statements 1-12 in order, the importance of "possible" and "necessary" are so crucial and have been so misunderstood (because they are very equivocal for Aristotle) that a

The "Not to Fear" Proof and Preliminary Remarks

preliminary introduction to them will be helpful. "Necessary" is given different senses in *Metaphysics* V 5 (1015a20-1015b16), but the most important from which the others are derived, Aristotle says, is "what cannot be otherwise" (1015a34-1015b1). The contradictory of necessary, if I might speak of a term rather than a sentence as being contradictory, is "non-necessary" or "not necessary," which itself includes either possible *or* impossible. That is, strictly speaking for Aristotle, if something is not necessary, it is because it is possible *or* impossible—and similarly if it is possible, it is because it is *neither* necessary *nor* impossible.[9] We will see in a moment that the Principle of Plenitude can be re-formulated in terms of necessity, that is, "what exists always, exists necessarily." However, because the account of the Not to Fear

---

9   Actually, even this account does not convey the fullest options, as I demonstrate throughout this book. It can easily be deduced that "not necessary" in Aristotle's thought is subdivided into (i) possible and non-possible (the latter of which is subdivided into impossible and non-impossible) or, alternatively, that "not necessary" is subdivided into (ii) impossible and non-impossible (the latter of which is subdivided into possible and non-possible). Aristotle holds typically at least three values—(a) necessary, impossible, and possible, or pairs of values (b) necessary and non-necessary, possible and non-possible, and impossible and non-impossible—rather than two values (necessary and possible) or three at the most (necessary, possible, and impossible); cf., for example, *On Interpretation* 12, 22a10-12, where "impossible and not impossible" and "true and not true" are said to be opposites along with the other dualities. This is similar to him typically speaking for the sake of elegance of true and false being the analogous two values of categorical sentences. Yet when it comes to certain cases he is clearer: True and non-true exhaust the category (as just noted for 22a10-12), and although false is often used by him for brevity or for any other reason to convey "non-true," strictly speaking "non-true" might convey "indeterminate" (like at the end of *On Interpretation* 9, of which more later) or might convey the kinds of sentences to which truth and falsity do not apply, for instance, interrogatives or commands, which are neither true nor false. Regarding *On Interpretation* 9, cf., e.g., Sarah Waterlow (Broadie), *Passage and Possibility: A Study of Aristotle's Modal Concepts* (Oxford: Clarendon Press) 1982, pp. 80 and 106-9. For a perspicuous explanation of the basics of the modal notions in Aristotle, see Jaakko Hintikka, *Time and Necessity: Studies in Aristotle's Theory of Modality* (Oxford: Clarendon Press) 1973, pp. 27-31.

Proof in Theta 8 is only partial and because an important *seeming* counter-example (which is crucial to this book) to the Principle that Aristotle furnishes in *On Interpretation* 9 is couched in terms of possibility, I phrase my version of the Principle of Plenitude and the Not to Fear Proof in terms of possibility, of something that might happen, rather than in terms of necessity, of something that must happen. The result, though, will be the same. It will not matter whether we argue that the Principle should be "in infinite time, any (kind of real) thing that exists always, exists necessarily" or, as I have it, "in infinite time, any (kind of real) possibility gets realized" or "in infinite time, no (kind of real) impossibility gets realized." Jaakko Hintikka gives four formulations of the Principle:

(T) each possibility must be realized at some moment of time;
(T*) that which is always, is by necessity;
(T**) nothing eternal is contingent;
(T***) that which never is, is impossible.

He adds convincing arguments for why Aristotle considered them equivalent, and states:

> It is not difficult to see that the four principles (T)-(T***) are equivalent **provided that one makes the same assumptions** concerning the interrelations of different modal notions as Aristotle does. All evidence for the acceptance of *one* of these principles by Aristotle therefore serves as evidence for the acceptance of *all* of them.[10]

A number of other notions of necessity in Aristotle's doctrines surface, showing how ambiguous the term is for him. For example, Richard Sorabji lists at least ten notions in discussing theories of determinism in human agency, in addition to the ones that he explicitly says Hintikka

---

10   Jaakko Hintikka, "Necessity, Universality, and Time in Aristotle," in *Articles on Aristotle 3. Metaphysics*, ed. by Jonathan Barnes, Malcolm Schofield, and Richard Sorabji (London: Gerald Duckworth & Co.) 1979, pp. 111-112; his own italics but my bolding. Broadie gives similar conversions, *Passage and Possibility*, pp. 1-3.

detects.[11] Moreover, in *Parts of Animals* I 1 (639b24-640a11) Aristotle distinguishes between the absolute necessity that is manifested in eternal phenomena and the hypothetical necessity that he says both natural things and human products have. He refers to two modes of necessity in natural or theoretical science without specifying what they are, and this topic is still debated.

I myself assume that part of his explanation might refer to (i) the necessity of certain things and events, which has been called *de re* necessity, and (ii) the necessity of certain sentences, which has been called *de dicto* necessity. That is, with respect to the latter, the modalities (of necessity, possibility and impossibility) are often discussed concerning Aristotle's formal logic, for instance, "A necessarily is B," in contrast to "assertoric" statements, "A is B." This book refrains as much as possible from delving into the complex and still debated issues of his modal logic, as given for the most part in his *Prior Analytics,* in which "necessarily" and "possibly" are at times seemingly applied directly to sentences rather than to events or objects in the world (which of course may be indirectly referred to via the sentences). Aristotle is perfectly at liberty to choose his meaning of necessity and possibility, and both will be disambiguated in this book. However, I will consider them primarily to be what Aristotle often considers them, as applicable first and foremost to the world and not to sentences, e.g.:

> of necessary things, some have an external cause of their necessity, and others have not, but it is through them [those whose necessity is internal] that other things are of necessity what they are" (*Metaphysics* V 5, 1015b9-12)... [and] therefore if there are certain things which are eternal and immutable, there is nothing in them which is compulsory or which violates their nature (*Metaphysics* V 5, 1015b15-16).

Ample evidence for the priority of "ontological" necessity, what some

---

11   Richard Sorabji, *Necessity, Cause, and Blame* (Ithaca, NY: Cornell University Press) 1980, pp. 222-4.

call "statistical" necessity, at least in some contexts for Aristotle, is forthcoming, and the foregoing suffices for my goals here.[12] I also take Aristotle at his word when he says that the primary sense of "necessary" is "what cannot be otherwise." Besides, he says at times and clearly implies at other times, in passages that I cite throughout this work and especially in the context of the absolutely crucial Theta 8, that eternal things are necessary (because they cannot be otherwise), intermittently-existing things possible (because if they are not omnitemporal they are thus not necessary), and never-existing things impossible (because otherwise, if they existed, they would be either possible or necessary), which is all we need to discuss the issues of the Not to Fear Proof.

---

12 For a different view, see Allan Bäck's "Aristotelian Necessities" (*History and Philosophy of Logic,* 16, 1995, 89-106). Bäck gives an impressive account of the kinds of necessity that Aristotle articulates and suggests an ingenious way in which they might be unified, one which, however, seems to prioritize propositional modality. It may be that Aristotle's most mature view matches Bäck's account, but the fact that, even according to Bäck, Aristotle explicitly says that the primary sense of necessity is that which cannot be otherwise and that Aristotle articulates three notions of necessity in *Parts of Animals* (or at least refers to two of them being in the philosophical texts), proves that at least at one stage in his thinking Aristotle understood and accepted that "necessity" (and by implication "possibility") were, like so many other words, ambiguous. In no way do I claim, therefore, that the ontological sense of necessity and possibility have to apply in all situations, especially in purely "logical" ones, that is, in modal logic, where necessity and possibility are "second-order," being applied to propositions that are often about the world. The goal of formal logic, whether assertoric or modal, is to establish valid forms of argumentation, not "soundness," which requires that one also evaluate the truth of the premises of a deduction. Validity, strictly speaking, is a matter of form, and only of form, and one can insert terms in a valid argument that are completely fictional, like Hamlet or The Pied Piper or Pegasus, which we will see are not Aristotle's concerns in the context of the Not to Fear Proof. This is all I need, but I would welcome a further discussion of this whole issue in the future were, e.g., Bäck or anyone else able to show that Aristotle could not have been employing ontological necessity and possibility when he composed *Metaphysics* IX 8. In doing that, however, they would go against the face-value reading of that chapter.

The "Not to Fear" Proof and Preliminary Remarks

All of this may strike modern readers as very unorthodox, given the tradition from Descartes, Hume and Leibniz onwards that often considers "possibility" to be simply that which is merely conceivable or distinctly conceivable, whether it ever comes into existence. These thinkers arguably inherit the tradition from thinkers going back to Parmenides.[13] In any event, Cartesian or Humean possibility does not *require* some existence, be it intermittently or not, during an eternity, in spite of Descartes's dictum "*cogito, ergo sum* (I think, therefore I am)." Aristotle's possibility (at least the type of contingency noted in Theta 8) does. Moreover, although we will see that Aristotle recognizes possibility *qua* conceivability in the so-called *Poetics,* we will also see that even in a treatise on fictional drama he prioritizes what I call real or genuine possibility (or, as just alluded to, what others have called ontological or statistical possibility). I myself cannot use the historically arbitrary title "*Poetics*" because the treatise has not one poem and because I have demonstrated that the better title is *Dramatics*, which is how I refer to the treatise from now on.[14] When out-

---

13   Three fragments of Parmenides that suggest thinking at least at times is identified with existence are:
[F2]... neither could you know what is not (for it cannot be accomplished), nor could you declare it [or: point it out].
[F3]... for the same thing is there for thinking and for being.
[F8]... The same thing is for thinking and is wherefore there is thought. For not without what-is, to which it is directed, will you find thought (transl. by Daniel Graham, *op. cit.*, pp. 213-7).

14   Gregory Scott, *Aristotle on Dramatic Musical Composition: The Real Role of Literature, Catharsis, Music and Dance in the POETICS* (New York: ExistencePS Press) 2018 (first ed. 2016), pp. 205-38. In short, the title *Poetics* drastically misrepresents what Aristotle examines in the treatise and has helped generate *and* perpetuate a number of perennial dilemmas that simply dissolve once we realize that he focusses only on three types of "musical" drama (tragedy, comedy, and epic). This is self-evident given that these are the only arts he covers in the book; given that these are the only arts he *intends* to cover (as explicitly said at the beginning of Chapter 6); given, to underscore, that there is not one poem in the treatise; and given that the *requirements* for tragedy include "music" and performance (including spectacle) in Chapters 1, 4, 6, 24 and 26, to list just the most important chapters.

side *or inside* the realm of drama or of fiction in general, and for very good reason, Aristotle holds the type of merely imaginative possibility that often characterizes modern thinking, and that characterizes some conceptualistic approaches stemming from Parmenides, in very low regard.

Because I cover in detail the different senses of possibility when examining Premise 3, let these preliminaries about necessity and possibility suffice. I now defend each of the statements of the Not to Fear Proof in order.

Statement 1

1) Motion has always existed.

The evidence for this premise for Aristotle is so weighty that I merely note some passages: *Physics* III 7, 207b25; III 8; VIII 1, 251b11-28; VIII 5, 256b13; VIII 6-10; and *Metaphysics* IX 8. Perhaps I should add that motion is meant typically by Aristotle in the sense of movement or of change, sometimes with respect to magnitude (e.g., becoming larger or smaller), sometimes with respect to "affection" or qualities (e.g., hot and cold, soft and hard), and other times with respect to place, i.e., locomotion. However, he considers this last to be the most noteworthy type of motion and change. As he says, "Locomotion is the primary motion (or change)"[1] and as he adds in *Generation and Corruption,* "we were also right when, in an earlier work, we called motion (not coming-to-be) the primary form of change."[2]

---

1 *Physics* VIII 7, 261a27-28. Cf. also, 260a28, 260b15, b24 & b29; transl. by R.P. Hardie and R.K. Gaye, in *The Complete Works of Aristotle*, ed. Jonathan Barnes (Princeton: Princeton University Press) 1984, as are all other translations of the *Physics* unless noted.
2 *Generation and Corruption,* 336a18-20; transl. H.H. Joachim, in *The Complete Works of Aristotle,* ed. Barnes, *op. cit.* All other passages from this text are also Joachim's translation, unless stated otherwise.

Aristotle's "Not to Fear" Proof

2) The physical universe has existed for infinite time because motion requires enmattered things.

This also seems to be Aristotle's doctrine if only considering *Physics* III 1, 200b32 (along with Statement 1): "There is no such thing as motion over and above the things."[1] However, matters now get more interesting for us because of the term "infinite" and because of the views of Sorabji and of the Christian theologian John Philoponus (c. 490–c. 570), for reasons I explain shortly. Let us begin, however, by making sure we use Aristotle's notion of infinity, and not a modern or different ancient conception:

> The infinite turns out to be the contrary of what it is said to be. It is not what has nothing outside it that is infinite, but *what always has something outside it...* what has nothing outside it is complete and whole... as a whole man or box... Nothing is complete which has no end and the end is a limit.[2]

Thus, infinity is not complete for Aristotle, strictly speaking, although there will be a different, *secondary* notion of infinity suggesting completeness that would be applicable for him, of which more later. Indubitably, infinity is not something best described as "that which contains everything," because the largest *finite* space would satisfy that description.

In Aristotle's physical and metaphysical discourses, infinity is typically discussed in relation to entities or substances, like physical constructs such as men, or to numbers (and geometrical figures) or to time. We will not concentrate on physical entities here, although it

---

1   Cf. also *Physics* VIII 1 251a10-11; a21-23, and *Metaphysics* IX 8, 1050a34.

2   *Physics* III 6, 206b34-207a14; my italics.

might help to understand Aristotle's overall perspective by contrasting his view briefly with other conceptions. For Aristotle in *Physics* III 5, no physical substance like a man or a box is infinite in size, because the person would be extended in all directions (the assumption being presumably that the bodily proportions would stay the same) and thus "overwhelm" or displace any other substance. The other reason is that a man, or any other physical substance, requires location and space, and for Aristotle infinite space cannot exist, one set of reasons pertaining to the Principle of Plenitude given by Hintikka.[3] Let this suffice, though, for this book with respect to extension of physical bodies, because the Not to Fear Proof focuses only on temporal or numerical infinity.

To be more precise, infinity applies to time, the *generations* of man (and not to the size of an individual), and division (although not addition) of magnitudes (*Physics* III 6, 206a26-7). The generations of man will be discussed in detail when examining Philoponus. Now I summarize the relevance of time and magnitude, starting with a prefatory remark by Aristotle:

> The infinite is not the same in magnitude and movement and time, in the sense of a single nature, but the posterior depends on the prior, e.g., *movement is called infinite in virtue of the magnitude covered by the movement* (or alteration or growth), and *time because of the movement*.[4]

Let us now focus on magnitude, which is "prior" in this passage, and let us start with the magnitude of a line. Asymmetrically, Aristotle allows infinite divisibility in a certain way (*Physics* III 7), but not infinite increase. As he claims:

> Our account does not rob the mathematician of their science, by disproving the actual existence of the infinite in

---

3   Hintikka, 1973, p. 117. As he concludes there: "Aristotle's universe is thus finite in an especially strong sense: no extension beyond it is even possible." See also Broadie, *Passage and Possibility*, p. 72, ft. 21.

4   *Physics* III 7, 207b21-7; my italics.

the direction of increase, in the sense of the untraversable. In point of fact they do not need the infinite and do not use it. They postulate only that a finite straight line may be produced as far as they wish.[5]

It is crucial to add that infinity in the context of mathematics—represented nowadays as ∞, which I call a drunken-eight because it looks like a number 8 that has fallen on its side—is not a number at all for Aristotle, even though there are times when the locution "infinite number" is for him a convenient *façon de parler*.[6] Certainly for him, infinity is not a whole number (3, 7, or 167954 and so forth) because numbers are countable and "infinity" by definition means that which always has something outside of it and which therefore cannot be counted (to completion). As he asserts: "The infinite cannot be quantity—that would imply that it has a particular quantity e.g., two or three cubits; quantity just means these."[7] All of this necessitates that any infinite mathematical series would not be countable, at least by a human being or a finite series of human beings, or even by a super-powerful computer, no matter how long it calculates, and no matter how powerful

---

5   *Physics* III 7, 207b2831.
6   Cf. Hintikka, 1973, pp. 118-124; also, Broadie, *Passage and Possibility*, p. 69. As Broadie also emphasizes, "infinite number" is sometimes used as an expression by Aristotle (pp. 69-70, *Passage and Possibility*), which has muddied the exegetical waters. Numbers are not real for Aristotle in the sense of existing "separately," but are created by thinking (even if they represent the quantity that exists and that would still exist were human beings not here); cf. *Metaphysics* IX 9, 1051a22-34, and especially 1051a31. An example of Aristotle using "infinite in number" as a figure of speech is at *Metaphysics* IV 4, 1007a16, when he discusses how arguing about the accidents of man would be "infinite in number." Aristotle thereby suggests that one could, if focusing on accidents, practically keep adding to the accidents, and this is easily seen: I could say that it is an accident of Plato that he was born before 100 CE, and before 100 CE plus one millisecond, and before 100 CE plus two milliseconds... The sense of the claim, though, is that accidents are not completely determinable and that we could keep adding until we get utterly exhausted or die, not that the infinite is truly a number *per se*.
7   *Physics* III 5, 206a2-4.

its processor. Moreover, to treat infinity as a number *per se* would destroy mathematics: "∞ + 1" would equal "∞ + 2," both totaling ∞, which means 1 and 2 are equal.

Likewise, infinity for Aristotle is not applicable to geometry in ways accepted today, when geometers often claim or imply, at least for heuristic purposes, that a line is comprised of an infinite number of points, a plane of an infinite number of lines (that are lying, as it were, side by side), and a solid object of an infinite number of planes (stacked on top of each other). Rather, very sensibly for Aristotle, a point has zero dimension and two points added together still give zero dimension. Adding more and more points, even an infinite number of points, still means adding zero's together and getting the sum of zero. Thus, strictly speaking, a line cannot be comprised of points in the sense that the points constitute the line.[8] Similarly, adding the zero-dimensional width of a 3-meter line to another 3-meter line and to yet another to get a plane that is 3 meters long along with some positive width, no matter how small, is nonsensical. One still only gets zero width. The same holds for adding planes with zero depth to build solid objects.

Rather, for Aristotle, the primary ontological and "geometrical" object is the three-dimensional solid. In *Physics* II 2, he makes the distinction between geometry and optics, with the latter investigating mathematical lines *qua* natural figures while geometry investigates lines as if they were separate from nature. He adds "natural bodies contain surfaces and volumes, lines and points" (193b24). We can abstract one side of, say, a box and arrive at a two-dimensional plane, without paradox. We can further abstract one edge of the plane and arrive at a line and, finally, take the endpoints of the line (or the intersection of two lines) to achieve position with no magnitude, a point *per se*.

---

8   *Generation and Corruption* 1.2 316a30-34, where Aristotle says "even if all the points be put together, they will not make any magnitude" (*The Complete Works of Aristotle*, ed. Jonathan Barnes, *op. cit.*). Cf. also Sorabji, 1983, p. 211.

By contrast with "optical" lines or planes, geometrical lines or planes, then, are mental constructs, even though in other places Aristotle recognizes the physical manifestations of lines and points, treating them differently (because sometimes without dimension one could not see the "point"). That is, when it is not the endpoint of a line, or an intersection of two lines, sometimes we use a circle for a point when drawing the point for purposes of explanation, and we conflate "optics" and "geometry."[9] Aristotle adds:

> The infinite and the void and all similar things are said to exist *potentially and actually* in a different sense from that in which many other things are said...to exist, e.g., that which sees or walks or is seen... [namely,] the infinite *does not exist potentially* in the sense that it will ever *actually have separate existence*; **its separateness is only in knowledge.** *For the fact that* **division never ceases to be possible** *gives the result that* **this actuality exists potentially**, *but* **not** *that it exists separately*.[10]

Let this suffice for this book with respect to extension and divisibility in geometry, because, again, the Not to Fear Proof focuses only on temporal and numerical infinity. Nevertheless, because time for Aristotle is a measure of motion (*Physics* IV 12, 220b32), because measure is a numerical concept, and because motion presupposes or "is posterior to" magnitude, the same principles above apply to time.[11] A duration cannot be created out of instants, which themselves each have zero duration. Rather we start with motion, like the sun going across the sky or a runner traversing a certain space or (in our case) vibrations of an electron, and take the duration as the difference between the starting and ending points, using whichever unit we find

---

9   I am grateful to Allan Bäck for bringing some of the additional aspects of the mental (or theoretical) physical distinctions in mathematics to my attention (at the SAGP, 2014). See also *Metaphysics* XIII 1-3.

10   *Metaphysics* IX 6, 1048b10-17, tr. W.D. Ross, *op. cit.*; my emphases, and my additional word in brackets.

11   *On Generation and Corruption*, 337a22-4.

most appropriate (nanoseconds or minutes or days) for the measure. An instant or "point in time" (I choose the phrase purposefully, given the geometrical view above) is merely the boundary of some duration, the point in time in this context itself having no (temporal) magnitude. Again, for Aristotle infinite time exists not "separately," like a commonly-understood substance (whether dog or lake or tree or, at least as a subject of a sensible sentence, energy that can burn one under a tanning lamp). Infinite time will not exist or be complete in the sense of having a definite beginning and corresponding end (because then it would be finite), no matter how massively large the numerical measurement. Moreover, an infinite boundary is a contradiction in terms—there is no place to begin (or end) measuring—and to say a finite plane of one-foot width is extended infinitely in terms of length is no counter-example because the boundary is of the two limited sides, not the infinite ones. In short, and to emphasize, infinite time will always have more *duration* outside of it for Aristotle, given his definition of "infinite."

To explain further the way in which infinite time can be "actual," the final fundamental consideration that should be recalled for Aristotle is:

> We say that the infinite **is** in the sense in which we say it is day or it is the games, *because one thing after another is **always** coming into existence*. For of these things too the distinction between potential **and actual existence** holds. We say that there are Olympics games, both in the sense that they may occur and that **they are actually occurring**.[12]

Thus, there is a sense in which the infinite is indeed actual, namely, it is "actually occurring" or is "one thing after another always coming into existence." This, I believe, negates what Sorabji says: "Even through [sic] the past years in a beginningless universe are not actual, their infinity must be. And for some purpose *Aristotle needs to avoid any*

---

12   *Physics* III 6, 206a21-26, my emphases.

actual infinity [my italics]."[13] How the past years, though, are not, or were not, actual (if Sorabji also implies "were") and yet how, he says, the infinity "must be [actual]" in some manner, when the infinity is presumably the infinity *of those years* (or millenia or days or minutes) is a baffling claim. Sorabji's claim is unsustainable given the rest of this book, especially because Aristotle says potentiality only applies to the future, not to the past: "No capacity (*dunamis*) relates to being in the past, but always being in the present or future" (*De Caelo* I 12, 283b12-13). That is, if the past cannot be potential (or have capacity, which is the same in this context, with *dunamis* meaning either), then presumably it must be, or have been, actual in some sense of that word. If, as is clearly the case for Aristotle, the past had no beginning, the implication surely is that the infinite past is, or has been, actual in a very real sense, even if not "separately" actual like a living person or a painting, the latter things being whole at any given moment (of their existence). Thus, it is false to claim that Aristotle needs to avoid "any actual infinity." Indeed, now that events have occurred, they are even necessary for Aristotle, one reason being given above: "Necessary" primarily means *what cannot be otherwise*. The events cannot

---

13   Richard Sorabji, *Time, Creation and the Continuum* (Ithaca: Cornell University Press) 1983 (second printing 1986), p. 217. The further sense in which the infinite can be actual, like the Games, also reveals what Gary Zabel misses, who claims wrongly in my view (in an otherwise enlightening article) that Aristotle only had potential infinity and no actual infinity *of any kind*: "...only the finite things are actual. The infinite is not found within the actualities..." Gary Zabel, "Excursus: A Short History of Infinity before Spinoza" (From Chapter 3 of *All Things in Common: Spinoza and the Collegiant Letters*), p. 7, published online (10/15/16) at:
https://www.academia.edu/19971501/Excursus_A_Short_History_of_Infinity_Before_Spinoza
We saw that the *potentiality* of infinite mathematical divisions is *actual* (in the mind) for Aristotle, just not "separate" like a dog. Also, Aristotle emphasizes that the infinite (which is presumably elliptical for infinite time) exists like the day or the Games, one part coming into existence as another part goes away. This type of existence, perhaps a process, is actual, not *merely* potential (or is both), as with a day or the Games.

be undone, and we cannot change the past or go backwards in time. The (years of the) past certainly were not fictional or merely potential (or merely possible), just as one's biological parents and their actions were similarly actual in the fullest sense, or senses, of the word, at least at one stage of the history of the universe. Otherwise, none of us would be here, reading these words. Another way of phrasing this is that infinity is a property of past years, e.g., "The past years are infinite" or "The time of the past is infinite," and the actuality of the infinite is meant in this sense. That is, in this context "infinity" does not subsist apart from the years or time to which "infinity" is predicated.

Temporal infinity is obviously not the same as an infinite physical object. As explained, Aristotle allows the first but rejects the second. To put all of this analogously in the context of art, infinite painting or sculpture cannot exist for Aristotle (unless we allow geometrical or mathematical *potential divisibility* of, say, lines within an art work), because then a complete infinite body would exist at one moment, which he emphatically rejects. However, if only theoretically, a temporally infinite symphony or vocal literary work could exist, because such a work, like "day" or "the Games," only shows a point-in-time, or better yet, a duration-in-time aspect of the work, or at any given duration only shows part of the work. The symphony could be continually played as long as new players kept the music going while old players dropped off for sleep, retirement or death (assuming not only Aristotle's view that the species is eternal but that civilizations did not go out of existence).[14] Naturally, this "infinite symphony" would not have the same finite structure as our normal symphonies because our symphonies have a recognizable beginning and end. On the other hand, the infinite one is unending and has no beginning. However,

---

14   Jorge Luis Borges wrote a short story, *The Book of Sand*, about a book that is infinite. Aristotle would reject such a possibility because the book described is a physical object but would allow that theoretically a spoken performance of the words could be infinite, as long as the readers were continually replaced.

the latter phenomenon would be just the peculiar nature of an infinite symphony. It would be no forceful objection to say, for instance, that, because we do not have the absolute first notes of the whole symphony, the current movement of the infinite symphony could not be enjoyed. In *The Greatest Arias of Opera*-type recordings, which are often best-sellers, listeners take an aria completely out of context without hearing the absolute beginning (of its full opera) and enjoy the aria tremendously. Moreover, we will see that "first" for Aristotle sometimes means merely first in comprehension, not necessarily first in terms of temporal occurrence. Nevertheless, I emphasize only the *theoretical* (call it *logical*) possibility of such an infinite symphony for Aristotle. Practically speaking, we will see that he notes that civilizations reach a peak and get destroyed before starting again, and so he, and I, are not claiming an infinite symphony actually exists or that in a sense of *real* possibility, the symphony could exist. Thus, the *merely* logical possibility of the infinite symphony would not counter, we will see, the best version of the Principle of Plenitude and it will not help the reader to use my words against me by saying that, according to the Principle, the merely logical possibility of the infinite symphony must be actualized in infinite time. Only real possibilities (that presuppose some material conditions including civilizations not disappearing) need be actualized in infinite time, of which more later, when we examine in detail the differences between genuine (or real) possibilities and (merely) logical, or so-called, conceptual ones.

Let this suffice, then, for a basic understanding of Aristotle's notion of infinity. Another way of putting this, perhaps, is that finitude and its opposite, infinity, do not exist in and of themselves like Platonic Forms. Instead, both are properties of boxes or other objects or of numbers or time and the like. Without those substances (including mental constructs), properties like finitude would not exist. Likewise, infinity: It is a property in this context for Aristotle of days or years, and without the years existing or having existed, it is absurd to speak of "infinity" existing or having existed (and again "years" and other constructs of time are "measures of motion"). Aristotle puts the matter very concisely: "the infinite...consists in a process of coming to be or passing away, finite, yet always different" (*Physics* III 6, 206a33). Thus, temporal infinity is a process, not a "separable" thing like dogs or lakes or paintings.

Even though it might seem now that Aristotle indubitably holds Statement 2—that the moving physical universe has existed for infinite time, especially because of the numerous passages that support it (e.g., *Physics* III 6, 206a9ff; III 8, 208a20)—Sorabji points to a difficulty that might throw the premise into doubt, pertaining to *De Caelo* I 12, 283a10: *to de pê apeiron out' apeiron outh' hôrismenon* ("As for that which is infinite in one direction, it is neither infinite nor limited").[15] Sorabji says of this passage:

> Aristotle...denies that what is infinite in only one direction really is infinite...[and] the reason, which is not given, may be that it [the one-sided infinity] has at least one boundary... [But Sorabji concludes], *at any rate, the implication is that* **the past is not infinite**."[16]

If Sorabji is correct here, then Statement 2 appears to be false, unless Sorabji is suggesting that the past is not infinite in "separation," like a substance, in which case everyone would agree with him. However, I see no evidence of that interpretation for him. Sorabji also says:

> Aristotle describes that which (like the future) is infinite in one direction only, and which ought to provide him with the clearest instances of potential infinity, *as not being infinite at all*.[17]

---

15   Transl. W.K.C. Guthrie, *Aristotle in Twenty-Three Volumes, VI, On the Heavens* (Cambridge: Harvard University Press) 1939, reprinted 1986. J.L. Stocks translates: "infinity in one direction is neither infinite nor finite." Broadie translates "what is infinite in one direction only is neither infinite nor determinate" (*Passage and Possibility*, p. 70). More on this translation later.

16   Sorabji, *op. cit.*, 1983, p. 218; my italics and bolding.

17   *Op. cit.*, 1983, p. 212; my emphasis.

Statement 2

What are we to make of Sorabji's remarks?

Aristotle, Philoponus, and Sorabji

Sorabji's comments occur in his discussion of how Philoponus not only drastically changed philosophy but effectively put an end to the ancient tradition of considering the past to be infinite,—a tradition that virtually all ancient Greek thinkers except Plato and perhaps a few other rare exceptions had held.[18] In order to argue that the universe had a beginning, Philoponus proceeds with a Socratic *elenchus* (that is, a *reduction ad absurdum* or "argument to absurdity") and tries to turn Aristotle's arguments about infinity against themselves. As Sorabji summarizes:

> My conclusion so far is that Philoponus's arguments are successful as an objection to Aristotle and the pagans... But the question remains whether *we* can answer his [Philoponus's] arguments by freeing ourselves in some way from Aristotelian ideas. To this question I shall now turn...[19]

Sorabji then discusses both the topic of *increasing infinity* (which Philoponus accuses Aristotle of being inconsistently committed to) and of Philoponus's rejection of an infinity that can be *not only actual but traversed* (all of which Philoponus also accuses Aristotle of being inconsistently committed to). Curiously, after supposedly "freeing ourselves from Aristotelian ideas," Sorabji gives, as one of his eight replies to Philoponus's position on increasing or traversing infinity, Averroes's view. The Arabic philosopher repeats Aristotle's point (as Sorabji explicitly acknowledges[20]) that ratios hold only between finitudes, which I show later is exactly the right retort to Philoponus,

---

18 Aristotle says in *Physics* VIII 1, 251b18-19: "Plato *alone* asserts the creation of time, saying that it is simultaneous with the world, and came into being (my italics)."
19   1983, p. 217.
20   1983, p. 218.

allowing Aristotle to evade the Christian's attacks:

> **Ratios only hold between finitudes** (*On the Heavens*, I 6, 274a8; I 7, 275a13)"
>
> [and]
>
> **"There is no ratio in the relation of the infinite to the infinite** (*Physics* VIII 1, 252a12-13; my boldings)."

Sorabji concludes:

> I have considered eight sources of resistance to the idea that an actual infinity of past years could have been traversed, and I have argued that they are all wanting. To that extent, then, I have come out against Philoponus, and maintained that the universe has not been proved to have a beginning. *I personally would leave it open whether the universe had a beginning or not.* None the less, I would recall that I have not altogether sided against Philoponus. *For I have maintained that his arguments do succeed ad homines against the pagans. Indeed, he has found a contradiction at the heart of paganism, a contradiction between their concept of infinity and their denial of a beginning.* This contradiction had gone unnoticed for 850 years. Moreover, the materials for beginning to answer Philoponus's puzzle about increasing infinity were not even assembled until Henry of Harclay and others, some 800 years later. We can therefore see Philoponus as being at the center of a 1600-year period. For the first time, he put Christianity on the offensive in the debate on whether the universe had a beginning. *This might well be called a turning point in the history of philosophy.*[21]

To my knowledge, scholars rarely discuss this turning point nowadays in the history of philosophy, at least in philosophy programs in the U.S. and Canada. Certainly, it was never mentioned in my own courses at the University of California, Columbia University and the Uni-

---

21   1983, p. 224; my italics.

versity of Toronto. I am therefore completely beholden to Sorabji for bringing it to my attention. Unfortunately, I cannot repay him with more than a sincere expression of gratitude and must argue against his conclusions. For the most part, Philoponus claims that infinity can be compared (as being larger, smaller or equal) with other infinities or with finitudes, ignoring Aristotle's view that ratios—in particular, comparisons in regard of magnitude—only properly exist between finitudes. If Sorabji reports correctly, this consideration was not even recognized by Simplicius himself when the renowned Aristotelian commentator tried to rebut Philoponus in the 6th century CE (but, again, Averroes did recognize it).

Once we see clearly that ratios only hold between finitudes, not only Philoponus's grounds but Sorabji's arguments in support of Philoponus fail, and the remaining ones can be easily found faulty. By explaining how Philoponus's *reductio* does not undercut Statement 2, we see even more evidence why Aristotle *sensibly* held such a premise, because the *reductio* does not involve any modern attitude about either mathematics or infinity. The *reductio* alleges only internal contradictions in Aristotle's doctrines. I explore these issues even though Philoponus came many centuries after Aristotle and even though his own view would not necessarily have shown what Aristotle wrote or thought. However, there may well have been colleagues of Aristotle who anticipated the same objections, especially because Aristotle's predecessor Anaxagoras had conceptions of greater and lesser infinities, all of which reflects a sophisticated understanding of infinity long before Aristotle's time.[22] Therefore, the exploration of Philoponus's *reductio ad absurdum* against Aristotle is probably not only justifiable here but required by rigor.

I start with Philoponus's arguments before moving to Sorabji's claims,

---

22   See also Zabel, *op. cit.*, for the Platonic views on infinity and for details of this very sophisticated understanding of infinity.

including the ones noted. By the end of this section, we will, I believe, be completely confident that Aristotle not only held Statement 2 but that we ourselves have very good reasons even today for holding it. The past indeed is infinite, and the universe (considered as *to pan*, "The All") had no beginning. Anyone who rejects this claim, including scientists who posit a Big Bang *ex nihilo*, arguably speaks very implausibly (Big Bangs from either singularity or Steady State, or brane theory, are different because those views entail something always existing before the Big Bang, which, e.g., exploded or expanded, and thus those cosmogonical theories also entail a universe without a beginning).[23] However, let us not try to guess what Aristotle would say to the modern variations on this whole topic.

Philoponus's Five Arguments

I follow Sorabji's translations, recounting the important premises or conclusions of the five individual arguments.

    I.   "...if the *kosmos* is uncreated, the result will be that there exists and has occurred an actually infinite number."[24]

This is clearly false from Aristotle's perspective, for whom numbers are created by mankind (as mental constructs), even if quantity exists in the universe apart from anyone counting any instance of it. Infinity

---

23   Some scientists say that the universe came from nothing, but in the next breath assert that the Big Bang presupposes a singularity. How they reconcile the singularity existing with absolute nothingness is beyond me, and saying the singularity was infinitesimally small only leads to absurdity. If infinitesimally small, the compaction would not have an end and any explosion at the "bottom" would take an infinite amount of time to occur and to reach our level of existence. Alternatively, the "bottom" could never be found or determined. The contradiction between claiming both an absolute nothingness and a singularity seems irresolvable. Modern science, or rather at least some scientists, cannot reasonably have both.

24   Sorabji, 1983, p. 214.

or the drunken-eight is simply not a number, strictly speaking, and treating it as such destroys mathematics. Again, "...the infinite cannot be quantity – that would imply that it has a particular quantity, e.g. two or three cubits; quantity just means these..." (*Physics* III 5, 206a2-4). Numbers are not mathematical Forms, as they are for Plato and for many modern mathematicians, existing eternally and separately apart from human thought. Because there was no beginning number (either 0 or 1, however one wishes to begin counting), there could be no *number* of years (or days or minutes or milliseconds) at, say, 2014 CE relative to the infinite past. At the best, we arbitrarily assign a year 0 or 1 to a certain event, e.g., the birth of Jesus for Christians, or some (apparently forgotten) event for the Chinese Emperor Huangdi and the first Han calendar in, roughly, 2637 BCE, or the founding of Rome for the Romans in approximately 750 BCE. From that arbitrary beginning—or "point-event"—we can begin counting and arrive at the calendar years just noted.

> II. "...it is in no way possible for the infinite to exist in actuality, neither by existing all at once, *nor by coming into being part at a time*, as we shall show more completely, God willing, in what follows... I say that the infinite cannot in any way exist in actuality, and I think this is clear from the following. Since the infinite cannot exist all together and at once, *for the very same reasons it cannot emerge into actuality by existing part at a time*. For if it were at all possible for the infinite to exist part at a time, and so to emerge in actuality, what reason would there be to prevent it from existing in actuality all at once?"[25]

I leave the "God willing" until a little later, when apparently for Philoponus God *cannot* will certain things, surely to the dismay of any

---

25   Sorabji, 1983, p. 215; my italics.

Christian followers. He himself presumably accepted, or should have accepted, a Christian God's omnipotence and omniscience were he a true member of the church. Now, although Philoponus indeed captures Aristotle's view that the infinite cannot exist all together and at once (what Aristotle calls "separate," in the way a substance with boundaries exists), he is utterly wrong in reporting that it cannot exist actually, as a series or a process. As we saw, the infinite for Aristotle exists in the same manner that the "day" or the "Games" can be considered potentially and actually to exist, leaving aside the difference between the latter being finite and the past having been infinite. In that sense, and in that sense only of "actual," the past is, has been or was infinite for Aristotle, part of it coming into being as (the previous) part disappears. Ironically, for reasons we see later, an eternal process for Aristotle is more important than a finite process, which disappears after a limited number of years. This is analogous to a point being less important ontologically than a solid object.

Philoponus's last question—What reason would there be to prevent it (the infinity) from existing in actuality all at once?—is utterly ridiculous. A painting, for example, the *Mona Lisa,* exists all at once. However, a symphony, or some kind of music that any thinker of Philoponus's day must have been familiar with, only exists like "the day," as a temporal sequence, or as an event. One cannot compress the symphony—as Philoponus suggests—into existence "all at once." What would one have or do? Count the occurrences of C notes, D notes, and B-flat notes in the composition, and then instead of playing them in sequence, play them all at once, one instrument per note, to claim that the orchestra has played the same number of notes and so exists "all at once"? Obviously, this would hardly be a symphony; it would be a monstrous cacophony. Hence, the "reason...to prevent it [any temporal sequence] from existing in actuality all at once" is simply the temporal nature of events themselves. Unlike a painting, the symphonies have different parts that go away when other parts come into being. Otherwise, one should expect everything to exist as a painting exists, symphonies to be monstrous cacophonies, and historical reality to be an absurd conflation of events with a duration of years collapsed into a single moment.

> III. "...even if [the infinite] does not exist all together at once (since some units will have ceased when others exist), none the less it will have come to be traversed. And that is impossible: traversing the infinite and, so to speak, counting it off unit by unit, even if the one who does the counting is everlasting."[26]

Philoponus obviously recognizes that others will accept that the infinite past did exist or has existed like "the Games," one part going away as another comes into existence. He introduces two new issues: traversing the infinite and counting by an everlasting being. Yet, the issue of counting is irrelevant and has been covered already with the discussion of infinite numbers.[27] The crucial new claim is whether an infinity is traversed. "Traversed" is something one does over distance or over time. Yet Aristotle reasonably says:

> ...there is no absurdity...in supposing the traversing of infinite distances in infinite time, and the element of infinity is present in the time no less than in the distance (*Physics* 8.8, 263a13-15).

Hence, traversing the infinite is perfectly possible, assuming that the series of individuals doing the traversing is also infinite (but this is different from counting from some ascertainable beginning like 0 or 1 or from the "very first event" in the history of the alleged whole universe). Indeed, for Philoponus to deny that an everlasting agent could not traverse an infinity suggests that even the Christian God is limited—that God cannot traverse an infinity—a rather precarious position for a

---

26 Sorabji, 1983, p. 215.
27 Those who believe in an omnipotent, omniscient and eternally-lasting Christian God might well wonder why such a divine being could not count an infinity, even if this idea is impossible for mere mortals to imagine.

Christian apologist to be in. This may have been the kind of doctrine that got his views declared heretical in 680 CE, although the general report has to do more, I gather, with his positions on the Christian Trinity. Whatever the reasons, he disappeared from the historical record for a long time and apparently is rarely discussed anymore, even by Christians, with Sorabji being an admirable exception.[28] I leave, though, these topics for specialists in medieval theology.

Another option regarding infinite traversal is that, for finite beings, Philoponus's past tense of "traverse"—namely, "traversed"—is not appropriate for an event that is still ongoing. "Traversing" or "is being traversed" or "has traversed" is more appropriate. Just as the day is not complete while we are still experiencing it, so arguably the infinite past is not "complete" but is always ongoing (and changing). Using "complete" here is a category mistake, just as calling a horizon "sad" or "enthusiastic" is such a mistake (unless one is speaking metaphorically). Even if one considers the present to be the "completed" endpoint of the past, still the beginning is forever unreachable, and thus forever untraversable, and in that sense "still ongoing" (at least in terms of comprehension of preceding events). What *is* complete is a finite demarcation or duration between two past instances: between a beginning—say, midnight on January 1, 2014—and an ending at midnight, 24 hours later. That particular day is indeed complete and truly traversed. However, the infinite past has and had no beginning and thus cannot be said to be "traversed" or "complete" in exactly the same way as this aforementioned day, even if the *type* of traversing is the same depending on the event or duration being discussed (one part going

---

28   I have no reason other than the obvious why Philoponus's doctrine on the limitation of God would have counted against him, no matter the historical record. That record is always incomplete. We do not need to have it written that Philoponus breathed, ate and slept, and, likewise, it hardly needs to be recorded that his suggesting that God had limitations adversely impacted evaluations of his related writings by those believing in God's omnipotence and omniscience.

away as another comes into existence).

One finds strong hints of Philoponus's argument (III) in Kant's so-called First Antinomy, but whether Kant knew Philoponus, or some medieval source like Bonaventure, who may have been influenced by Philoponus,[29] I cannot say. In my view Jonathan Lear reports and correctly concludes in at least one respect:

> Kant thought that reason could construct two equally valid arguments, one to the conclusion that the world had no beginning in time, the other to the conclusion that the world had a beginning... The proof that the world had no beginning is similar in structure to Aristotle's. To prove that the world did have a beginning, Kant supposes that the world had no beginning and then infers that an [actually] infinite extension of time must have passed before the present moment, which he takes to be impossible. Aristotle would accept both that the world had no beginning *and* that it is impossible that an actual infinity of time should have elapsed, but he would reject the inference and thus the argument as invalid. **From the fact that the world had no beginning, all that follows is that there can be no measure of a first change.**[30]

---

29   I am grateful to Calvin Normore, with whom I studied at Columbia University and the University of Toronto, for dissuading me at the SAGP 2014 from inordinately asserting the influence of Philoponus over later Medieval theology. Normore also assures me that at least one of Philoponus's arguments can be found in Bonaventure.

30   Jonathan Lear, "Aristotelian Infinity," *Proceedings of the Aristotelian Society*, (1980) 80 (1): 187-210, p. 208; his italics but my bolding. Also at: https://doi.org/10.1093/aristotelian/80.1.187 (as of 8 September 2015). I completely agree with the bolded conclusion. However, depending on what one means by "actual infinity," which Lear recognizes is very ambiguous (pp. 188, 190, and 194), the implications may or may not be as Lear wholly gives it. The passage we saw above—"there is no absurdity...in supposing the traversing of infinite distances in infinite time, and the element of infinity is present in the time no less than in the distance" (*Physics* 8.8, 263a13-15)—seems to permit that Aristotle would deny the second conjunct that "it is impossible that an actual infinity of time should have elapsed." In a certain sense, the

IV.   "...the succession of the race would not have come down as far as each of us, since it is impossible to traverse the infinite."[31]

This is simply a variation on (III) above. Yet, if the race were infinite also, as it is for Aristotle, the traversing would indeed be possible, given his statement above from *Physics* VIII 8. There would be no reason humans could not have continued begetting other humans until 3000 BCE and then again until 528 CE (Philoponus's era) and then again until 2014 CE and then again until this moment and then again for another trillion years (assuming the race continues) and then again, *ad infinitum*. As unlike this view is to our modern one(s), Aristotle has no dilemma regarding, e.g., which came first, the chicken or the egg. There was never a first and there was always an antecedent because of the doctrine of the "eternal species."

V.   "Moreover, suppose the *kosmos* had no beginning, then the number of individuals down, say, to Socrates will have been infinite. But there will have been added to it the individuals who came into existence between Socrates and the present, so that there will be something greater than infinity, which is impossible."[32]

This fifth argument is arguably Philoponus's most compelling one. He adds two variations on the general theme that the infinite past

---

infinite past (has) occurred, actually, and is still occurring, just as yesterday actually occurred. Thus the infinite past (has) "elapsed" (unless, e.g., by definition "elapse" can only apply to finite durations). More on this when we get to "one-sided infinities."

31   Sorabji, 1983, p. 215.

32   Sorabji, 1983, p. 215. Broadie has noted a phrase in *De Caelo* where Aristotle speaks *as if* infinity can be augmented, but she incisively gives the reasons why this is a *façon de parler* and I refer the reader to her two pages of detailed explanation (*Passage and Possibility*, pp. 70-2).

entails infinity being augmented (that is, "added to") or multiplied, which should be impossible on Aristotle's own account. The first variation involves adding infinite men to infinite dogs and getting a double infinity. The second variation involves a case of different rotational speeds of heavenly spheres, some slow ones taking years and some fast ones taking days. The infinity of the slow ones will be multiplied by the number of fast ones to arrive also at a plurality of infinities, again, a seeming absurdity on Aristotle's own account. However, if one answers the case of Socrates, one can also easily handle the variations, so for the most part I concern myself here with the number of men to Socrates and whether Aristotle is committed to the position that a supposedly infinite number gets augmented when we consider the number of men to us, as Philoponus claims.

In reply to the Christian theologian, on Aristotle's view numbers (and addition and multiplication) only apply to finitudes. With respect to temporalities, we must have a beginning point and an ending point. Thus, given that there simply was, and is, no infinite number *per se*, and given that there was no beginning, whether or not counting is occurring at this moment, no proper way exists to add to, or to multiply, that ostensibly infinite "number," the drunken-eight. In other words, no *proper* way exists to say the infinite past is being added to or augmented, in spite of the seeming impression that it is. Another manner of putting this is that an *infinite* series of men, even if they are not being counted, *cannot be greater even if more men are added to the series*. The result is still an infinite series, and if one ignores Aristotle's principle about only comparing finitudes, one could say at best the two infinities are equal, which still leads to paradox (because one infinity would have more members than the other infinity). One of the infinities is not "greater than" the other, even if you add more to it. Again, *when adding to infinity one still has infinity*. To reiterate—and this point is absolutely crucial for this book—for Aristotle you cannot even properly say the infinities are equal. That is the strange nature of infinity, given Aristotle's sensible approach that it *always* has something more outside of it. Ratios (including equality) *only* apply to finitudes.

I venture to assert that the apparent force and success of Philoponus's argument comes from the *impression* that people have that the past to, say, our year 2000 CE is *longer* than the past to Socrates in 400 BCE. Philoponus takes the past to be the same in both cases—i. e., the "beginning" to 400 BCE and the "beginning" to 2000 CE—and then compares the two durations, with "beginning" having the implication *of a definite point*. In that case, one indeed has the mental impression that one period (to 2000 CE) is longer than the other (to 400 BCE). Yet, this is misleading if "beginning" means "the infinite past." Analogously, we have the impression that we are at rest when on a moving train, viewing what seems to be a landscape rushing by us, although the latter case is one of perception while the former case, of comparing infinities, is of mental calculations or intuitions. In other words, Philoponus and others like him assume the following (and here the ellipsis "..." stands for the infinite past, that is, for ∞):

(i)   ... -> 400 BCE
(ii) ... -> 400 BCE plus 2400 years (= 2000 CE)

Clearly, it *appears* that the second is longer than the first, considering that the past as "..." is the same or "equally" long for both. The ellipsis for the infinite past, namely, for the drunken-eight, functions as the so-called "beginning" and functions *on the surface* as "x" does in mathematical expressions, "x+400" or "x+(400 + 2400)" or "x+2400" or "x+1/x+2." Thus, Philoponus deduces that there is a *definite* "beginning" that ends in 400 BCE and the *equally definite* "beginning" ending in 2000 CE, thereby treating these infinities as if they were actual finitudes, having a set, originating boundary. Yet as we saw before, for Aristotle, adding any finite number to infinity destroys mathematics, whether we add 1 to ∞ or 2 to ∞ or 2400 to ∞. All sums still equal infinity, and if the rules of mathematics apply, then

Statement 2

1=2=2400, which is absurd.

A more extreme example follows, which I note for emphasis, because I have read modern mathematicians who think that they can with a mere mathematical solution resolve Zeno's paradox of pedestrians having to reach ½ the distance to their goal repeatedly before reaching the goal, *ad infinitum*. The pedestrians never actually reach the goal but come infinitesimally close and that is good enough for the mathematicians. However, surely, we want to know that we can get all the way, not just almost there, no matter how small the final distance is that we cannot traverse. The mathematicians simply do not know that arguably the only solution to allow us to reach the goal is to make the distinction that Aristotle makes in solving the problem, between potential and actual infinity (and to permit potential infinities but not actual infinities to be traversed by finite beings).[33] The modern mathematician, then, might think that "1" or "2" or even "2400" in the context of infinity is essentially inconsequential, so let me take a large number that is not inconsequential, with the understanding that we could employ much, *much* larger ones in lieu of this example (were we willing to keep writing zero's at the end of the number):

$\infty + 1 = \infty$
   and
$\infty + 200{,}000{,}000{,}000{,}000 = \infty$

Therefore, both 1 and 200,000,000,000,000 are not only equal *but are both equivalent to zero*, having no impact on the original "number" ∞ when added to it. Just as "x+0=x" is a mathematical truth, similarly "$\infty + Y = \infty$" (where Y is *any* number), *if* one treats ∞ as a number (which, again, Aristotle would *not* do). Likewise, we can "subtract" 2400 years from infinity, but we still necessarily have infinity. Therefore, claiming that "∞ - 2400" is shorter than "∞ - 400" equally de-

---

[33] *Physics* VIII 8, 263a4ff.

stroys mathematics, because both results of the "shorter than" calculation are still infinity and are thus still equal.

Multiplying infinity by any number results in the same absurdities, since multiplication is simply a faster, or more compact, way of addition (and hence the reason we need not go into the variations of multiplying infinity that Philoponus gave above). These are, of course, merely some of the paradoxical and unpalatable consequences of treating infinity as a number on classical approaches, *as if* it had a beginning; of either adding to, or subtracting from, it, or multiplying infinities; or, and this is the most relevant point for this case, treating infinities as if they are "equal." Some might appeal nowadays to Cantorian mathematics and infinities, but this is irrelevant to Aristotle's view, and, at any rate, Cantorian mathematics is replete with its own unpleasant paradoxes concerning infinity. Our focus is on Aristotle and, again, concerning him, ratios only apply to finitudes, and "larger" or "longer" or "equal" are comparisons or ratios. This is why it is perfectly legitimate to compare Socrates to 600 CE and Socrates to 2015 CE, and to say that the second "past" is longer than the first "past" (of Socrates to 600 CE) because now we are comparing two *finite* past durations.

Although the *infinite* past may *appear* to be the same in both cases to Socrates and to us, that past, insofar as it is treated as infinite, is best thought of as an incalculable quantity that cannot be used for comparisons,—*even for comparison to a seemingly identical drunken-eight*. We can say one "unknown" is the "same" as another "unknown" but it is typically not advisable then, Aristotle would claim, to make quantitative comparisons about the two, whether by themselves alone or if they are part of a combination. The primary reason Philoponus was, or has been, convincing is that human cognition needs something that functions as a finitude to calculate and to make comparisons. Thus, I venture to say, people mentally assume that the "infinite past" or drunken-eight is equivalent to one trecentillion (=10^{903}) BCE and then we *seemingly* get properly to the conclusion that the past from one trecentillion BCE to us is longer than the past (from one trecentillion BCE) to Socrates. The drunken-eight morphs cognitively into a fantastically large finitude automatically.[34]

Sorabji recognizes some of the perils of entering into discussions of "mathematical infinities," saying with respect to Philoponus:

> In order to answer the adding and multiplying objections [of Philoponus against Aristotle], we must see what is right and what wrong about them. We can do so without entering at all into the complication of transfinite numbers. There are *perfectly good analogues* of adding and multiplying in relation to infinity. The only restriction is that in a certain sense these processes will not have the usual consequence of making the collection larger.[35]

Presumably Sorabji is being diplomatic, because surely the incredible paradoxes of Cantorian mathematics and transfinite numbers are more than just a "complication," and I for one would like to know what the "good analogues" are, and more importantly what both the literal examples are and the "certain sense" in which the collection does not get larger when something relevant is added to it, unless the result, as suggested, always just stays "infinite." (This assumes that the something being added is not just zero, because in this case the addition is an addition in name only, not in reality.) Zero is the only (non-negative) "number" that could be added to a collection without making

---

[34] Trecentillion is not determinate in the sense that a typical person could determine what it really means in terms of everyday considerations,— or if you can grasp it then multiply it by yet another trecentillion to get a result for the example. I was tempted to use Quattuornonagintanongentillion, which is 10 to the power of 2985, but it is so awkward to write and pronounce that I decided to make the same point with the easier and smaller number, given how vast it still is. The multiplied numbers would be so large, especially if we continued the process, that even the best computer could not calculate it in our lifespan. One would be long dead before others, and even others with computers, could count all the zeros in the number. Yet it is still finite.

[35] 1983, p. 217; my italics.

it larger in classical mathematics, assuming we allow zero to be a number, which only happened historically with the Arabic scholars, hundreds of years after Aristotle.[36] In short, if we accept Sorabji's under-emphasized "only restriction" we might as well accept that we can add any number to infinity in the relevant sense of "add" and ignore the consequences for mathematics, however absurd they are. At any rate, transfinite numbers are irrelevant to this discussion of Aristotle, and thus the foregoing must suffice on this topic.

Were Aristotle alive today, he would presumably argue that, like Riemannian geometry, these kinds of mathematics (with infinity or negative quantities being considered numbers) are fictional constructs, like certain forms of logic, with no intention to match the physical, real world, and that these systems change the meaning of "number" as commonly understood.[37] They may be "consistent" and "coherent,"

---

36   One reason that 0 (zero) is not a number for Aristotle: He speaks of a unit, and then a number, with the smallest number being two (as "there are a *number* of people in this room," implying more than the single unit) (*Physics* IV 12, 220a27). He also says that "Number...is a plurality of 'ones' and a certain quantity of them" (*Physics* III 7, 207b7). I leave aside "negative numbers" as not being something the Greeks around Aristotle's time would have considered. Negative numbers are known to have occurred in the Han Dynasty in China, circa 200 BCE. However, the first Westerner to consider negative numbers was apparently the Alexandrian mathematician Diophantus (200 - c.284 CE), who described a collection of problems in which he developed a series of symbols to represent the "unknown" in a problem. In one case, he wrote the equivalent of "4 = 4x + 20" which would give a negative result, and he called this result "absurd." In India, negative numbers appeared in the work of Brahmagupta (598-670 CE) who used the ideas of "fortunes" and "debts" for positive and negative numbers, but possibly earlier works use negative numbers. In Baghdad, Al-Khwarizmi (c.780 - c.850 CE) described equations using algebraic methods and geometrical diagrams. In his algebraic methods, he acknowledged the work of Brahmagupta. Later Middle Eastern scholars developed theories of negative numbers, and in the 1400's European scholars took up the concept, some calling them "imaginary numbers." (In part this history comes from https://nrich.maths.org/5961.)

37   A professional mathematician and professor in Montreal once ex-

perhaps, "in a certain sense," to use Sorabji's qualification, which is perhaps all these mathematicians care to be at times, but they are very different from classical mathematics and the related tradition, just as Riemannian geometry differs from classical, Euclidean geometry. Recall Aristotle's statement that the mathematicians act as if they use infinity as a number but actually just give it the sense of the largest possible number. This is in effect the same phenomenon I described in comparing the past to Socrates and then to us: The drunken-eight in order to become *seemingly* part of a proper mathematical calculation, *or comparison*, takes on the sense of trecentillion. To put this in another way, for Aristotle some forms of modern mathematics would be analogous to the form of the bivalent propositional calculus that takes the whole conditional "if p, then q" to be true no matter whether q is true or false, *as long as p is false*. This approach is opposed to the arguably more sensible trivalent forms, in which the whole conditional is indeterminate if the antecedent, p, is false. The latter is how computer science typically treats the conditional and is how in my view Aristotle himself seems to argue when using conditionals, as he frequently does in his corpus. His statement in *On Interpretation* of "true" and "not true"[38] as being the opposites seemingly involves

---

pressed his annoyance when I, as a Ph.D. student, had the temerity to suggest that mathematics should have a connection to reality. He indicated that it should have no such thing and tha it was a study of quantitative properties in whatever way the mathematicians found rewarding. I myself see no difference, then, between his field and fictional literature, except that the latter convey stories and the mathematicians symbols that represent imaginary quantities. More important is what Aristotle has to say on the subject in *Metaphysics* XIII 1-3 and 6-9 and XIV 1-4.

38   As alluded to, Aristotle analyzes the semantic concepts and their opposites in two chapters, *On Interpretation* 12-3, and concludes: "We must take the opposite expressions to be these: possible—not possible; admissible—not admissible; impossible—not impossible; necessary—not necessary; true—not true" (*On Interpretation* 12, 22a10-12). I noted this once before, but it bears repeating because of the glass-eyed stares I have encountered from ancient Greek specialists trained in modern logic. The strict contradictory of "true" is not "false" but "not true," which could mean false or indeterminate,

trivalence, because false and indeterminate would be sub-categories of "not true," assuming truth to have primacy.[39] In the case of bi-

---

even if for ease of speech Aristotle often considers false to be the opposite of truth). Further proof that Aristotle has a trivalent system *underlying any seeming bivalent one* is this: "That is why not everything is either equal or unequal, but everything is equal or is not equal" (*Prior Analytics* I 46, 51b27-28).

[39]   Additionally relevant is what Aristotle says at the end of *On Interpretation* 9, and I report Bäck's account (*op. cit.,* 1992), because Bäck denies that Aristotle accepts a third truth-value (indeterminacy): "When Aristotle says at the end [of Chapter 9], 'it is not necessary of every affirmation and opposite negation that one should be true and the other false' (19b1-2), he is however thinking of several features of future statements at once..." (p. 143). I address the "several features" in a moment, but it is important to say first that Bäck then rejects J.L. Ackrill's interpretation of this statement, which is that Aristotle accepts a third truth-value. Bäck writes that Ackrill:

> holds that future statements [such as there will be a sea battle tomorrow] originally do not have a truth value, and then come to have one. So there would be three truth values: true, false, and indeterminate. Again, I do not think that there is much evidence that Aristotle has a three-valued logic. I hold that future statements do have truth values, *but just do not make non-modal, categorical claims.* It might be said that future statements would have an indeterminate truth value, if they made categorical claims, which they do not (p. 144; my italics).

Bäck's claim stems from his ingenious attempt to solve the problems of Chapter 9. Part of his solution is that we read Aristotle's claim "it is necessary that either a sea battle will occur tomorrow or not" as elliptical for "it is necessary that either a sea battle will occur or it will not occur, *when it occurs*" (p. 140; my italics). Thus the "several features" mentioned above include at least an additional, suppressed phrase "when it occurs," which Aristotle omitted for the sake of brevity. I rush to no conclusions here and merely note that settling these difficult issues would involve understanding why, if Bäck is right, Aristotle did not say "it is not necessary of every *categorical* affirmation and opposite negation that one should be true and the other false." Rather Aristotle says more broadly, "it is not necessary *of every affirmation and opposite negation* that one should be true and the other false (my italics)." If Bäck responds that, just as the Principle of Plenitude is elliptical, so is this claim in Chapter 9, we might reply in return that other passages in the corpus suggesting *bivalence* are also elliptical, for the sake of brevity, and that Aristotle really does accept "indeterminacy" as being applicable to future contingent statements (although admittedly not to *necessary* propositions, which

valent conditionals for some modern logicians, the use of "false" and "true" no longer matches the sense used by most people in common discourse, which Aristotle describes as follows: true is "to say of what is, that it is," with false being the opposite.[40] Similarly, Sorabji's "multiplying…infinity" no longer matches common discourse.

At any rate, whether Cantorians and modern mathematicians not following classical models can evade, or would even care about evading, Aristotle's criticism of treating infinities like numbers, or whether they use the symbol ∞ but actually treat it, the "number" infinity, as if it were the "maximal finite number," and whether they have simply traded one group of paradoxes for another, are fascinating questions but ones outside the scope of this book. Suffice it to say that, *contra* Philoponus and Sorabji, Aristotle's view does not commit him to augmented infinities, and his view that the past was, or is, infinite and

---

could include propositions that are true at *all* times and which Bäck properly explains can be said to be true even if they involve the future tense, p. 150). More reasons why modal claims involving necessity are at least sometimes reducible to categorical claims are given later, when I discuss Hintikka's concern that modal and non-modal generalizations collapse for Aristotle.

40   *Metaphysics* IV 7, 1011b25. Future contingents on some interpretations of *On Interpretation* 9 are, as we just saw, indeterminate, but a purposefully fictional statement, with no intent to capture reality, might be claimed to be neither true nor false nor even indeterminate. There is no intent of say of what *actually* is that it is. Franz Brentano was correct in saying:
> The harmony or disharmony between our thought and the thing has no influence whatever upon the existence of the latter; they are independent of our thought and remain untouched by it. He [Aristotle] says in *Met.* IX. 10: "you are not white because we believe *truthfully* that you are white." Conversely, our thought depends upon things, and must agree with them in order to be true. "Rather because you are white, we, who say it, speak the truth." Similarly, in the fifth chapter of the *Categories*: "we say of a statement that it is true or false *because* something is or is not the case." (Franz Brentano, *On the Several Senses of Being in Aristotle,* ed. and transl. by Rolf George, Berkeley: University of California Press) 1975, p. 19; my italics.

actual in the sense that an ongoing event like a day or the Games is actual seems very tenable, indeed perfectly sensible. Denying that the past was actual in that sense puts one arguably in worse straits than accepting it, for then how was it real? All hands agree it is not actual "in separation," like a man or dog. No other reasonable manner presents itself, and, to repeat, if readers deny that the (infinite) past was actual (for Aristotle or anyone else), then they seemingly deny the reality of the causes that bring those self-same readers and this article into being. One might say all those causes and the events existed or have existed but that "the past" is something different, but presumably the Aristotelian reply to this is that "the past" is simply a locution for the totality of those series of events (even though we understand that a *finite* total *per se* cannot be calculated). Clearly, Aristotle holds that infinity exists in some sense with respect to the past because he states emphatically that denying infinity means accepting the beginning of the universe, which he indicates is absurd; the relevant sense is "one thing after another is always coming into existence" (*Physics* III 6, 206a22-23). That this sense is not merely potential, as it might be with respect to division, is clear, I trust from the above. Again, we must keep in mind which arena of discourse Aristotle engages in when discussing these issues: physical bodies, temporality, or mathematics (including geometry).[41]

---

41   All of this is perfectly consistent with Aristotle rejecting actual infinities when, to add to my earlier introduction to this topic, he solves Zeno's famous paradox, about having to reach ½ the distance before reaching the goal, *ad infinitum* (or first reaching ½ the distance when starting, but before reaching half reaching first ¼ of the distance, and then first 1/8 of the distance before getting to the first ¼, *ad infinitum*). The result for Zeno, of course, is that one never reaches the endpoint or worse, on the second interpretation, *never even gets started*. Aristotle claims (correctly) that only a *potentially* infinite series of points in the finite distance that Zeno postulates is traversed. No actual infinity exists, as Zeno requires for the dilemma to have force. Yet the finite distance, which is bounded on both sides, is different from the past, which has no boundary at least on the side of the "beginning," and again Aristotle has stated, very reasonably, that infinite traversal is possible as long as

Statement 2

We can now easily see also why Aristotle does not worry about "parts" of infinity being infinite, one of Sorabji's concerns. As Sorabji says:

> Before I finally leave Philoponus's problem about increasing infinity, I should point out one extra way in which it is wounding to Aristotle. For in effect Philoponus is arguing that the pagan denial of a beginning gives us the very thing which Aristotle called impossible: an infinity whose *parts* are infinite. At least it will do so, **if the period down to yesterday is a *part* of the period down to today.**[42]

Even though Sorabji ends with a conditional, the fact that he states Aristotle had been wounded strongly suggest that he accepts the protasis, "(if) the period down to yesterday is a *part* of the period down to today." Why Sorabji's (and Philoponus's) account fails, however, is merely a variation on the theme seen a few times already.

Strictly speaking, a part is a ratio and only applies to finitudes. A part of a month is a day or "half a month," because it has a definite size in relation to the encompassing whole, which also has a definite size, a beginning and endpoint. In other words, a part is a fraction of a whole, e.g., 1/4 of the box, 1/8th of the pie; 3/10th of one's annual income, 15 of 30 days. As Aristotle says "'Part' means...that into which a quantity can be in any way divided" (*Metaphysics* V 25, 1023b12-13). What though would a specific, "partial" infinite duration of a temporal infinity be,—say, 24/∞ hours? How would this really differ from 8/∞ hours or 1024/∞ hours, given that ∞ *always has something more outside of it* and is indeterminate? The infinite past to yesterday, or as Sorabji put it, "the period down to yesterday," is like a fraction with the drunken-eight as the denominator. No sensible answer, at least from the Aristotelian perspective, can be given to these claims about these alleged "parts" (one side of which is infinite). As the Northern Greek says in

---

that which does the traversing is infinite too.

42   Sorabji, 1983, p. 218; his italics but my bolding.

Physics III 5, 205b29-30, trying to divide the infinite in half is absurd. In short, there are no (infinite) parts *of something infinite*. The only types of parts of the infinite past are the finite ones, e.g., the complete and definite day January 1, 2012 and *only* those type of (finite) parts can be sensibly compared.

Claiming that the infinite past to yesterday is a part of the infinite past to today is superficially sensible only because "the past" is considered not as something truly infinite but relative to some beginning, like the "maximal finite number" in history or the Big Bang or something functionally equivalent to trecentillion years, as I already explained. Any immediate cognitive impression in support of Sorabji's claim, analogous to the impression that the sun goes around the earth, is simply wrong on reflection.

This finishes the arguments of Philoponus against Aristotle. Sorabji makes additional claims in his chapter entitled "Infinity Arguments in Favour of a Beginning," that result more from his perspective, or from modern perspectives, even if inspired by Philoponus. However, I only note a few of them, because this section is not intended to address the truth and falsity of the claims from all perspectives, including the medieval or modern ones, but simply to support that Aristotle held Statement 2 and that we can find more evidence that it is true than not, given the arguments of classical mathematics up to the time of Philoponus. Nevertheless, Sorabji makes other claims about Aristotle that might be considered for a fuller understanding of the topic at hand (justifying Statement 2). Sorabji writes:

> If Aristotle's view of infinity is finitist [in the sense of being an *extendible finitude*, as Sorabji's phrases it], I believe it will be perfectly adapted for some cases, but inadequate for others. If, for example, we take pairs of whole numbers, they will never be separated from each other by more than a finite number of whole numbers. *The most we can do, by selecting pairs still further apart, is to obtain an*

> *extendible finitude of Aristotle's sort*. On the other hand, my view would be that the totality of whole numbers is *more than finite*. I shall later suggest that there may be an asymmetry between the past and the future, in respect of years traversed: that the series of future years traversed, starting from now, may best be viewed as an extendible finitude in Aristotle's manner, while the series of past years, if there was no beginning, should be viewed as *more than that*.[43]

To begin with, it is not clear what Sorabji really means by "finitist" or "extendible finitude," but this description could not apply to eternal time, unless he is simply reporting Aristotle's view that the "parts appearing always" as "*other* parts go away" refer to finite parts. The past is undoubtedly not finite for Aristotle and thus the present and future are not merely extending a finitude in such a way that the past, as "the totality of whole numbers," would be "more than that," i.e. more than that extended finitude. Infinity for Aristotle *always, always and still always* has something outside of it. We do not "build" infinity out of finitudes, even if something finite undergoes infinite time. Rather, the reverse is the case. We can demarcate part of infinity by selecting a finite beginning and finite endpoint, like "last week." This is the only way that infinity is "finitist."

Regarding Sorabji's pairs of whole numbers, imagine the pairs are 4&7, 9&20, and 100&121. We easily see the numbers that separate them (3, 11, and 21). However, what if we now take in addition 222&333, 500&775, and 1000&2000. What does it mean to say that the most we can do is "to obtain an extendible finitude of Aristotle's sort"? Unless I am completely missing Sorabji's point, we simply need add the whole numbers, namely, 111, 275, and 1000. We get a definite sum, 1386, whether or not the sum is "extendible." Maybe Sorabji is implying that we could continue the process *ad infinitum*, which leads us to the second point in italics, where he holds that the "totality of

---

43   1983, p. 212; my italics throughout and my bracketed comment.

whole numbers is more than finite." This makes no sense to an Aristotelian, though, because, first, you could never establish a *total* for something that you have not finished enumerating, and if the total can be calculated then it is finite and is at best a sub-total. You would have ongoing and changing sub-totals, without end, if you actually had an infinity. If Sorabji means the total amount of numbers (such as those going from one to ten, so ten total), rather than their sum-total (1+2+3+4+5+6+7+8+9+10, or 55), the same criticisms apply. If you stop at some point in order to have the total, then you have a finitude, which contradicts his own claim that they are "more than finite." Aristotle allows that *potentially* one could always increase (at least conceptually) a number (or a line in the case of the geometers noted above), so Sorabji's first point is empty. If not, and if Sorabji is claiming that the whole numbers are *actually* more than finite, they must be infinite, and he is saddled with all of the paradoxes above. Another reply is that the numbers, strictly speaking, throughout human history are still finite, no matter how incredibly large (given some chosen starting point and not allowing the drunken-eight to be a number). They might function *as if* they are infinite (recall Aristotle's claim about not robbing mathematicians of their science) but they are nevertheless finite. You can raise 10 to whatever exponent you wish (I used 903 in the case of trecentillion) or multiply any massive number by another massive number as many times as you wish, with a computer as powerful as you wish, perhaps with the new DARPA terahertz chip from 2014. You will still always have a finite number or an incomplete calculation, if the computer has not finished the processing.

On the third and final point in italics in the passage above, Sorabji tries to compare past and future infinities, using Philoponus's approach; thus, the past is "more" than the future. However, this again abrogates the sensible Aristotelian rule. We should not compare infinities, when comparisons instead only apply to finitudes, and any time an author uses "more than" in conjunction with "infinity," as Sorabji does, we can reasonably expect that some untenable conclusion will appear very soon. Thus, leaving aside the issue that the past is both completed in a certain sense and *necessary* for Aristotle, as we see more in a moment, and the future primarily *potential*, we cannot sensibly compare the size of the (necessary) past with the (potential) size of the future, for each is a drunken-eight, and not sensibly comparable, at least in terms of measurement.

We can now return to the two comments that Sorabji made, which started this whole discussion:

> "As for that which is infinite in one direction, it is neither infinite nor limited." [Sorabji says of this passage:] "Aristotle...denies that what is infinite in only one direction really is infinite... the reason, which is not given, may be that it [the one-sided infinity] has at least one boundary... But [Sorabji concludes], *at any rate, the implication is that the past is not infinite*..."[44]

> Aristotle describes that which (like the future) is infinite in one direction only, and which ought to provide him with the clearest instances of potential infinity, *as not being infinite at all*.[45]

Let us address both of Sorabji's claims, which are given out of the context of *De Caelo*, from which the passages arise. The latter claim is the easiest to rebut and follows from the just-finished, related discussion. The future for Aristotle does not exist *yet* in the *fullest* sense of "actual"—it is always potential and always potentially infinite (but with *real* and not merely conceptual potentiality being assumed). He states

---

44 Sorabji, *op. cit.*, 1983, p. 218; my italics. Curiously, Sorabji had said in *Necessity, Cause, and Blame* (*op. cit.*, 1980) that "The sun and stars last for the whole of time, and for Aristotle the whole of time is an infinite amount of time. One would expect, on the other hand, that an infinite amount of time (e.g., the past) need not add up to the whole of time; but at *Cael*. I 12, 283a10, Aristotle says of time which is infinite only in one direction that it is infinite only 'in a way' (p. 128, footnote 3)." "In a way" is not discussed in the book from 1980, to my knowledge.

45 *Op. cit.*, 1983, p. 212; my italics.

in many places that the universe will have no end, which necessitates that motion and therefore time likewise will have no end, e.g. *De Caelo* I 12; II 1, 283b27-32. Why then the future is not a clear example of *potential infinity* for Aristotle is baffling, unless Sorabji is appealing to the same consideration that ostensibly infects the past: because the future is one-sided (with "now" or the present being one boundary) it is not truly infinite at all (because the assumption appears to be on Sorabji's perspective that the infinite must be unbounded in *all* ways for it to be infinite). Take, however, the case of Aristotle resolving Zeno's paradoxes, in particular the one where we cannot reach the end point without having first reached the halfway point and then the ¾ point and so forth, *ad infinitum*. Aristotle is obviously willing to accept a *starting point* and also a *potential infinity* of divisions to the ending point. Moreover, he claims a potential, and only a potential, infinity can be traversed when one truly reaches the end point, as we do many times an hour. Only were there an actual infinity would one not be able to arrive at the end. Surely, then, this is a case for Aristotle of a one-sided "potential infinity," with the beginning point being one boundary. Indeed, the potential infinity (in terms of divisibility) exists even when *both* sides are bounded! Recall, however, that this type of infinite divisibility exists (actually) in thought; as we saw Aristotle saying, *its separateness is only in knowledge*. Nothing, then, about the five-foot distance I must traverse to get to the goal, the door, is *actually* infinite, and the *potentially* infinite half-way markers only exist, strictly speaking, in our minds, as far as our minds can and do take them (which will never be more than finite). Thus, clever Zeno actually reaches his home after slinking away, defeated.

The future is similar to the past in one way, being always open-ended, despite the vast difference between the actual(ized) past and the still yet-to-be determined future. The actuality of the infinite past is like the actuality of a past year or past Games that are still occurring; still, the past, insofar as it is finished, has no potentiality *per se*, although, in a different way, we might say that the past has potential. The present "now," *considered as a boundary of that past*, might be argued properly to have potential, just as the rest of today or of the current Games, if we are in the middle of them, also involve potentiality. "Now" shares a common boundary and a common potential with the future, just as a wall and a door share a doorjamb. Aristotle is unambiguous at *De Caelo* I 12, 283b13: "No potential (*dunamis*) relates to being in the past (but only to the present or future)."

Let us now switch from Sorabji's remark about the (potentially infinite) future to the past, and whether the past itself is infinite. I have already addressed this issue to some extent but another solution to Sorabji's worry about a one-sided infinity being not infinite, or at least confirmation for my previous remarks, follows. Aristotle's comment about one-sided infinities not being infinite does *not* support Philoponus's view, which Sorabji ignores. That is, even granting Sorabji that the one-sided infinity (like the past) is not infinite or is not fully infinite, it does not follow, as Sorabji and Philoponus would want, that the past is "limited" (or finite), and thus that the universe is created. Aristotle also excludes that in the same breath: it (the one-sided past) is neither infinite *nor limited*. Sorabji does not consider this aspect, but he should. Somewhat surprisingly given his claim about the one-sided past not being infinite, he usually and properly recognizes in other passages throughout his chapter that Aristotle had no doubt that the past was infinite, in the proper sense of the word when applied to temporal history, even if occasional statements suggest a particular perspective that triggers a dilemma. In brief, Sorabji should not imply that the baffling statement about one-sided infinities is support for the past being finite and for the universe being created, backing Philoponus, even if Sorabji then himself sits on the proverbial fence about whether the past is infinite or not. I gather Sorabji imagines that the fence is very rounded and comfortable; I take it instead to be philosophically jagged and razor-sharp.

The rest of this section on one-sided infinities applies to both of Sorabji's claims, whether to the past or to the future. A penultimate solution to one-sided infinities not being infinite—outside the context of *De Caelo*—is to suppose that Aristotle is speaking elliptically, and that he means more precisely "one-sided infinities are neither (fully) infinite nor (fully) limited." "Fully infinite" means *unbounded* in both or all pertinent ways; "fully limited" means *bounded* in all pertinent ways, like a day or a week. The past, or one-sided infinities, are bounded in some respect and unbounded in another crucial respect. Otherwise, the only way in which Aristotle's claim (that the relevant one-sided infinities are neither infinite nor limited) can be made sensible seems to be because they are non-existent, for then they need not have either property. Otherwise, the (one-sided) past is finite but he has indubitably rejected that option, as we saw before.

Aristotle occasionally uses a shortened expression for the sake of rhetorical effect or for simplicity, as we all do on occasion. Consider a similar example from the *Dramatics*. Aristotle says:

> We have laid down that tragedy is the representation of a complete (*teleias*) i.e. whole action which has some magnitude (*megethos*) *(for there can be a whole with no magnitude)*. A whole is that which has a beginning, a middle and a conclusion.[46]

Aristotle adds that if the magnitude is too small or too large the whole cannot be perceived well or easily remembered, as in the case with a huge animal a thousand miles long (1451a1-6). The crucial point for us is this: The claim in this context that a whole can have no magnitude is impossible, especially given that Aristotle's whole tragedy must have parts, namely, a beginning, middle, and end. One cannot have parts of zero. Aristotle only means, therefore, by "no magnitude" such insignificant size that *for all practical purposes* involves no magni-

---

46   6.1450b24-26; Richard Janko, Aristotle *Poetics* (Indianapolis: Hackett Publishing Company) 1987; my italics. Thus, something with only a beginning or an end (but not both) is not a whole; cf. 1450b28f-33.

tude. This is suggested further by his following remark about animals so tiny as to be imperceptible. Thus, "with no magnitude" is merely elliptical for "with no (discernible) magnitude" or something similar, and, analogously, a "one-sided infinity not being infinite" is elliptical for a "one-sided infinity not being (fully) infinite."

My final solution to the current problem of one-sided infinities: As noted, Sorabji quotes Aristotle out of context. Examining another statement in the chapter containing Aristotle's baffling comment may shed more light on the problem or at least counter Sorabji's two suggestions that "the past is not infinite" and the future is not "infinite at all" (i.e., not even potentially). The statement occurs shortly after the passage about one-sided infinities just discussed. I offer a neutral party's translation, that of W.D. Ross: "*anything which exists for a time infinite* either absolutely *or in one direction*, is in existence either always or usually" (*De Caelo* 283b1-2; my italics). Thus, Aristotle suggests that one-directional (and absolute) infinities exist, and that they exist *usually* or *always*. I stress the "suggests" because strictly speaking we can interpret this statement in nine ways, taken out of the context of that chapter (because it is in the form "**A** or **B** is **x** or **y**").

(1)   **A** (but not **B**) is **x** or **y** (exclusive disjunction holds for the subject but inclusive disjunction is allowed for the predicate).

(2)   **B** (but not **A**) is **x** or **y** (exclusive disjunction holds for the subject but inclusive disjunction is allowed for the predicate).

(3)   **A** is **x** (but not **y**) (exclusive disjunction holds for both the subject and the predicate).

(4)   **B** is **x** (but not **y**) (exclusive disjunction holds for both the subject and the predicate).

(5)   **A** is **y** (exclusive disjunction holds for both the subject and the predicate).

(6)   **B** is **y** (exclusive disjunction holds for both the subject and the predicate).

(7)   **A** or **B** is **x** (inclusive disjunction holds for the subject but

exclusive disjunction for the predicate).
(8)   *A* or *B* is **y** (inclusive disjunction holds for the subject but exclusive disjunction for the predicate).
(9)   *A* or *B* (or both) is **x** or **y** (or both) (inclusive disjunction holds for both the subject and predicate).

Spelled out, the options become:

(1)   **Absolutely infinite existence** exists *always* or *usually*.
(2)   **One-directional infinite existence** exists *always* or *usually*.
(3)   **Absolutely infinite existence** exists *always* (but not *usually*).
(4)   **One-directional infinite existence** exists *always* (but not *usually*).
(5)   **Absolutely infinite existence** exists *usually* (but not *always*).
(6)   **One-directional infinite existence** exists *usually* (but not *always*).
(7)   **Absolutely infinite existence** or **one-directional infinite existence** (or both) exists *always*.
(8)   **Absolutely infinite existence** or **one-directional infinite existence** (or both) exists *usually*.
(9)   **Absolutely infinite existence** or **one-directional infinite existence** (or both) exists *always* or *usually* (or both).

Is Aristotle really expecting us to mentally calculate nine options, including the fact that only two of the theoretical options do not involve one-sided infinity? Or should his view about one-sided infinities be gleaned from the three options—2, 4, and 6 — that have only "one-directional infinity" as the subject, all of which involve existence for it *always or usually*? At any rate, it seems clear from the context that he is arguing *against* chance or fortune occurring *always or for the most part* and it would be very odd that he adds "or one-directional infinity" if he thought it did not *function* somehow the same way as "absolute infinity." The implication, then, is that both absolute infinity and one-directional infinity could exist or, better yet, do exist in a certain sense (and the reason why infinity is inconsistent at least at times with the subjunctive "could exist" will be clear when we examine possibility and necessity more later, especially in the setting of Theta 8). That is, Aristotle seemingly holds the subjects to be part of an inclusive disjunction. Thus, when he says, "anything which exists ***for a time infinite*** either ***absolutely*** or ***in one direction***...," he does allow that "time infinite" in one direction exists, and we need not determine whether it is "always" or "usually," although intuitively the latter option might be most reasonable. However, depending on what he means by "exist," he might even allow the one-sided infinity to exist "always." If actual existence is meant, then because the past as a one-sided infinity is necessary insofar as it is past and cannot be changed, and because the future is only "potentially existent," then the actual existence of the past is *all* that has ever been actually existent *per se* (in the sense of "actual" that is most real and most complete). In short, Aristotle means option (9) because he says it, and if he had wanted a more restricted meaning, he would have written one of the other eight sentences.

To return to the issue of chance in this context in *De Caelo*, Aristotle argues that an ungenerated universe could not be destroyed and that a generated universe could not be indestructible. In arguing for this bifurcated point, Aristotle appeals to this distinction—namely, that by nature what exists always or for the most part is opposed to what exists rarely, which he says exists by chance or luck. For our purposes, we only need focus here further on what Aristotle resists: First, he does *not* indicate that "always" is *more* than the "one-sided infinity," even if "usually" might appear to be less than "always," which may or may not set up a tension for him.[47] Second, and more importantly,

---

47   What would the difference be between, say, numbers that happen

the crucial point is that one-sided infinities are not like chance and luck. Aristotle thereby suggests that both "one-sided" and "absolute" infinities exist and implies that each could have actual existence of a certain sort, as a process or series of events, just not existence like a horse, with "separateness" that is complete at any moment.

Sorabji notes that Broadie herself has pinpointed the worry with one-sided infinities in *De Caelo* I 12.[48] Yet he ignores in this context her own solution to this problem, and her ingenious interpretation in no way causes us to think that the past was finite or limited in a temporal sense (and thus in no way gives support to Philoponus's views).[49] As noted, she translates *hōrismenon* as "determinate" rather than "limited" and, in a dense six-page explanation within the context of Aristotle's whole argument in *De Caelo* I 12, shows other places in which *hōrismenon* is used also as "determinate." The word does not necessarily suggest mathematical quantity, in spite of Aristotle having

---

"usually" in an infinity (say, every tenth number in a sequence) and those that "always" happen (every number in sequence without a gap)? Why would the latter sequence (which is open-ended) be more than the former (which is also open-ended)? Better, it appears to me, not to get involved in such a comparison of infinities, which is the approach that Aristotle recommends. *Ratios only hold between finitudes.* Alternatively, he might be suggesting that the one-sided infinite past is "usually" but still infinite, insofar as common speech suggests that the other type of infinity including past-present-future is "always." More on this when covering Statement 9.

48   Sorabji, 1983, p. 212.

49   Later in his book (1983, p. 277), Sorabji does discuss Broadie's solution to one-sided infinities in *De Caelo*, and says "the whole of time can, for this purpose, be viewed as definite **in a way** (*hōistai pōs*). But a period which is infinite in only one direction **is not definite in any way at all**. Presumably, Aristotle is thinking that, for example, an infinite future is of no *single* length, since one that begins in 1980 is longer than one that begins in 1981 [my bolding but his italics]." Why the boundary of the present is not something "definite in any way" is puzzling. The present *seems* to be the definite boundary of the past or the future. In any event, Sorabji continues to ignore that ratios like "longer" for Aristotle only hold with finitudes.

suggested first that infinite time is an *amount* of time.⁵⁰ The full explanation is beyond the scope of this book, but suffice it to say that Aristotle has been arguing that everything relevant to the current problem exists "for a finite time" or "always." No other option is available (with luck or chance only existing rarely and so not being relevant now or, if being relevant, then being finite). To put the matter extremely summarily, perhaps the comment about one-sided infinities excludes from consideration those one-sided infinities, at least at this moment, just because they do not fall cleanly in the options he is considering.⁵¹

However one resolves the mysterious passage in *De Caelo* about one-sided infinities being neither infinite nor determinate, indubitably in the *Physics* Aristotle maintains that the past was or has been infinite. Also, the past, which cannot be finite for Aristotle, is necessary while the future is potentially infinite.⁵² What is necessary cannot be (merely) potential, so there must be some aspect of actuality that is relevant to the past. If a solution that would reconcile *De Caelo* and the *Physics* with respect to the tensions generated by "one-side infinities" is impossible, or if Sorabji could rebut the arguments above and sustain his claim that the one-sided infinity (especially the past) is not actual in *any way*, it appears we have to say that at least parts of the *Physics* were later and that Aristotle dropped the view that a one-sided infinity could not be (actually) infinite in at least one relevant sense. Be all of this as it may, whatever the solution to the problem of how to read "one-sided infinities are neither infinite nor determinate," we must conclude, to reiterate, that because the (one-sided) past is not

---

50   Broadie, *Passage and Possibility*, pp. 69ff.

51   Broadie, *Passage and Possibility*, p. 69. Moreover, as indicated, Broadie shows Aristotle treating "always" and "infinite" to be the same.

52   Cf. Sorabji (1983, p. 211-2 and 216-7) for the differences in views on infinity between *De Caelo* and the *Physics*. Also, see Guthrie's introduction to his translation of *De Caelo*, esp. pp. xxviii ff. Broadie too discusses the relation, and puzzles, of infinity in *De Caelo* versus *Physics* (*Passage and Possibility*, p. 76, ft. 27).

infinite in the sense of being potentially infinite, it must be actually infinite *in some sense*. Thus, Sorabji cannot be right when he says that for Aristotle "*the implication is that the past is not infinite.*"[53]

This concludes the arguments why Aristotle indeed holds Statement 2. The physical universe has existed for infinite time because motion requires enmattered things.

---

53 *Op. cit.*, 1983, p. 214.

3) In infinite time, any (sort of genuine) possibility is actualized (the Principle of Genuine Sortal Plenitude).

This section is probably the most important one of the book, in part because of the controversy and confusion surrounding the Principle of Plenitude and how Jaakko Hintikka and Broadie have championed it on behalf of Aristotle. The Not to Fear Proof has not been seen, I believe, in large part because many excellent scholars have doubted that Aristotle advanced the Principle. Yet for me it is the Philosopher's Stone, as it were, with all the other premises being well understood doctrines for Aristotle and with any deductions for intermediate conclusions in the Proof being trivial. Even the two aforementioned philosophers who have advocated the legitimacy of the Principle for Aristotle did not enter the realm of theological metaphysics when dealing with the various related issues. Their concern, even when metaphysical, was in the relation to modal logic and other issues like determinism. I discuss later in great detail why other scholars have not recognized or accepted that Aristotle held the Principle and why for still other reasons no one noticed the Proof.

For the moment, suffice it to say that Hintikka, Broadie, and some other ancient Greek specialists have grasped that the simple (short) formulation of the Principle is merely elliptical for Aristotle, and with good reason. Three other formulations can, and will, be constructed. I start then by presenting the core part of Hintikka's insights, and afterwards I disambiguate the Principle, clarifying all four versions. I subsequently analyze the notion of "possibility" because that notion, too, has been the source of much controversy and confusion in this setting.

After this prefatory work, we can most effectively examine the criticisms of Hintikka's interpretation as given by other scholars, notably Jeroen van Rijen and Jonathan Barnes, in order to see that they do not undercut Hintikka's ground-breaking work in the most crucial ways, even if they properly forced Hintikka to renounce his overly-optimistic attempt to maintain that Aristotle uses the temporal modal conception embedded in the Principle in *all* contexts, be they ontology, logic, epistemology or aesthetics. In other words, the modal terms are very equivocal for Aristotle, not univocal, just as *logos* and *mimēsis* and other rich terms are equivocal. Those who do not understand the different conceptions of the terms in the different contexts will distort Aristotle's thought, no matter which side of the debate they are on, just as those who think that "play" is univocal would make hash of most of the statement "Nick will play Creon tonight in the play *Antigone*, but his wife Barbara cannot attend because she has to play her tennis match, nor can their oldest daughter because she has to play the violin in her concert."

Finally, I present the views of Broadie, along with my own supplementary arguments, concluding that Aristotle indeed accepted the Principle at least in the ontological context of Theta 8. The scope of the Principle covers only eternal things or kinds that function like eternal things, including so-called artificial kinds like cloaks or clothing in general that, like art or other human production and human activity, are just as eternal as the species for the ancient Northern Greek. Human beings are not just statues. As texts like the *Dramatics* easily reveal, we act and produce, and thus, if we are eternal, our actions and productions *qua* classes are eternal too. The way afterwards to the conclusions of the Not to Fear Proof will be clear sailing, with only a few jibes or tacks needed for the other statements.

Statement 3

Hintikka and the Principle of Plenitude

The name of the Principle of Plenitude in its most elliptical form—"Any possibility will be realized in infinite time"—was coined by Arthur Lovejoy in 1936 in *The Great Chain of Being*, even though Lovejoy thought that Aristotle rejected it.[1] Hintikka takes the opposite position and offers a series of arguments to handle possible objections, explaining away texts by Aristotle that might seem to support Lovejoy, which are unnecessary to reproduce here. We examine some of the passages of Hintikka below, to introduce his arguments, and after go into great detail. The arguments provide ample evidence that Aristotle truly accepted the Principle *but insofar as it is elliptical*.[2]

For Hintikka, Aristotle's support for the Principle is made immediately clear for at least some circumstances in *Physics* III 4, 203b30: "In the case of eternal things, what may be is." It is also found, Hintikka says, in *Metaphysics* IX 4, 1047b3-6, when Aristotle writes: "If, as we have said, that is possible which does not involve an impossibility, it cannot be true to say that a thing is possible but will never be."[3] Equally important for Hintikka is that possibility *in the relevant sense* for Aristotle has temporality built into it, that of realizability at some moment, and this temporal notion of possibility will be crucial, at least

---

1   Hintikka, 1973, p. 94. On the surface, as stated in its elliptical form ("Any possibility will be realized in infinite time"), the Principle is indeed absurd. Otherwise the possibility of Aristotle becoming a Spartan hoplite will be actualized, even if Aristotle is sixty years old when he imagines this possibility. It also means Aristotle's possibility of flying to the moon will be actualized, long before the flights are commercially available. Lynne Spellman correctly says, in evaluating the *Passage and Possibility* of Broadie, that the premise is "*prima facie* implausible" (*Philosophy and Phenomenological Research,* Vol. 46, No. 4, Jun., 1986, pp. 688). More on this topic soon.
2   Hintikka, 1973, pp. 99-105.
3   Hintikka, 1979, p. 112. Jonathan Barnes denies that this passage supports the Principle, as we see below.

for the context of Theta 8 and of the Not to Fear Proof.[4] Even though for some people laws of logic and laws of mathematics are timeless in the sense that they are out of time, or have no relevance to time, I myself follow Hintikka in holding that for Aristotle those laws also involve a temporal notion in that they *always* hold in time. They are not *divorced* from time. They simply as a result do not need a temporal index (e.g., "2+2=4 at noon today"). The reason is not because the index changes the truth-value of the claim but because the index is redundant and might suggest that at other times 2+2 is not equal to 4. Mathematics and logic, at least as conceived by the Northern Greek, derive from phenomenal reality and are not Platonic phenomena that exist in some other reality.[5] Timeless just means in this context that we need not pick a time at which laws are true, unlike a statement that depends upon a time when it is uttered or thought, e.g., "Gloria is running." We can utter one and the same proposition (with respect, say, to laws of logic or to necessary truths) at any time, and it will be true, unlike the statement about Gloria's motion. To emphasize, one sense of "timeless" is "at *all* times."

---

[4] See especially Hintikka's chapter "Aristotle on the Realization of Possibilities in Time," *op. cit.*, 1973, pp. 93-113, even though, to reiterate, Hintikka never considers anything like the Not to Fear Proof.

[5] For Aristotle, laws of logic are ultimately based on nature for him, given the importance of proving those laws and given his notion of truth as a semantic concept that grounds truth-functional statements in physical reality. The proofs in *Prior Analytics* themselves involve deductions and counter-examples (or not) from the real world, such as the use of "movement, animal, white" or "animal, man and white" in *Prior Analytics* 1 9-10. Therefore, the Law of Non-Contradiction insists that x cannot be y and not y at the same time and in the same respect. It cannot be the case that George is alive and not alive at the same time... For Aristotle, this is intuited based on experience, as axioms of geometry are simply grasped. The Law and the axioms are not proved in any other way—in fact, the Law, like axioms, form the basis of proofs. Cf. *Metaphysics* IV 4, especially 1006a2-11. That proofs are dependent on axioms or on what is intuited immediately is also shown in this context in *Physics* II 1, 193a4: "That nature exists, it would be absurd to try to prove..." More on the grounding of logic in physical reality for Aristotle when we discuss Broadie's views.

Statement 3

Hintikka also says that Aristotle "accepted the principle that every genuine possibility is sometimes actualised or, possibly, another form of the same principle according to which no genuine possibility can remain unactualised through an infinity of time."[6] Notice that "genuine" is now added to the Principle. The reason for Hintikka comes from the famous passage in *On Interpretation* 9:

> "For example [Aristotle says], it is possible for this cloak to be cut up, and yet it will not be cut up but will wear out first." Here we in fact have a clear instance of possibility that according to Aristotle will not be realized. *It does not go to show that the principal forms of the principle of plenitude cannot be attributed to Aristotle, however.* The possibility of a particular cloak's being cut up is a possibility concerning an individual object, *and not a possibility concerning kinds of individuals or kinds of events.* Nor does the unfulfilled possibility Aristotle mentions remain unfulfilled through an infinity of time, for when the cloak wears out, it goes out of existence, and no possibility can any longer be attributed to it. Thus Aristotle's example does show that the "genuine" possibilities which the principle says are actualized *do not for him include possibilities concerning individual objects which only exist for a certain period of time.* However, it does not show that Aristotle did not believe in some other forms of the principle which prima facie are much more plausible anyway.[7]

In short, the simplest version of the Principle of Plenitude is contradicted by the example of the cloak being worn out before it can be cut, and yet for the reasons that Hintikka gives above, Aristotle does not give up the Principle.[8] Any correct interpretation of the Princi-

---

6   Hintikka, "Aristotelian Infinity," *op. cit.*, 1979, pp. 115 and 125.

7   1973, pp. 100-1; my italics.

8   I do not like the example of the garment being worn out before it is cut, because "worn out" often means for us that it is badly frayed, with clasps missing, etc. Nevertheless, it still could be worn in dire circumstances or cut to be used as rags. The better example would be to say the garment is burned to ash, and thus could not be cut in any way whatsoever, which is how I trust

ple, therefore, will have to handle this seeming exception of the uncut cloak, and one way to handle it is to restrict individual objects to those existing for infinite time (and we saw that in the *Physics* Aristotle plainly says that for eternal things, presumably objects like eternal planets, what may be, will be). This, then, allows us to evade the problem with the item going out of existence when the item is the subject of the possibility. Then Hintikka states:

> His [Aristotle's] formulations suggest, moreover, that the version of the principle involved is just our (T) [the principle of plenitude], that is, the version that rules out an infinitely long frustration of a possibility. *Even possibilities concerning individual objects fall within the scope of this principle, provided of course that the individual in question does not pass away* [such as the eternal planets], *for there are in Aristotle's view no possibilities concerning non-existent particulars*.[9]

However, Hintikka adds further:

> ...it is not clear what kind of possibility is intended in it [the Principle]. Possible events? Possible courses of events? Possible kinds of individuals? Possible individuals (particulars)?[10]

I will address this issue in detail, because these questions are absolutely crucial in my opinion for the fullest understanding of the issues of this book, but let me put this in the terms of an example that I used to hear in my youth. If you put a monkey on a typewriter and it started typing randomly for an eternity, it would compose *Don Quixote*. For Hintikka, this could not happen, because the monkey would be dead after a few years. It would not be a "genuine" possibility.

---

the reader interprets the example. I will therefore sometimes use "burned up" rather than "worn away," for clarity, but they amount to the same, namely, "to be destroyed."

9   1973, p. 105; my italics and my example in brackets.
10   1973, p. 94.

Statement 3

Now, if the *imaginary* monkey lived an *imaginary* eternity, then I myself imagine that an *imaginary* novel, in fact all novels by all writers throughout Spanish history, would be composed through sheer luck by the imaginary random keystrokes. Eternity is an awfully, *awfully* long time, and it wouldn't matter whether the monkey typed one character an hour or whether it was a simian speed-typist doing a thousand words a minute. However, let us return to more sensible cases, because once one starts down the path of mere imagination over the course of an eternity one could, dare I say?, go on forever. I assume that by the end of this section we need to be very clear on the scope of "possibility" for the Principle, as Hintikka suggests. For him, the Principle's scope requires either eternally existing individual subjects (unlike a cloak) or, to highlight the second way in which he protects the Principle, "kinds" that exist in and of themselves for an eternity for Aristotle, which is seemingly standard Aristotelian doctrine. As Hintikka adds:

> A statement as to what is possible in a given moment to a given individual must be taken as an elliptical statement *which really says something about all the similar individuals at all the different times*. A mere generalization [in equating possibility] with respect to time [or with respect to "sometime truth"] is not enough; Aristotle apparently has to generalize also with respect to individuals. That this is what he does is strongly suggested by *An. Pr.* I 13, 32b4ff.[11]

This passage of the *Prior Analytics* I 13 says that possibility can have two meanings:

> [i] to happen for the most part and fall short of necessity, e.g. a man's turning grey or growing or decaying, or *generally what naturally belongs to a thing...* [ii] In another way it means the indefinite, which can be both thus and not thus, e.g., an animal's walking or an earthquake's taking place while it is walking, or generally what happens

---

11   *Op. cit.,* 1973, p. 172; my italics. Cf. also p. 115.

by chance; for none of these inclines by nature in the one way more than in the opposite [my italics].

Although Hintikka does not explain exactly how this passage supports his point, I take it that he means something along the following line, referring to meaning [i]: "Generally what naturally belongs to a thing" captures the thought that an individual *is an individual of a kind or of a species* (which exists eternally for Aristotle and which then satisfies that seeming condition of temporal scope of the Principle of Plenitude). If this is correct, and Hintikka's statements in other place indicate that it is (e.g., 1979, p. 115), then Hintikka believes that to speak of an attribute x generally belonging to an individual without presupposing that it "similarly" belongs to other individuals of the same kind would be unAristotelian.

It is a platitude that individuals for Aristotle come from other individuals of the same species, and, having the same nature or essence, entail in general the same *specific* or *generic* capacities, potentialities and thus possibilities. Alternatively, if the individuals are things that are not organic and thus do not propagate, and are made by human beings, then they have the same properties as given by the definition of the relevant class. For example, in the *Posterior Analytics* and other places, Aristotle indicates that the essence is necessary and that all members of a kind then have those essential characteristics, insofar as they are member of that kind.[12] Man begets man, and the son is formally identical to the father.[13] Thus, what one individual *as a member of a species* has or can do (like walking or speaking) the other members could do also similarly, although Hintikka does not extend this to my knowledge to what the individuals can make (as artwork or craft) that is is *explicitly* eternal. Yet all tragedies have the essential conditions given in the definition of *Dramatics* 6. I address this issue

---

12   *Posterior Analytics* I 6, 74b; *Metaphysics* V, 1017b22; *Metaphysics* V 8, 1017b19.

13   *Metaphysics* VII 7, 1032a26; IX 8, 1049b28-29.

more later, but for the moment, suffice it to say that just as color or texture belongs to all (kinds of) cloaks (and to all clothing), by nature, so does being "cuttable" belong to them. Of course, cuttable is simply the possibility of being cut.

If this is correct, then for Hintikka Aristotle's Principle is better understood as being elliptical with *sortal* presuppositions. That is, making this presupposition explicit, we would arrive at what I call The Principle of Sortal Plenitude: Any *kind* (that is, sort) of possibility will be actualized in an eternity. The instance of a particular worn-out but uncut cloak of *On Interpretation* 9 does not function, therefore, as a counter-example to the *sortal* principle; rather what is in scope of the Sortal Principle is cloak as a (cuttable) *kind*. A particular cloak considered as a "particular accident," one which might have a peculiar wine stain at the bottom right of its front, is *not* within scope. That cloak *qua* particular accident does not exist for eternity, whereas cloak as a kind for Aristotle does provide the temporal requirement. Hence, one requirement for Hintikka for the Principle is that Aristotle treats a relevant individual *in general*, as a member of species. If this condition is not met, the Principle is not supposed to apply *unless the individual itself is eternal*. The reason that an individual cloak's cutting was a legitimate possibility, even before it got dissolved or burned up first, is that for Aristotle the possibility holds for the kind (which had existed before the particular cloak). In summary, the accidental particular's existence (or lack of existence) is not at issue for the *sortal* possibility covering many individuals and thus the example of what happens or not accidentally to a particular cloak, considered as the accidental particular, in no way undercuts the sortal form of the Principle of Plenitude.

I discuss this all more fully below in considering the objections to Hintikka, but let this suffice as an introduction. To summarize and to conclude this section: If the original Principle is elliptical for "genuine possibilities" that implies "*kinds of* possibilities," we can resolve the problem of the individual cloak being worn out before it gets cut.[14] Treating the individual cloaks as stand-ins for a species rather than as "accidental particulars" makes the Principles much more palatable. Analogously, for Aristotle there is no science of accidents and one should not expect scientific knowledge to apply to *accidental* characteristics or events.[15]

---

14   Sorabji says that the principle is "slightly less implausible" in this form, with its sortal restriction (Richard Sorabji, *Necessity, Cause and Blame*, London: Duckworth, 1980, p. 131). It is not plain, however, why then he would still deny the truth of the claim; he gives no counterexample. At any rate, because I am only concerned here with providing the evidence that Aristotle supports the Principle, I leave aside whether it is persuasive for modern sensibilities, which typically find eternal species foreign to their default conceptual frameworks.

15   *Metaphysics* VI 2, 1026b2-3.

Statement 3

Different Versions of the Principle of Plenitude

Let us start afresh and clarify what the Principle of Plenitude might mean and has meant, in order to help evaluate not only the responses to Hintikka but other discussions of whether Aristotle accepted the Principle, such as by Broadie and Barnes.

The Principle of Plenitude: "In infinite time, any possibility is actualized."

This is Hintikka's first version, and the way in which the Principle is generally phrased by proponents and critics alike. Read literally, and assuming that "possibility" means what some thinkers from Parmenides onwards have thought, namely, that which is merely conceivable, this version of the Principle would require the following possibilities to occur during infinite time:
- autumn leaves to float in winter back to the twigs and re-attach themselves;
- dogs (or werewolves) to turn into human beings and vice-versa;
- philosophers to sprout wings in order to fly to the moon and back in five seconds but ministers and popes to fly to Pluto and back in three seconds;
- Martha to cut her coat tomorrow at 14:00, even if it gets burned first in a fire at noon (because she will travel backwards in time to cut it); and
- assuming matter and energy are eternal and have different forms, one or both to be combined in any way that can be imagined.

It is hard to accept, though, that Aristotle assumed the Principle should be interpreted so simplistically and without reasonable presuppositions. We ourselves often speak elliptically and chide anyone who takes us at our word, ignoring the reasonable presuppositions for any given case. For example, while driving on a freeway, we see signs sometimes saying "No Stopping (Anytime)." Every driver immediately realizes, however, that the sign cannot disallow stopping in an emergency, with other cars stopped in front of oneself, and therefore drivers fill in the rest of the meaning. They understand the sign must mean "no stopping anytime *under normal conditions*." Aristotle likewise very reasonably presupposes certain assumptions for the Principle. This takes us to the other formulations of the Principle, with the presuppositions made increasingly more explicit.

Principle of Genuine Plenitude: "In infinite time, any *genuine* possibility is actualized."

This is Hintikka's first modified version. As we saw him writing:

> the "genuine" possibilities which the principle says are actualized do not for him [Aristotle] include possibilities concerning individual objects which only exist for a certain period of time.

In short, genuine in this context for Hintikka seems to indicate only infinitely existing objects or objects as members of kinds that function like infinite objects. If the object is real but only temporarily existing it is not "genuine." I myself assume that "genuine" rather means something like "real," "ontological" or "following natural laws," whether or not it is existing at the time a claim is made about it, but let us not get ahead of ourselves and let us stick for the time being with Hintikka's view. Obviously, Hintikka's use of genuine disallows (and correctly) not only the fantasy cases given in the simplest formulation of the Principle but even future contingents that are indexed for a particular time, such as Martha's coat being cut at 14:00 tomorrow even if it is burned at noon. Time cannot be reversed for Aristotle, and therefore we cannot make sensible claims about non-existent coats in this context without being absurd. As Hintikka says: "...*there are in*

Statement 3

Aristotle's view no possibilities concerning non-existent particulars." I trust we should interpret this to mean that no relevant possibilities exist at the moment when a particular is non-existent, although I will question later whether a soon-to-exist individual as a member of the species might not be a proper subject of the relevant possibilities.

In short, the first modified version of the Principle restricts the scope of the realizable possibilities to eternally existing individuals, on Hintikka's reading, or to anything that functions like eternally existing individuals, which takes us to our next formuation. For the sake of utmost clarity, I present this version while examining only Hintikka's considerations regarding "kinds" and while leaving aside for the moment the previous addition of "genuine." "Kinds" for Hintikka at times seems to function like the qualification "genuine," both triggering the need for sufficient temporality on the part of the subject of possibility. However, the two concepts are different, and thus it is important to clarify them individually before using them together.

Principle of Sortal Plenitude: "In infinite time, any *sortal* possibility is actualized."

As we saw, Hintikka writes:
> The possibility of a particular cloak's being cut up is a possibility concerning an individual object, and not a possibility concerning kinds of individuals or kinds of events... Aristotle apparently has to generalize also with respect to individuals. That this is what he does is strongly suggested by *An. Pr.* I 13, 32b4ff.

As we also saw, *An. Pr.* I 13 indicates that possibility can have two meanings, one being to happen for the most part and to fall short of necessity, e.g. a man's turning grey or growing or decaying, or *generally* what naturally belongs to a thing.

As noted, "sortal" here just marks what something has *in general*: A sort, type, kind, or class, with no other technical meaning. A *kind* of possibility is a *sort* of possibility, and for additional reasons I soon give, these are really the possibilities with which Aristotle is concerned, even if he speaks elliptically. Read literally, however, this sortal version is subject to the same criticism that the simplest version is subject to. In saying this, by the way, I have just given an immediate example of how in English we speak elliptically, too, of "types," because I simply said "...subject to the same criticism..." rather than "...subject to the same (type of) criticism...," which is what I really mean. Nevertheless, every reader has probably taken the point to be the same.

Hence, *kinds of* fantastical possibilities like "Certain kinds of golden retrievers could sprout wings, catch bats, fly to the moon to bury the bats there, and return with a satisfied grin" would be realizable in an infinity if Aristotle intended the Principle merely to be elliptical for the Sortal Principle. Naturally, this is absurd. Thus, as Hintikka and I read Aristotle, we need to combine the two preconditions, both with respect to being genuine and to being sortal, and make them explicit. This takes us to the final and best version of the Principle.

Principle of Genuine Sortal Plenitude: "In infinite time, any *genuine sortal* possibility is actualized."

Obviously, by adding "genuine" (or "real") to "sortal", we restrict the domain of the Principle much more plausibly—indeed extremely powerfully I would argue—to things or events that could exist, given "laws of nature" or natural history or the like. Aristotle's way of putting this in the *Dramatics* is "possibility in accord with probability and necessity," as we see shortly with citations when disambiguating the notions of possibility for the Northern Greek. In cases without eternal individuals, Hintikka's further underlying assumption is that the type of thing or of event (for which the possibility is relevant) is eternal even if members of the type are finite; otherwise we run into the same absurdity we saw above, where we make claims about possibilities of things that do not or could not exist. The Genuine Sortal Principle, therefore, does *not* cover cases of real but "accidental individuals (of finite duration)" that are supposed to actualize a *particular* possibility, e.g., being cut before burned or vice-versa in the case of a particular cloak. Rather, this final and best formulation of the Principle only entails that at least one member of the kind actualizes the possibility at some point in time, not that every member of the kind does (which Hintikka emphasizes at 1979, p. 115). Some pertinent examples might be:

- (Cloth) coats (as kinds) are cuttable.
- Animals can run.
- Broiled fish can be eaten with gusto.
- Teenagers can dance.
- However, not: Beth may have a stomach-ache tomorrow, or angels can both dance on the head of a pin and simultaneously debate the Ontological Proof (this would not count as "genuine" because angels are, like witches and warlocks, presumably only figments of our imagination, of which more later).

It will be helpful and at times crucial to keep the best version of the Principle in mind as we discuss the issues, although the most elliptical version can be used if an object or event is eternal. Otherwise, one of the other versions, and ideally the last, must be used, or at least must be implied even if an elliptical version is employed. I explain the Principle more as we go through the historical discussion, starting with the reactions to Hintikka. Before doing that, however, let us cover the different senses of "possible" for Aristotle, because, as mentioned, the word is also a source of confusion and of arguments at cross-purposes.

Aristotle's Senses of "Possibility"

Hintikka speaks of the definition of possibility but all he really means by that is a "working characterization" (p. 110, *Time and Necessity*).

It is the tautological description stating, in short, that possibility is whatever is not impossible. To my knowledge, Aristotle never defines possibility the way he defines, say, tragedy, following biological-type definition, similar to the definitory approaches outlined in the *Posterior Analytics*.[16] At least six senses or descriptions exist, along with two other, broad formulations from the already-mentioned *Prior Analytics*, and I describe them from what appears to be the widest span to the narrowest.[17]

I should first indicate that "possibility" is not a substance, strictly speaking, for Aristotle, and functions as an elliptical expression at times for, say, "possible event." We will see the text for this in, e.g., *On Interpretation* 9, when "possible events" are discussed. In other words, "possible" (*dunaton/endecheston*) is often an adjective or an accident, in his terminology. Given his metaphysics, one cannot have an event without a subject to act or be acted upon, so "possible things" must also be an appropriate combination and presumed source of the simpler term "possibility." The abstracted form that is treated as if it were a substance (but in the sense of being a subject of a proposition) is given in *Prior Analytics* 1.13, 32a18-20, when Aristotle writes: "I use the *terms* 'to be possible" and 'the possible' (*to endechomenon*) of that which is not necessary, but, being assumed, results in nothing impossible."[18] I discuss this sense more within the context of the upcoming various senses of possibility for the Northern Greek, but the crucial point for the moment is that "possible" and "possibility" are

---

16   Cf. Scott, *Aristotle on Dramatic Musical Composition*, 2018, especially pp. 153-4, for a summary of the differences of these types of definition for Aristotle.

17   I mean "widest to narrowest" from the perspective of thinking. From the standpoint of reality, however, the widest may be "according to nature," because there are obviously many aspects of reality that no one has ever thought about and that no one will ever think about.

18   Translation by A.J. Jenkinson, in *The Complete Works of Aristotle*, ed. Jonathan Barnes, Vol. 1 (Princeton: Princeton University Press) 1984, as are other passages from the *Prior Analytics* unless noted; my italics.

used in a variety of ways by him, and we cannot mechanically establish in advance what one meaning the terms will always have in his corpus. We can only pay close attention to the context and purpose of any argument within which the terms are applied. With these caveats, then, we can speak for the sake of brevity of (mere) "possibility" and "possibilities."

(1) *Conceivability*

As noted before, possibility means, or is entailed by, "conceivability," as it often does for us and as it has meant for some philosophers going back at least to Parmenides.[19] We sometimes call this fictional possibility or story-telling, especially insofar as a thought or tale does not obey laws of nature (cf. *Dramatics* 25.1460b11). An example would be that Cyclops is a half-god, and eats, or will soon eat, some Greek sailors, or that autumn leaves float upwards en masse and re-attach themselves to the twigs of trees from which they originally fell. Another would be that Aunt Barbara sprouts wings, flies to Mars in two seconds, and returns to the dinner table with red rocks to entertain some bored nieces. Conceivability may be impossible in nature.[20] Hume's

---

19   To augment my previous comments in this regard, I should add that G.E.L. Owen, in a seminal article "Plato and Parmenides on the Timeless Present," makes a seemingly stronger claim about Parmenides: "...he wants to reason about whatever it is that can be a subject, whatever it is that can be talked and thought about. And he contends that if we have such a subject it *must* exist, since if it did not exist we should not have anything to talk about [my italics]" (*The Pre-Socratics: A Collection of Critical Essays*, ed. by Alexander P.D. Mourelatos, Garden City, NY: Anchor Press/Doubleday, 1974, p. 272; orig. published in *Monist* 50, 1966, 317-40).

20   As Hintikka says:
>For him [Leibnitz], "possible" meant the same as "distinctly intelligible." [*Nouveaux essais sur l'entendement humain*, II, xxx, Sec 4]. Of course, the mere fact that things of a certain kind are distinctly intelligible does not suffice to guarantee that there is, has been or will be things of this kind (1979, p. 116).

One might think that Hintikka recognizes then the difference between a merely conceivable possibility and a truly realizable one, which I discuss in a mo-

case of the billiard balls, which I discuss more below, is a famous, or infamous, historical example in a philosophical setting. There is, of course, also conceivability that does follow natural law, such as "Eva might take a trip next year to China," and this will take us to the next sense. However, before moving to that topic, I should emphasize that Aristotle himself is not sympathetic to mere conceivability entailing in and of itself true or real possibility. As Hintikka recounts, Aristotle mentions a geometrical case where we might *say* that the sides and the diagonal of a square *can* have a common measure but that this will *never* occur (given, presumably, the Pythagorean theorem).[21]

(2) *Believability*

Possibility means, or is entailed by, "believability," for example, to return to the just-mentioned example, "Eva may go to China next year." This shows an overlap with conceivability and how the notions can be synonymous at times. Another example is "Joey, who is very greedy, may murder his very wealthy, old father." This is a notion found in *Dramatics* 9, when Aristotle says:

> it is the function of a dramatist to relate not things that have happened, but things that may happen (*dunata*), i.e. *that are possible in accordance with probability or necessity... What is possible (dunata) is **believable** (pithanon);* we do not believe that what has never hap-

---

ment, and at times he suggests a difference. For example, he says "by 'possible' he [Aristotle] understood more than merely 'conceivable'. He seems to have thought of 'possibilities' as something not unlike 'natural tendencies'" (1979, p. 113). These seem to become the "genuine possibilities" for Hintikka, ones that could be realized given ample time and nothing preventing them. However, Hintikka will ignore some of the conceptions of possibility that I list, and concentrate, e.g., on logical and physical possibility (and conceivability) in the modern sense, concluding that "conceivability implied for him [Aristotle] realisability somewhat in the same way as it did later for Descartes" (1979, p. 137). Missing some of the other meanings of possibility is one reason, I believe, that Hintikka takes a difference stance on some related issues from my stance, as this section on Statement 3 later demonstrates.

21   Hintikka, 1979, p. 113.

> *pened is possible, but things which have happened are obviously possible—they would not have happened, if they were impossible...* there is nothing to prevent some of the things that have happened from being *the **sort** of things* that may happen according to probability, i.e., that are possible.²²

First, if an imaginary event has never happened or at least has never been experienced (like Aunt Barbara sprouting wings and flying to the moon), then it may be conceivable but it probably is not believable. Second, "the *sort* of things" is important here because if a real-life Oedipus killed his father, he cannot then kill again the same father now or in the future. Aristotle thereby indicates that a son killing his father is the *sort* of thing that can happen. (Notice, by the way, how effortlessly Aristotle glides from "some of the things" to "the *sort* of things.") Clearly, this kind of possibility *qua* believability is more grounded than mere conceivability, which can be as fantastical as anything one can imagine. Aristotle obviously realizes that people believe many things that have not occurred in nature, such as stories about the gods, which, to emphasize, means that sometimes conceivability and believability overlap and get confused with one another (cf. *Dramatics*, 25.1460b30-61a2). This takes us to the next notion of "possible."

(3) *Permitted by nature*

Possibility means, or is entailed by, "allowable given the laws of nature." I assume that Hintikka intuited this when he said, as noted, that possibility for Aristotle was more than just conceivability but also suggested "natural tendencies." This common use of possibility actually can include things or events or states that in other contexts are *necessary*. In this context what is necessary is also possible *in the current sense*. As Aristotle says at *Prior Analytics* I 13, 32a20: "We say indeed, homonymously, of the necessary that it is possible."²³

---

22   1451a36-b33; my translation following Janko, and my italics and bolding.

23   Transl. A.J. Jenkinson. Homonymous means for Aristotle the same

This notion of possibility is what I assume Aristotle may also mean in the passage in the *Dramatics* just examined: "*possible in accordance with probability or necessity.*" If the possibility is not in accord with natural necessity and probability, we hardly grant that the possibility is realizable (although gullible teens growing up on a steady diet of comics and fictional movies may grant differently). I assume here that this sense of possibility could be a subset of "believability," given that the contexts we are concerned with in this book are ones that involve discussions and hence beliefs. Nevertheless, I grant that natural possibilities exist which have not been recognized and which will never be recognized. Thus, those possibilities will never be believed, but they will be irrelevant for our purposes, and consequently I do not insist that this third notion of possibility is a subset of believability from *all* perspectives.[24]

(4) *Contingency*
Possibility in the sense of contingency is "to be or not to be," as Shakespeare says. In *Metaphysics* IX 8, in the middle of the (partial) Not to Fear argument, Aristotle says:

> Every potentiality (*dunamis*) is at one and the same time a potentiality for the opposite; for, while that which is not capable of being present in a subject cannot be present, *everything that is capable of being may possibly not be actual. That, then, which is capable of being may either be or not be; the same thing, then, is capable both of*

---

term being used to mean something different in different contexts. He gives the example of "sharp" in *Topics* I 15, 107b24-6, and states:
> Sharp differentiates sound from sound, and likewise also one body from another [dull] body... it forms differentiae of genera that are different without being subordinate to one another [because a material body is not in the same genera as that of sounds].

24   This is one reason the narrowing of scope in the senses of possibility I list are said to be "from one perspective." There may be other perspectives in which the natural possibilities are wider than the conceivable ones. "Truth is stranger than fiction."

being and of not being. And that which is capable of not being may possibly not be; and that which may possibly not be is perishable [my italics] (1050b8-13).

An example of this would be Randy, who is sleeping, possibly running for exercise after he awakes and eats breakfast. He may not run. Aristotle's passage not only shows that potentiality (as capability) is related to possibility, at least in this context, but that the meaning of possibility *qua* contingency is different from the third sense of possible as merely allowable by the laws of nature (including laws of science that might be accurately called necessary). The reason is that Aristotle immediately adds: "Nor can anything which is of *necessity* be *potential*" (1050b18).

The reader might complain and say that Aristotle is using "potential" rather than "possible," but we will see a number of times in which possibility and potentiality are treated interchangeably by Aristotle, as they are here.[25] Like contingency, potentiality is said to be at one and the same time a potentiality for the opposite, and the ontological nature of the context is confirmed when Aristotle says at the end that "that which may possibly not be *is perishable*." Only things that are real (and that have potential or not) are perishable, and the comment would be absurd if Aristotle were presupposing fictional constructs. All of this follows, perhaps, the sense of possibility that Broadie highlights. As she reports, "In *Prior Analytics* 1.13, 32a18-20 Aristotle writes: 'I say that the *possible* (*tò èndechómenon*) is that which is not necessary, but which, if we suppose it the case, has no impossible consequences" and she adds "what the sentence just quoted explicates is **'possible' in the sense of 'contingent'**, i.e. 'neither necessary nor impossible'."[26] The rest of I.13 supports her claim (e.g., 32a37).

---

25 See Makin, *op. cit.*, pp. xxii-xxvii, for an in-depth discussion of the use of potential, capability, possibility and the like, and how they are sometimes different and sometimes overlap.

26 *Passage and Possibility*, p. 16; my bolding. Brentano seemingly thought this passage meant something wider, more akin to my "conceivabil-

All of this in effect captures what I claimed earlier, that the contradictory of necessary is "non-necessary." Again, "non-necessary" can be sub-divided into "impossible" and "non-impossible" with the latter containing "possible" and "non-possible." As Aristotle suggests in the *Analytics*, start with the contradictory of necessary; rule out then the path that is "non-impossible (and its consequences)"; and you are left with "possible" (or "non-possible," but since we are dealing with possibility then considering something under the rubric of "non-possible," whatever that might be, is irrelevant at the final step). Whether or not, however, the formulation in the *Analytics* necessitates temporal existence or not for the modals, as in Theta 8, is an interesting question that I shall not pursue. Aristotle may well have used a more general sense of the modals in the logical treatise than in Theta 8, one which still follows, though, his core notion of necessity as "that which cannot be otherwise." Suffice it to say that with the notion of perishability, as noted in the passage we just examined, and the focus on the sun and stars, clearly there is a temporal, ontological aspect to the modal notions in Theta 8.

What needs emphasis now is that in this sense of possibility qua contingency, less common in everyday discourse, **it is confusing or incorrect to say** *"It is possible that (vital) George will die."* An exception would be if one intends to mean that he might die at a very definite time, say, tomorrow at noon by a firing squad because an intended reprieve is denied. Saying without qualification that "George might die" while using "might" *in the sense of contingent* or "It is possible *qua contingent* that George will die" is improper, because one thereby suggests he might not die (given the meaning of contingency). This is obviously improper because we know that all human beings—indeed, every kind of animal—*must* die. More properly, then, a specific temporal reference or equivalent qualifying context should be expressed or assumed when one says or hears "George might die."

---

ity." I address this more in discussing his position with respect to possibility and potentiality.

Statement 3

Again, possibility *in the sense of contingency* assumes that both options—"x" *and* "not x," that is, "to be *and* not to be"—are open.

Presumably, given Aristotle's typical examples, both sides of a contingency still follow laws of nature. Some earthly substances move (or not). The man *qua* "prime mover" hits a stone with a stick (or not). If contingency does not assume laws of nature and is used in cases of mere conceivability that can include supernatural fantasies, Aristotle's (and our) senses of "possible" get even more ambiguous. Take a modern case: "It is (contingently) possible that Wall Street will be flooded by a hurricane." Although this sense of possible *qua* contingent is, on the surface, not exactly the same as the second sense of possibility above (meaning "believable"), nevertheless, it is consistent with that second sense (and with the third sense, obeying natural laws). Whether the flooding occurs or not depends on the future interplay of the very complex natural laws and meteorological circumstances. Moreover, although we know now that it is improper to say simply "It is (contingently) possible that dogs will die," it is debatable whether we can say, strictly speaking, whether a particular street in lower Manhattan contingently gets flooded 50 years from now. The whole area may be razed by a new construction project 20 years from now, and the street disappears before the next hurricane or heavy rain. After the razing and street removal, contingency, or the two contrary options suggested by contingency, presumably become irrelevant for the object that no longer exists. The flooding of the street in the remote future may only be therefore a possibility in the first three senses—conceivable, believable, or allowable (by nature)—which takes us to the next notion of possibility.

(5) *Immediately realizable*
Possibility means "immediately realizable (although not yet realized) given relevant conditions or requirements" such as a certain street existing and a storm approaching. Another example is that Michael possibly becomes a concert pianist, after he has studied and performed for

many years. Strictly speaking, it is incorrect to say that a baby is possibly (or potentially) a professional musician, perhaps to the despair of professional musicians who are new parents. The reason comes from the example that Aristotle himself gives in Theta 7, that earth is, strictly speaking, not possibly or potentially a man—too many intermediate steps remain unfulfilled, one being that earth becomes sperm first.[27] Aristotle even shows that a series of possibilities (or potentialities) is serially needed when he describes learning and applying knowledge:

> One who is learning a science knows potentially in a different way from one who while already possessing the knowledge is not actually exercising it... the learner becomes from one potential something another potential something (for one who possesses knowledge of a science but is not actually exercising it knows the science potentially in a sense, though not in the same sense as before he learnt it)."[28]

Similarly, if Henry is beginning to be quartered by the King's knights on horseback, and nothing arises to stop the knights as they begin to race in separate directions and the very strong, correctly tied ropes begin to tighten, we do not say while speaking sensibly that Henry might die (or it is contingently possible that he will die), but that, indeed, he will or must die (and in about two to five seconds). There seems to be no immediately realizable condition, or set of conditions, that would allow him to live, and so we would only unreasonably or metaphorically say "He *might* (contingently) live," as in "His soul will live in heaven (rather than in hell)." If this were a fictional scenario, as in a Hollywood film, of course four marksmen could kill the four horses before they really begin to accelerate, but the assumption is that this is a real case with no fantastical Robin Hood-type scenario in play. This fifth sense of "immediate realizability" could be a refined category of the third and fourth senses of possibility (permitted by nature and contingency), because the conditions are such that the

---

27   Theta 7, 1049a1-3; a14-15.
28   *Physics* VIII 4, 255a33-b4.

possibility indeed truly gets fulfilled, if nothing blocks the realization. That is, a child prodigy named Wolfgang Gregory Brahms may fail at the last moment and not become a concert pianist for any number of reasons. Perhaps he wins so much money in a lottery that he decides to live a decadent life travelling for decades or his hands get mangled in a horrible accident immediately before his first professional concert. Thus, this fifth sense arguably presupposes at least some of the others in the ways noted, whereas the more basic, or broader senses, like "conceivability" do not necessarily presuppose the more restricted sense like "immediately realizable." Mere imagination not only displays great leaps of logic but an immense lack of concern for practical considerations. However, explaining deeply any mutual interdependence of these varieties of possibility is a project for a later date, if ever.

(6) *Permitted given a maximum power*
A sixth sense of possibility exists, which continues the relation of capability (or potentiality) to possibility suggested already, and I am indebted to Broadie for exploring it in enlightening ways. Possibility means, or is determined by, "maximum capacity" (*De Caelo* I 11.28b12-20). The person who can lift 100 talents, Aristotle says, has the capacity to lift 2 talents, but, he implies, not 175, if 100 is truly the maximum. Thus, it is possible the person could lift 2 talents but not 175. Capacities and their related possibilities in this sense are natural, and are in some ways restricted by natural considerations. This may be a sub-category of the fourth or fifth sense above, although it might be incumbent on the person expressing this type of possibility to say in what respect the "maximum" holds. Aristotle states, quite aptly, that in terms of sight the person who can see the smallest grain is actually the one who has the relevant maximum capacity. "Superior sight is of the smaller body" (*De Caelo* I 12 281a26). Is the "maximum capacity" for concert pianists a capacity for more works in their repertoire or for the fastest tempo that they can play or for any other number of less mechanical but artistically important matters, e.g., the ability to inter-

pret musical compositions in the most varied or stylistically appropriate ways? Perhaps the relevant maximum is a capacity of all or most of those considerations or perhaps a multitude of relevant maxima exist. Since the Principle of Plenitude does not seem to require this notion of capacity and its related possibility, I leave this topic and the related questions as is.

Recall the two meanings of "possibility" in *Prior Analytics* 1.13 discussed with respect to Hintikka because he explicitly relies on them: (i) to happen for the most part but to fall short of necessity and (ii) to be indefinite. Aristotle also might be thought to imply by contrast indirect meanings to possibility when he states that "impossibility" has two senses: "First, where it is untrue to say that the thing can ever come into being, and secondly, where it cannot do so easily, quickly, or well" (*De Caelo* I 11, 280b12-14).[29] The first sense of "impossible" appears to correspond (in the sense of being the opposite) to the sense of not "allowed by nature," my third sense of possible above, and the second sense of "impossible" roughly (as an opposite) to "immediate realizability," my fifth sense.

Mere Conceptual Versus Genuine Possibility

I apply now some of the insights above and then assume throughout this book that mere conceptual or fictional kinds of possibilities are a different matter from genuine possibilities. Insofar as merely conceptual ones do not reflect natural possibilities they are not covered by the Principle of Plenitude.

Modern scholars, who have grown up with possibility *qua* (distinct) conceivability as their notion of possibility, in accordance with Leib-

---

29   Transl. J.L. Stocks, op. cit., *Complete Works*, Barnes.

nitz, Hume and Descartes,[30] have assumed that Aristotle likewise meant conceivability by possibility. It is unsurprisingly, then, that the scholars would find the Principle unpalatable. Recall Descartes's famous "cogito, ergo sum" ("I think, therefore I am"). This dictum is ambiguous and on one reading is perfectly natural. If someone thinks, he or she must exist. However, on another reading, it prioritizes the thought rather than the existence, and reverses the true ontology. For Aristotle, merely conceiving of something in and of itself does not lend credence to the possibility of its existence. As he says:

> To rely on thinking is absurd: ...One might think that one of us is bigger than he is and magnify him *ad infinitum*. But it does not follow that he is bigger than the size we are, just because some one thinks he is, but only because he *is* the size he is. The thought is an accident."[31]

Therefore, Aristotle's better dictum is: "I exist; therefore I think, and

---

[30] Hintikka (p. 116, "Necessity, Universality and Time in Aristotle," in *Articles on Aristotle: 3. Metaphysics*, ed. Barnes *et al, op. cit.*) gives the source for Leibniz, and also ironically establishes *in Aristotle's thought* the root of possibility as "conceivability" for subsequent thinkers like Aquinas, Kant and Bertrand Russell. As I have begun to show, though, this is merely one of the senses of possibility for the ancient Northern Greek and is more Platonic or Parmenidean.

[31] *Physics* III 8.208a14-19 (transl. R.P. Hardie and R.K. Gaye, in *The Complete Work,* ed. Barnes, Vol. 1). It might be replied that this example is not conclusive because Aristotle is apparently arguing only against the view that a potential infinity is possible while the actual, separable infinity is not. Given this, it might be said further that thinking a potential infinity creates that possibility and thus that conceivability does create possibilities. However, Aristotle immediately adds that magnitude is not infinite in the way of magnification in thought, and, moreover, he has said that even a potential infinity in terms of addition of magnitude does not exist "separately" (cf. 206b20). No one denies that *imaginary* possibilities are created when imagination is at play. The issue is whether real possibilities result, and I do not believe we can ever arrive at a simple principle to determine in advance when the imagination is coupled with enough justified pragmatic memory to claim that a thought is a real possibility. Sometimes it is; sometimes not. The conceptual and practical combinations are too immense, and creativity too wide-ranging, to establish limited patterns in advance.

therefore the idea (as an idea) exists." Equally well Aristotle could say "I eat (or walk or dance or sing or sleep), therefore I am." Cartesians prioritize thinking because of concerns with sense data, mistakenly feeling pains in a foot that had been amputated, and immaterial souls, of which more later. Yet people exist when only sleeping and not thinking, so conscious thinking cannot be prior to existence, ontologically, although it might help establish numerical identity. A fetus might be in a drug-induced state for medical reasons until it is born and then held in an incubator for months, at which point it slowly starts living independently and then consciously thinks for the first time. Surely we would say that the individual existed before the intellect.

Leaving aside Leibniz for later, I now contrast Aristotle's approach with Hume's (in)famous example, according to which thinking that a normal billiard ball could strike another normal billiard ball and *not* cause the stationary one to move under normal conditions is a possibility for Hume, the mere conception of which counts as evidence that such a strange event could happen.[32] Considering additional passages

---

32   Hume says:
The contrary of every matter of fact is still possible; because it can never imply a contradiction, and is conceived by the mind with the same facility and distinctness, as if ever so comformable to reality.
  [He adds:]
Motion in the second billiard ball is a quite distinct event from motion in the first: nor is there anything in the one to suggest the smallest hint of the other... When I see, for instance, a billiard ball moving in a straight line towards another; even suppose motion in the second ball should by accident be suggested to me, as the result of the contact of impulse; *may I not conceive, that a hundred different events might as well follow* from that cause? May not both these balls remain at absolute rest? May not the first ball return in a straight line, or leap off the second in any line or direction? All these suppositions are consistent and conceivable. *Why then should we give the preference to one which is no more consistent or conceivable than the rest?* (*An Enquiry Concerning Human Understanding*, as reprinted

in Aristotle's texts that I examine shortly, Aristotle would reject that the billiard balls ever act this strangely in typical circumstances, at least given natural capabilities as we know them, and by "striking" I do not mean that the first ball comes perfectly to rest just as it touches the stationary ball, leaving no force to cause the stationary one to move. Nor are we considering the type of case where the stationary ball is pinned by the cushion(s) so it cannot move. Nor, to take another more obvious example, will the following (conceptual) possibility be actualized: The billiard balls by mere contact simply by themselves cause under normal conditions an atomic explosion that destroys half of the earth. If one can imagine the first conceptual possibility and claim that the imagination is evidence that the event can occur, why not the second? Why stop there? Why does the collision not destroy our whole solar system? Nor, to revise an earlier example, would a conceivable possibility ever occur in which Jeff in California turns into a werewolf, hurdles the Pacific Ocean in a leap, turns into an opera lover looking like Russell Crowe wearing formal attire, attends a performance at the Sydney Opera, reverts to a werewolf, and returns home with a second leap, no matter what the temporal duration of the universe and despite someone's ability to depict this episode in a film.

Here I diverge from Hintikka, whose views on natural or genuine possibility strikes me as foreign to good Aristotelian empiricism, for rea-

---

in *The Empiricists: Locke, Berkeley and Hume*, Garden City, NY: Anchor Press, 1974; pp. 322 and 325-6; my italics).

Hume will then seemingly reverse himself and emphasize experience as the way to give preference to one of the thoughts, but the crucial point here is that possibility appears to be most fundamentally represented as conceivability, with the results of previous ball-collisions giving no special precedent, *in this passage*. For Aristotle, the previous results of billiard balls colliding *would* give a very strong preference to the second billiard ball being moved or not, in a certain direction or not; recall, e.g., the discussion in the *Dramatics* of believability because of historical events. More importantly, the *Mechanics* 24 (855b35-856a1) and 31 & 33 (858a3ff), even if it came from another Peripatetic, shows the type of Aristotelian thinking that would consider Hume's remarks utterly preposterous.

sons I relegate to a footnote.[33] In any event, as emphasized and as I

---

[33]   Recall my comments above on Hintikka focussing on conceivability in a number of passages from different Aristotelian texts except for the *Dramatics*. In part I am sympathetic to what he has to say, but I believe one has to be more careful of the context. For example, he gives an example of Aristotle's psychology and how in thinking, or conceiving, of something the mind actualizes the form (p. 125, *Time and Necessity*). We must be very wary, though, of how we extrapolate that kind of comment on Aristotle's part (assuming it was his settled doctrine) to his mature metaphysics. Consider the following.

Hintikka says that "the Aristotelian view is foreign...to the modern way of thinking of natural necessity and natural possibility...[for] there is nothing... physically impossible about golden mountains nor (apparently) anything biologically impossible about unicorns; and *yet we certainly do not expect ever to find them actualised*" (p. 117, "Necessity, Universality...", *op. cit.*; my italics).

Now, maybe I do not have a modern way of thinking, but I find this comment of Hintikka's puzzling because we might indeed expect to find golden mountains and unicorns actualized *somewhere in the universe over infinite time*, admittedly if not in our lifetime, while being very faithful Aristotelians. What amounts to the same, we would not be unduly surprised if we discovered that golden mountains and unicorns existed at some point in the distant past, maybe on a heretofore undiscovered island or planet. If a rhinoceros (which of course also has one-horn) and a gigantic diamond can exist, surely unicorns and golden mountains *could* exist, at least at some point in the history of the entire universe, unless I am unaware of scientific laws that rule out the formation of such massive amounts of gold. Indeed, it might have been, or might be, not only that unicorns and golden mountains existed or will exist, but that *the self-same unicorns capered, or will caper, on these self-same golden mountains*. A large part of the whole planet might be gold, although it would not have the kind of life we have on earth, exactly.

The other option is that the objects are conceived as more generic kinds: four-legged with a single horn, like a rhinoceros, which certainly exist. Nevertheless, this is a significantly different case from Hume's billiard ball scenario, because there has never been evidence for such an event (properly described even at a more generic level as one object forcefully hitting another, unfixed one of the same weight, etc., and not causing it to move). Thus, allowing for past or future unicorns on Aristotle's view does not commit us to allowing freakish Humean scenarios, including one billiard ball causing an atomic explosion during a normal game of billiards. Why the existence of rhinoceros and other horned animals is enough to ground the natural possibility of unicorns but why the imaginary billiard balls is not enough to ground Hume's case as a real possibility, and in general what precisely distinguishes logical or fictional possi-

trust is amply clear by now, Hintikka also realizes that Aristotle could not have accepted the Principle of Plenitude without qualification, although the reason Hintikka gives is not related at times to "realizable conceivability" versus "purely fictional (i.e., contrary-to-natural-law) conceivability." Rather for him "genuineness" pertains to the length of existence, that is, unless I misread him, eternal existence for an individual thing or sufficient existence to have a possibility genuinely attributable to it.[34] For me, a subject, or more importantly, a kind of a subject may be "genuine" even if one of its members has not yet started to exist, as long as its existence would be natural (such as prospective baby that has not been formed yet even as a zygote). I discuss this later.

Support for my views about possibility, and the importance of real possibility and contingency over merely fictional and contrary-to-nature conceivability, occurs in the *Dramatics*. There, in Chapter 9, Aristotle argues that dramatists have the function of expressing what might happen (1451a36-37) and that they may invent entirely, an example being Agathon's *Antheus*, in which the incidents and names are

---

bility from real possibility, is beyond the scope of this book. It is enough to say here that events which disobey laws of nature are excluded from the Principle of Plenitude.

Recent experiments in quantum mechanics show that some particles apparently begin existing out of nothing. Such experiments might be considered evidence that things in general can appear from nothing, because the implication is that new forces, and thus new laws, could just appear, as if by magic. Thus, it might be said that the stationary ball could just "spontaneously" attain a certain force, without changing its weight, etc. However, the technology measuring these sub-atomic particles is still too new, and the findings too recent. When the technology gets better, we will find that the particles come from something already existing. They do not come from (absolute) nothingness.

34   To underscore: One of the reasons I believe Hintikka takes a slightly different approach is that he never appears to pay attention to the *Dramatics*. See, e.g., his section entitled "Conceivability and realizability in Aristotle," (1973, pp. 124-127) in which he cites often very illuminatingly, different doctrines from a variety of different texts but not one from the *Dramatics*.

entirely invented, he says. They do not deal primarily with what has happened historically. Nevertheless, Aristotle does not imply that the invented incidents are contrary-to-fact or merely conceivable, like humans sprouting wings and flying to the moon. The invention of *Antheus* is specified by Aristotle to be in terms of names and natural incidents, not in terms of mere conceivability. "Although only the title of Agathon's *Antheus* is known, the play was thought to be the first tragedy whose characters *did not originate in mythology*."[35]

Aristotle adds that the dramatist can, and by suggestion should, at times incorporate previous actions in their plots. The reason, he says, is that what has happened *could happen*, and, to repeat the passage we saw once before in articulating possibility *qua* believability:

> We do not believe (*pisteuomen*) that what has never happened is possible (*dunata*), but things which have happened are obviously possible—they would not have happened, if they were impossible.[36]

Aristotle does not say that the dramatist *need only imagine a plot* to make the plot possible (or probable), which arguably distinguishes him from some modern artistic figures, including some science fiction writers, with their emphasis often on conceivability (although some science fiction is truly based on science). Unsurprisingly, Aristotle does not in the *Dramatics* speak about the need to know that some plots run counter to scientific laws while others do not. Having common experience seems to suffice, which is to be expected given that drama was created for the Athenian citizens and not only for a highly educated and specialized subculture. The fact, then, that Aristotle emphasizes possibility in terms of what has happened rather than in terms of imagination, gives us another clue that possibility for him is *temporal*, pertaining to realizability at some time, rather than

---

35 John E. Thorburn, *The Facts on File Companion to Classical Drama* (Infobase Publishing / Facts on File, Inc.; New York) 2005, p. 23; my italics.

36 Janko, *op. cit.*, 1987, 1451b16-18.

to mere conceivability, *contra* Parmenides *et al*. Likewise, Aristotle stays away in his recommended dramas from unnatural solutions to endings, like the *deus ex machina*, in part because these solutions are merely imaginary and hence unbelievable at least to those with empirical persuasions. He also distinguishes himself from dramatists of his day who would represent anything fantastical, like visiting the dead in the Underworld, conversing with them, and then returning.[37]

Aristotle also speaks of possibility in the *Dramatics* 9 in a way that does not suggest mere conceivability, as we saw once before from another perspective, but in a way that deserves repeating. As he says, "...it is the function of the dramatist to relate not things that have happened, but things that may happen, i.e. that are possible *in accordance with probability or necessity* [my italics]" (1051a38-b1). There would be no reason for him to add "in accordance with probability or necessity" unless he were trying to exclude conceivable possibilities like fantastical fiction, such as returning from Hades or billiard balls colliding and thereby causing an atomic explosion.

This is all more support for why we should take "genuine" (or "real") possibility in my sense of the word for Aristotle, as being aligned with natural considerations or laws. In short, the Northern Greek prudently excludes from the Principle of Plenitude supernatural or impossible things or events, such as Judith having wings at the same time and in the same respect as not having wings, which even "conceivalists" like Hume would exclude anyway because of the Law of Non-Contradiction. However, Judith sprouting wings (and flying) in and of itself is not a contradiction and so would count as a possibility for Hume, as explained. However, the situation is obviously as improbable as anything one could imagine.

---

37   See, e.g., Aristotle's types of "discoveries" in Chapter 16 of the *Dramatics*; the discussion of how believability is attained in tragedy versus epic in Chapters 23-25; and the final chapter in Scott, *Aristotle on Dramatic Musical Composition*, 2018, for the detailed justification of these claims.

Final Thoughts on Possibility

Possibility is without question a very ambiguous term for Aristotle, and, to emphasize, one must be careful of the sense being used not only in any given argument *but in any given passage.* The Greeks were as capable as we are in allowing a word with different senses to be used even in one sentence (and I gave the example of "play" earlier). At times Aristotle writes as if the necessity of something could be possible (as we saw above when he noted that this use is "homonymous") and other times not. Again, in *Metaphysics* IX 8, he says "... Nor can anything which is of necessity be potential," which given the association of potential with possibility in the same chapter, entails that what is necessary is not possible. This seems paradoxical, because if it is necessary that the planets always move or motion always exists, as Aristotle asserts, is it not potentially the case, that is, possible, that next month planets move or motion exists?

If we disambiguate the meaning of possibility we see that no confusion surfaces. Necessity here in IX 8 is contrasted with possibility *qua contingency.* Yet this is perfectly compatible with the statement that motion (of any eternal planet) is possible next month, if "possible" *there* is being used in the sense of "allowed by natural law," what is functionally equivalent to "homonymous" in *Prior Analytics* I 13. If "possible" is not used in this sense of "natural permissibility" but in (the fourth) sense of contingency above, it is bad English as well as bad Greek, to say "Motion of the outermost stars is (contingently) possible next month." This requires that motion is also not possible, in virtue of the meaning of "contingency. Yet if that motion is eternal and necessary, as Aristotle believes it is, for reasons we will see in great detail, then a contradiction ensues. Never-ending motion cannot be contingent for him. Therefore, we should really say "The motion (of the stars) *must* occur next month" or "The motion can (but in the sense of 'as allowed by nature') occur next month."

Statement 3

We can now make good sense of a troublesome passage regarding the different senses of "possible" that has vexed commentators on Aristotle's modal logic. I offer this merely as an aside, because modal logic is emphatically not my primary concern in this book. Richard Patterson states:

> One final comment on a curious and stubborn textual question: The passage in which Aristotle first begins to discuss possibility propositions (*Pr. An.* A.3, 25a37-b14) is, as Ross remarks, a "very difficult" one. Aristotle says, first, that possibility is said in several ways (*pollachōs legetai to endechesthai*, a37-39), for we call the necessary, the not necessary, and the potential possible (a38-39).[38]

Patterson now impressively goes into a very detailed examination of the various types of logical conversions, which is outside the scope of the Not to Fear Proof. Given, however, my list of six "major" senses of possibility, I believe that the passage above is not problematic, even if the related and subsequently examined logical conversions in the *Prior Analytics* might well be extremely vexing. However, I leave that latter issue to the experts like him. Aristotle here on my reading simply indicates that possibility is an equivocal term, and gives three senses. We already saw above that a natural opposition to "not necessary" is "possible" (and vice-versa), which covers one of the three senses. We also saw that the oddity of using possibility "homonymously" with necessity follows the common practice of people saying that what is necessary (for instance, that I'm going to die) is also possible, whereas to use "possibility" in the sense of contingency in that case is unwelcome. It would mean that what might be the case (that I die) also might not be the case (that I do not die), a fanciful but impossible option because of my mortal nature. This covers the second sense. The only

---

38 Richard Patterson, *Aristotle's Modal Logic: Essence and Entailment in the Organon* (Cambridge: Cambridge University Press) 1995, p. 256. Because I agree and disagree on various claims that Patterson makes in the rest of this book, I should acknowledge in the interest of full disclosure that I studied under him (with great pleasure) at Columbia University.

oddity, then, with the "very difficult" remark that Patterson notes is that Aristotle mentions that "potential" is also used in the sense of "possible" (and vice-versa) but we have just seen some evidence from *Metaphysics* IX 8 that Aristotle treats the two terms to be functionally equivalent at times and we will see Aristotle making that identification other times throughout his corpus. It is just the way the Greeks used the terms, and English speakers often treat them similarly, too. "The drug has the potency for curing you" often just means the drug has the possibility of curing you or, depending on the kind of drug being mentioned, of putting one in a very different psychological state. Of course, there are differences between the two terms at other times. To say that a drug is potent is to suggest it is not merely possible but powerful but this just shows the richness of related terms or of one and the same term. Brentano recognized the identification at times of "potency" and "possible," while noting that in some circumstances they were different. Possibility could be merely "logical" or "rational" or "of thoughts," roughly what I am calling conceivability, whereas potency as the phenomenon associated with actuality had a more definite implication of possible *real* being, with the implication even more strongly that wildly fantastical cases are not at issue.[39] Thus, as

---

39 Cf. pp. 27-30, Brentano, 1975. I present one passage here for convenience, which may suffice for readers interested in what he has to say:

> There is a great difference between what we here mean by the potential [the *dynaton* or *dynamei on*] and what in more recent times is meant by calling something possible **in contrast with real, where the necessary is added as a third thing**. This is a possibility which completely abstracts from the reality of that which is called possible, and merely claims that something could exist if its existence did not involve a contradiction. It does not exist in things but in the objective concepts and **combination of concepts of the thinking mind**; it is a merely rational thing.
>
> Aristotle was quite familiar with the concept of possibility so understood, as we can see from *De Interpretatione*, but it bears no relation to what he calls potential being, since otherwise it would have to be excluded from the subject of metaphysics along

Statement 3

I read the "difficult" passage that Patterson highlights, Aristotle may be suggesting that it is important to cover the conversions for all three senses. However, modal logicians presumably have settled, or will settle, whichever sense(s) he intended to cover and how, if the issue can be resolved given the texts we have. More on this below when discussing van Rijen.

One final preliminary remark: As is clear from *Prior Analytics* I 8 when Aristotle discusses the logical modalities, "there is a difference according as something belongs, necessarily belongs, or may belong..." Aristotle seems to give no priority to one of these three modes. Yet

---

> with being as being true. So that no doubt may remain, he mentions in *Met.* V. 12, as well as in IX. 1, the impossible whose contrary is necessarily true [*adynaton hou to enantion ex anankes alethes*] (*Met.* V. 12. 1019b23). The possible object [*dynaton*] which is associated with this impossibility is distinguished from the potential object [*dynaton*] which bears this name because it stands in relation to a power [*dynamis*]. **It is the same only in name and must be distinguished from this potentiality along with the powers of mathematics, a^2, b^3, etc., which are powers only in a metaphorical sense** [*kata metaphoran*]. Thus he speaks here of something which really has potential being. This is based upon his peculiar view that a non-real, something which has, properly speaking, non-being (*me on*), in a manner or [sic] speaking exists insofar as it is potentially, and it is this which leads him to a special wide sense of real being, which comprises as well that which potentially is.
>
> Now, what is this potential thing which, being real, belongs to the object of metaphysics, and which has potential being as opposed to actual being? Aristotle defines it in the third chapter of the ninth book as follows: **"a thing is possible if there is nothing impossible in its having the actuality of that of which it is said to have the potentiality..."** (pp. 27-28; my bolding).
>
> To see more citations for how "possible" and "potency" sometimes overlap for Aristotle, cf. "Potentiality," *Aristotle: Selections,* Translated with Introduction, Notes, and Glossary by Terence Irwin and Gail Fine (Indianapolis/Cambridge: Hackett Publishing Company, Inc.) p. 606.

consider the context and other statements of *Metaphysics* IX 8, when Aristotle argues that actuality is prior in substance and in time:

> ...actuality is prior [to potentiality] in a higher sense also; for eternal things are prior in substance to perishable things, and *no eternal thing exists potentially* (1050b6-7)... Nor can anything which is *of necessity* be potential; yet these [eternal] things are *primary; for if these did not exist, nothing would exist* [my italics] (1050b18-19).

Note also *Metaphysics* XI 7, 1063a13-16:

> ...*in pursuing the truth one must start from the things that are always in the same state and suffer no change.* **Such are the heavenly bodies**; for these do not appear to be now of one nature and again of another, but are manifestly always the same and share in no change [my emphases].

These two passages prioritize necessity and equate it with omnitemporality. Thus, by implication, modal logic in the modern sense with "necessity" is arguably primary and more important than both (i) the basic syllogism and (ii) deductions pertaining to mere possibility or to mere assertoric ("to be") statements, at least from one perspective. The basic syllogism is normally taught first in universities and refers to things belonging (to something), not to things *necessarily* belonging or to things that *may* belong. Again, as Aristotle claims, "in pursuing truth one must start from things that are always in the same state..." Here we see Plato's influence on Aristotle, without Aristotle accepting in any way Platonic Forms. Plato avers:

> I take it that anyone with any share in reason at all would consider the discipline concerned with being and with what is really and forever in every way eternally self-same by far the truest of all kinds of knowledge.[40]

More on this topic later in Part 2, but for the moment suffice it to say that possibility and impossibility might be characterized in terms of

---

40   *Philebus*, transl. by Dorothea Frede (Indianapolis: Hackett Publishing Co.) 1993, 58a-b.

necessity, with no circularity. The last, necessity, is arguably fundamental.[41] Again, it is the eternal phenomena that are primary.

Let us continue, now that we have covered the various senses of "possibility," while keeping in mind that in Theta 8, and by extension in both the Principle of Plenitude and the Not to Fear argument, the sense of possibility is clearly the sense of "contingency" that also suggests adherence to nature, or, as Hintikka put it, "natural tendencies." For those fascinated by fiction or drama, it is the kind of possibility "*in accordance with* necessity or probability." It is not contingency as a subset of mere conceivability.

---

41   This is obscured by various passages in the Aristotelian corpus, one of which we already recalled, in which Aristotle says: "We say that that which cannot be otherwise is necessarily so" (*Metaphysics* V 5, 1015a34-34). It seems as if necessity and possibility then are simply defined in terms of each other, and in a circular fashion, but if I am right they are grounded in temporality, or more precisely, omnitemporality, which breaks the circularity. As we just saw Aristotle putting it: "Nor can anything which is of *necessity* be potential; **yet these things are primary**; *for if these did not exist, nothing would exist.*" As both Hintikka and Broadie confirm, for Aristotle "*that which is always, is by necessity.*" As Hintikka acknowledges, "hence the attributes 'necessary,'... 'omnitemporal,' and 'eternal' become virtually equivalent" (p. 111), which means of course that that which is always, cannot possibly be otherwise. Possibility is secondary. Cf. also the end of *Metaphysics* V 5, in which Aristotle suggests that necessity is most primitive because of its simplicity, of not being "two-sided," as it were (sandwiched between necessity and impossibility or involving both to be and not to be, as contingency is). Also see Bäck, 1995, *op. cit.*, p. 90, and Jeroen van Rijen (*Aspects of Aristotle's Logic of Modalities*, Dordrecht/Boston/London: Kluwer Academic Publishers, 1989). Van Rijen also indirectly confirms that necessity is more primitive, although he considers this within the context of modal logic. After noting that necessity is defined in terms of possibility and vice-versa in *Metaphysics* V, van Rijen says: "Be this as it may, if we look at the way in which Aristotle actually works with these definitions or descriptions when showing something to be impossible or necessary, we get a clear view of their meaning and finally a confirmation of the primitivity of the necessity operator" (p. 31).

Reactions to Hintikka's View

According to Jeroen van Rijen's noteworthy history, Hintikka discovered Lovejoy's "The Principle of Plenitude" after Hintikka's initial forays into the topics of necessity and universality, which were inspired by G.E.M. Anscombe's own insights and queries about Aristotelian necessity.[42] Hintikka then continued to use the label, although in his case, as in mine, the Principle carries no theological coloring.[43] Let us start to examine van Rijen's account:

> ...in 1957, Hintikka advanced the hypothesis that the idea that no genuine possibility can remain unrealized forever [the Principle of Genuine Plenitude] was *the main root* of Aristotle's modal concepts... On the logical level, this principle seems to amount to the statistical interpretation of modal operators... (p. 5; my italics & bracketed comment)

By "statistical interpretation of modal operators," van Rijen means that a temporal aspect is implied, which is to say that "possibility" and any opposite such as "necessity" are to be understood as what happens in reality, throughout time "statistically," the former at least once in the history of the universe and the latter always.[44] I should also

---

42   van Rijen, *op. cit.*, 1989, pp. 60-5.

43   I follow Hintikka in this respect, who explicitly cautions of the "Principle of Plenitude" being misleading but uses it as a *"terminus technicus"* (1973, p. 114). Broadie also warns of the theological import of the phrase (*Passage and Possibility*, p. 14), but the reader will observe by the end of this book the irony of the Principle demoting the need for an Unmoved Mover or a god of any anthropomorphic kind on Aristotle's side. Hence, in part because a bit of irony might add some desirable texture to a dry metaphysical discussion, I follow Hintikka's use of the phrase as a mere technical one.

44   Later, van Rijen lays out precisely the Principle of (Genuine) Plenitude as involving at least one occurrence of possibility throughout time, although he phrases it in terms of truth of a sentence that involves the possibility operator; conversely, a sentence that is necessary in the relevant way is "true at all times" (p. 63).

Statement 3

add that van Rijen's statement is ambiguous and implies two different claims for Hintikka: (1) Aristotle held at *some* times the Principle of Plenitude or (2) Aristotle held at *all* times the Principle. In this book, I do not argue at all for the second point, and it suffices for my purposes that only (1) is true. Indeed, Aristotle held different conceptions of possibility and necessity that I have already started to demonstrate are not integrated systematically into one and only one overarching notion, and the rest of this book will provide more evidence for this view. Depending on the context, the modals have different meanings, even if a thinker like van Rijen can demonstrate or has demonstrated that in *some*, or perhaps even in a *majority*, of the domains of discourse, be they logic, epistemology, science, metaphysics, dramatic theory, or what have you, Aristotle had a systematic and unified view. That Aristotle did not have one and only one meaning for all the modal terms in *all* contexts is immediately shown in my list of six senses of possibility where possibility in the sense of "following natural law" allows the general categorical "animals possibly die" to be true whereas possibility in the sense of contingency (where both x *and non-x* must be able to occur for Aristotle) does not allow the statement to be true. Hence, it is very improbable that one over-arching sense of possibility could ever be found that applies to all contexts for Aristotle, both for indexed-to-a-time (particular) claims and for universal ones.

At this point, before examining the evidence for Hintikka's view in the Greek texts, van Rijen cashes out the Principle so that truth becomes integral to the discussion, thereby complicating the matter for us, even if the complication is necessary for his own, logical purposes. The Not to Fear Proof has no concern for truth, which itself, strictly speaking for Aristotle, is a property of categorical sentences. Again, truth is defined as "to *say* of what is *that it is*."[45] Van Rijen then adds that he

---

45   This is not to deny that sometimes Aristotle speaks of the truth of the Principle, only that we can discuss the Principle without complicating the matter by adding truth to it. Van Rijen himself gives three passages where Aristotle speaks of the truth of the (sentence that expresses) the Principle—*Top-*

shall try to give an exposition of Aristotle's modal notions such that modal and temporal notions in *On Interpretation* 9 and *De Caelo* I 12 become clear; Aristotle's notion of necessity in *Posterior Analytics* I 4-6 fits in; and the consistency of Aristotle's intuitions concerning validity of the apodeictic syllogistic moods is preserved as much as possible (pp. 11-2). More precisely, van Rijen specifies that he is committed to five numbered points.

> ...in this study I shall try to give an exposition of Aristotle's modal notions such that[:]

> 1. The exposition is in line with *all* of Aristotle's transparent and unproblematic remarks about and explications of those notions [my italics];"

> 2-5. [in the aforementioned points 2-4 van Rijen notes his planned focus on *De Interpretatione* 9, *De Caelo* 1 12, *Posterior Analytics* I.4-6, along with preserving the validity of the apodeictic moods "as much as possible," while finishing with the bulleted point (5), namely, the maxim that "mistakes may only be imputed to Aristotle's theory if his words admit no other natural meaning"] (pp. 11-2)

Curiously, when then discussing Hintikka, van Rijen ignores the stress on "genuine" that I showed is crucial to Hintikka's stance and that van Rijen had at least noted in passing, as we saw at the beginning of this section. As I have begun to show, Aristotle himself omits what is possible *qua* merely conceivable and implicitly considers the scope of the Principle of Plenitude to apply only to *genuine possibility,* actualizable by real things or real events, at least if they last infinitely via a kind. Thus he would only accept the two versions of the Principle of Plenitude that have "genuine" in them. Again, this is not to say that van Rijen has completely missed Hintikka's use of "genuine," only

---

ics VI 6 (145b27ff), *Metaphysics* IX 3 (1047a12-14), and the opening sentence of *Metaphysics* IX 4—but van Rijen also gives a number of passages where the Principle is expressed more simply, only in ontological terms (pp. 70-1). I examine these passages later, especially with respect to Barnes's discussion of whether Aristotle actually held the Principle.

that he under-emphasizes the relevant scope of possibility, namely, to what is real or possibly real, whereas logic, whether assertoric or apodeictic, is concerned primarily with validity and with how terms in general can be used in forms of reasoning. Thus, terms in merely fantastical imaginations might be used in reasoning, but may never be actually referring to a being that has, does or will exist. For example, the following is valid: "All minotaurs are killers of centaurs; All killers of centaurs are lovers of Athenians; therefore, All minotaurs are lovers of Athenians" which is bArbArA,[46] and perfectly valid, although of course not sound. In some ways, then, logic for Aristotle has a broader scope than metaphysical discussions and one should not be surprised if Aristotle's modal senses change (say, to *de dicto* from *de re*).

Van Rijen also ignores the types of possibility given in the *Dramatics*, as noted in my list of six major senses. Hence, although he might be very successful in his enterprise with respect to modal logic, given its typical scope, he has hardly given a *complete* assessment of the uses of possibility in the Aristotelian corpus, if that was his purpose and, on at least one reading of his aims, it is (note again his first bullet point). Moreover, while complimenting van Rijen on the excellence of his analysis of *De Caelo* and *De Interpretatione* (which was used by van Rijen to undercut part of Hintikka's overly optimistic argument that the type of possibility in the Principle of Plenitude is the basis of *all* modal contexts), Patterson states that van Rijen's:

> treatment of modal syllogistic is very selective, however, covering only the "apodeictic" moods of *Pr. An.* A.8-11, and these not in great detail. More important to him is the reconciliation of the *Prior* and *Posterior Analytics* on a certain point about the requirements of scientific demonstration, namely, that whereas in the latter an apodeictic conclusion requires two apodeictic premises,

---

46   "BArbArA" is the form "All a's are b's; All b's are c's; therefore All a's are c's." "All" or a universal affirmative statement is abbreviated by "A," and the three "A" statements are given the mnemonic "bArbArA" or "Barbara."

the former allows that in some cases an apodeictic conclusion is obtainable from one apodeictic and one assertoric premise (as in Barbara *NAN*).[47]

Patterson goes on to demonstrate how van Rijen's reconciliation is not necessarily completely successful, for reasons that are much too detailed to try to summarize here (cf. Patterson, pp. 102-6). I mention all of this now because it helps show that van Rijen's attempt to establish a new systematic use of modals across *all* contexts in Aristotle, at least on one reading of van Rijen's explicit goals, is yet again unsuccessful, following the centuries of thwarted attempts to achieve this Holy Grail.

However, even if van Rijen can resolve the difficulties that Patterson mentions, which may or may not be orthogonal to the issue of a single use, or to a single set of consistent meanings, of the modalities across the whole corpus, I myself have given already *prima facie* evidence against anyone ever showing Aristotle to be using the modal terms univocally in all contexts. I say this in spite of my admiration for Aristotle as a thinker who tries to systematize *as much as possible*. However, (i) the complexity of reality, (ii) the various disciplines in which the terms are used, and (iii) the manner in which people in general and philosophers in particular use the terms ambiguously do not permit a single, unified meaning. A related attempt at a similar Holy Grail in aesthetics, to show that Aristotle had one meaning of *mimēsis* across his dramatic theory, much less across his whole corpus, has been shown recently to be probably equally unobtainable.[48] The forced attempts to come up with a single meaning across domains

---

47   Patterson, *op. cit.*, p. 102. Given the explanation of bArbArA just provided, I only need add here that "NAN" means that the first premise is said to be Necessarily the case, symbolized by "N"; the second is the typical assertoric "All," symbolized by "A"; and the conclusion is also "Necessarily" the case.

48   Cf. Scott, *Aristotle on Dramatic Musical Composition, op. cit.*, 2018, esp. pp. 250-66.

have caused great difficulty in understanding the related theories. There are too many contexts, problems and different historical uses of the Greek term at Aristotle's own time to allow one to pick, say, "imitation" as the one and only correct translation of *mimēsis*. It will simply make hash of, for example, the discussions of music, which has nothing (other than at times other music) to be "imitated"; likewise, when a dramatist creates a play with no historical character and with everything made up, no or very little "imitation" *per se* occurs. All of this strongly suggests that "express," one of the original meanings of *mimēsis* in the 5th century BCE, is the better translation in the musical discussions, and "impersonate" is better in other, especially dramatic contexts. To give another example that returns us to "play": The attempt at the Holy Grail for a unified approach to modalities no matter what the context would be similar to readers in 3025 trying to make systematic and univocal sense of "play" as found in the example already introduced, in a theory of culture written before 2025, when most other texts were destroyed because of nuclear war: "Nick plays Creon tonight in the play *Antigone*, but his wife Barbara (named by her parents in honor of formal logic!) cannot attend because she has to play her tennis match, nor can their oldest daughter attend because she has to play the violin in her concert." I defy any reader to establish a univocal sense of "play," even when the three occurrences as a verb are used in one sentence, which means we are ignoring "play" as used in other books and contexts. Instead, the individual settings and usages, including here the direct objects of the verbs, give the different meanings in a nanosecond and no English-speaker is confused a jot; likewise with the Greeks and *mimēsis* or the modalities.

To summarize: Given everything I have seen in Aristotle's texts and in the secondary literature, and given the outright inconsistency between, for instance, the sense of possibility as "allowed by nature" versus the sense of contingency, as explained amply, I doubt that anyone will ever establish one over-arching univocal sense for each of the respective modalities, or even a set of compatible and consistent set of senses, as van Rijen seems committed to finding in all of the various disciplines in the Aristotelian corpus. Moreover, to reiterate, given van Rijen's lack of analysis of possibility as used in the *Dramatics*, even his first bullet-point-goal was not fulfilled. Let us grant that his other explicit goals (in bulleted points 2-4) were satisfied, *contra* what Patterson suggests and merely for the sake of argument. Still, they leave open whether Aristotle had in metaphysical or meteorological settings a temporal sense of possibility, involving kinds (over an eternity). Some of van Rijen's own remarks indicate that this was how Hintikka ultimately settled the matter, as we shortly see.

Let us, though, first address van Rijen's more detailed treatment of Hintikka and the Principle of Plenitude:

> ...Hintikka's interpretation of Aristotle's modal logic, as sketched above, lends itself to a neat and simple formulation. In its ontological version, its kernel is formed by a temporally relative version of the *Principle of Plenitude*:
>
>> (34) If something is possible at a time t_i it is actual at t_j for at least one time $t_j \geq t_i$, with '$t_j \geq t_i$' as short for '(is) identical with or later than t_i'.
>
> This principle and the common interrelations between the modal notions of possibility, necessity and contingency make the whole story. As one of its consequences it has the already noted corollary
>
>> (35) what is the case at all times $t_j \geq t_i$ is necessary at t_i.
>
> The *Principle's* counterpart **on the semantic level** obviously takes the [following] form [where M means the possibility operator and φ is any sentence]
>
>> (36) if M_ϕ is true at t_i then φ is true at t_j for at least one time $t_j \geq t_i$.
>
> Given definition 6 [which was given by van Rijen as "necessarily φ if and only if not possibly (that) not φ," and which was symbolized by him as follows, with "L" as the

necessity operator, with "-" as negation, and with "<—>" as "if and only if": $Lf <—> -M-f$], we get the following truth condition for apodeictic sentences:

(37) L_ϕ is true at t_i if ϕ is true at all times $t_j \geq t_i$.

Together with their converses, (36) and (37) amount to the so-called *statistical interpretation of modal operators*... On the ontological level, this seems to square with Aristotle's remarks to the effect that **the past is necessary**.[49]

Again, for this book we need only focus on the ontological formulations, but I mention van Rijen's "semantic" version in order to help the reader make sense of his next remarks, which contain the critical statements that I demonstrate below do *not* undercut Aristotle holding the Principle of Plenitude in ontological discussions.

...a modification...must be introduced that has been proposed by Hintikka himself in order to clear away a too overt discrepancy between what [van Rijen's interpretation of] the model [described above] says in its present form and the explicit affirmation of the existence of never actualized possibilities in Aristotle's work. A notorious example of the latter is *De Interpretatione* 9, 19a12ff., where Aristotle says that it is possible for a particular coat to be cut in two halves even if it will actually not be cut but wear out. The patent defect of the model is repaired by restricting the reach of the *Principle of Plenitude* to *kinds* of beings [with van Rijen citing Hintikka, 1973a, p. 100, namely, *Time and Necessity*]. Then the *Principle* becomes:

(38) no possibility with respect to a being of a certain kind can forever remain unrealized with respect to every being of that same kind.

---

49 Pp. 62-3; his italics but my bolding and bracketed explanations. Van Rijen does not give the reason why the past is necessary for Aristotle but the obvious reason is that the primary notion of "necessary" for Aristotle is "what cannot be otherwise," and for Aristotle one cannot go back and change the past. Time is uni-directional.

In that case, a specimen of a particular kind of coat may be said to have the possibility of being cut if and only if there is or will be a specimen of **the same kind of coat** that is or will be cut.

This new version of the model was formulated by Hintikka in ontological terms. The parallel alteration of its semantic counterpart is absent in Hintikka's work. Yet, it is clear that the required adaptation cannot be brought about without a considerable loss of the simplicity in which the original version excelled. To begin with, there are no truth conditions available for modally qualified sentences if no further structure is assigned to them. The adapted model seems only to account for the logic of modal operators as far as they are prefixed to categorical sentences, and thus loses a considerable part of its original scope. **Besides, it is not immediately clear how, in the adapted model, one can still account for the alleged necessity of temporally definite, true sentences.** For why should the sentence 'it is necessary that coat $\underline{a}$ is cut at t_i' be true if coat $\underline{a}$ is cut at t_i, when other coats of the same kind are not cut at t_i so that it is possible for coat $\underline{a}$ not to be cut at t_i according to the revised version of the *Principle of Plenitude* [what I, Scott, have called the Principle of *Sortal* Plenitude]? **Since Hintikka did not raise this question, he did not answer it.** What we do know is that...Hintikka has become more reserved as to the role of the *Principle* in Aristotle's thought. In *Aristotle on Modality and Determinism*, for example, he even went so far as to abandon every attempt to construe Aristotle's modal theory as a closed or coherent doctrine, but proposed rather to approach **it in terms of competing paradigms of which the statistical model is one**. In the same work Hintikka also appears to consider another way of dealing with Aritotle's [sic] never realized possibilities by distinguishing *total* from *partial possibilities*. Total possibilities, being those possibilities for the realization of which all the conditions are fulfilled, cannot remain unrealized. Partial possibilities, being those possibilities for the realization of which not all the conditions have been satisfied, may remain unfulfilled. The case of the uncut coat can now be resolved by classifying its possibility of being cut as a partial possibility only, a knife and/or an agent wishing to cut the coat being absent.[50]

What I show now is that these critical remarks miss a better interpretation of Hintikka's, or Aristotle's, view about kinds of possibility, an interpretation that, once recognized, makes the Principle of (Sortal Genuine) Plenitude extremely powerful, and impervious to van Rijen's objections. Again, this is not to claim that Hintikka was, or should have been, successful in his initial attempt to demonstrate that the Principle was "the main root" of *all* the modalities for Aristotle, no matter the context, merely that, as van Rijen himself recognizes, the ontological Principle could have been **one of the paradigms** that Aristotle holds in *some* contexts. Indeed, as van Rijen proceeds in his book, he gives (especially on pp. 70-1) a number of passages in the Aristotelian corpus that he admits are strong evidence that Aristotle holds the Principle but in restricted domains. Thus, successful as van Rijen was in arguing against a couple of passages that Hintikka claimed presuppose the Principle, and as successful as van Rijen was in undercutting Hintikka's initial project pertaining to the Principle being the main root of all the modalities in all circumstances, his final conclusion with respect to the concerns of the Not to Fear Proof is that Aristotle could still be holding the Principle in ontological contexts. Indeed, others like R.M. Dancy have seen that the Principle of Plenitude is embedded in the part of the Not to Fear Proof that is explicitly given in *Metaphysics* IX 8, even though Dancy in no way explored the theological ramifications of that Principle, especially concerning the

---

50   Pp. 64-5; my bolding, but van Rijen's own italics. In my view, Hintikka is (if anachronistically) conflating, or restating, possibility *qua* "immediately realizable" with "total possibility," because they amount to the same thing. They both require that certain conditions must be fulfilled before a possibility can be actualized.

conclusion that we should not fear the sun and stars stopping.[51]

Let us start at the top of van Rijen's critical remarks and proceed through them or at least through the important ones. First, the formulation he gives as "(38)"—"No possibility with respect to a *being of a certain kind* can forever remain unrealized with respect to every being of *that same kind*"—is a fair representation of Hintikka's position, if we do not mind that van Rijen uses "kind" in lieu of "genuine" (recall how "genuine" and "kind" seemed to perform the same duty for Hintikka at times, even if, at other times, "genuine" suggests sufficient temporal existence). As we saw, this means for Hintikka that, if something is possible for X, it must occur at least once in eternity with respect to a member of the kind that X properly belongs to, even accepting that X and the other members have finite existence. Otherwise, if X existed always, or any action it engages in is eternal, it would be necessary, and if it never existed, it would be impossible. That is how simple (and yet powerful) Aristotle's notion of necessity is in this (ontological) context, and, as van Rijen acknowledges, it then allows Hintikka and Aristotle to evade any criticism based on the cloak not being cut in *On Interpretation* 9.

A brief excursus, which will confirm all of this, might be useful while on this topic of kinds. Patterson himself gives a similar reading in mentioning in passing Hintikka's Principle of Plenitude, although Patterson, like van Rijen, does not emphasize the importance of "genuine-ness" for the kind of possibility (but perhaps they both assume it): "Any *kind* of event that can occur will occur at some time [his own italics]" (p. 180). This is the Principle of *Sortal* Plenitude. Patterson

---

51   R.M. Dancy, "Aristotle and the Priority of Actuality," in *Reforging the Great Chain of Being: Studies in the History of Modal Theories,* ed. Simo Knuuttila, 73-115 (Dordrecht: D. Reidel) 1980, pp. 102 and 107. As Dancy reads Aristotle in IX 8: "(P5) Everything that can be ϕ at some time is ϕ, where 'ϕ' is replaceable by anything or nothing. (P5) is the Principle of Plenitude" (p. 102).

Statement 3

adds:

> It is obvious by now that I do not believe that *any temporal definition of Aristotelian modalities* can be correct. The basic notion of necessity involved in the understanding of Aristotelian necessity statements of the *Prior Analytics* has to do with the relations of entailment and (in)compatibility among the natures and attributes introduced by subject and predicate terms. So, for example, *cloaks can be cut up, because there is nothing about being a cloak that precludes being cut up*. This holds for any particular cloak whether or not it is ever cut up, and *even if it happens that no other cloak is ever cut up. Facts of this sort will explain the omnitemporality (or non-omnitemporality) of various statements,* **and not vice versa** [my italics and bolding] (pp. 180-1).

Now, if Patterson is only concerned about logical entailments and the use of necessity in a temporal sense in the *Prior Analytics*, then I may have no disagreement, although, given the precise goals of this book, I have not needed to examine those very complex and very precise entailments. However, if he intends to claim, as the example of cloak suggests, that no temporal notion of necessity exists in Aristotle in other arenas, then I must point to a discussion already mentioned of the sense of possibilities found in the *Dramatics*, where believability and possibility not only arise because of what Aristotle says has happened in the past, but where possibility is said to be "in accordance with probability and necessity." That is, Aristotle even in a treatise about drama or fiction is not considering merely logical (and sometimes fantastical) possibility but the type of possibility in accordance with what we would call natural law, i.e., in accordance with the temporal past. Morever, and what is more important, in Theta 8, as we see amply throughout this book, actuality precedes potentiality more fundamentally than the reverse (because Aristotle recognizes that both can be said to be primary).[52] Thus, I must contest the italicized

---

[52] Makin confirms this in great detail in *Aristotle Metaphysics Book Theta* (2006), *op. cit.*, saying: "The discussion of priority in substance start-

claims in the above quotation of Patterson. Cloaks can be cut *for Aristotle* because at least one cloak in eternity has been, or will be, cut. In other words, *because* of their actual nature (being made of cloth, etc., one point that Patterson agrees with) and having been cut at least once as members of a kind, or to be cut at least once in the future, they *can* be cut up, not the other way around. By "other way around" I mean that taking into account some cloaks during some finite durations does not necessarily convey all of the relevant possibilities, because none of *those* cloaks may have been cut. I cover this issue more when discussing Aristotle's evidence for the ingenerability of the universe.

The paradox of how cloaks can they be cut if they do not *first* have the potential to be cut is resolved by Aristotle in the middle chapters of Theta (because in one way the potentiality does precede the actuality). However, as this book hopefully makes clear, if no cloak *ever* (and this truly means "ever," in infinite time) were to be cut up, then it would be *impossible* that a cloak could be cut up for Aristotle (and this entails that some cloaks, no matter how many, exist across infinity and are obviously different numerically if the same in species). Facts that are seen in a finite duration do not explain omnitemporality for Aristotle, or at least in the way Patterson suggests, who focusses at the end of the passage above on the omnitemporality of *statements*, whereas Aristotle is focussing on the omnitemporality of the things themselves. That is, finite facts do not explain, or are not prior to, omnitemporal facts; it is just the opposite, *contra* Patterson. Analogously, as we saw briefly before, and as we see much more in Part 2 regarding this whole issue, Aristotle follows Plato in terms of the primacy of eternal things and the associated best kind of knowledge. A day can (like a finite action) be abstracted or derived from infinite time, but one cannot

---

ed at 1050a4 has covered three instantiations of the actual-potential schema: change-capacity, substance-matter, and eternal-perishable. Aristotle has sought to show that in each case the item which is an actuality is prior in substance to the item which is a potentiality" (p. 217). Thus, actual cutting is prior, in at least one very important way, to potential cutting.

Statement 3

"construct" as it were, infinite time from days (because the infinity is always "open"). Another way of putting this is that "must be"-claims for Aristotle are prior ontologically to "is"-claims, even if logicians for heuristic purposes start with the easier "is"- or "to be"-claims. However, let us wait until Part 2 to address this issue with the precise textual evidence.

Since Patterson does not discuss the Principle of Plenitude or its ramifications for the issues of this book in any more detail, I turn to Sorabji for the remainder of this excursus, who similarly understands that the issue at hand is about kinds, and explores more the topic, although he phrases the issue instead as "cloaks in general" (rather than "kinds of cloaks"). Despite the faulty positions that Sorabji had pertaining to related matters, as discussed throughout the last section on Statement 2, he gleans correctly the relevance of kinds, saying:

> ...the important thing to stress is that Aristotle refuses to apply the principle of plenitude to things of finite duration. The evidence for this is abundant. We have already noticed that at *Int.* 9, 19a9-18, he distinguishes between things which are for ever active and things like a cloak. The latter is capable of being cut up, even if it never will be. We have also observed that the argument for plenitude in *Cael.* I 12 is not *intended* to be applied to transient things, even if Aristotle's oversights would leave room for an unintended application... Aristotle's view is stated particularly clearly, though representatively, at *Phys.* III 4, 203b30: 'In *everlasting things*, there is no difference between being possible and being the case.'[53]

> ....he [Hintikka] claims that Aristotle would still apply the principle of plenitude in a way to non-everlasting things, such as particular sea battles and cloaks. And he suggests

---

[53] Sorabji notes other passages, but the ones given suffice, although because the Not to Fear Proof is mostly given in Theta 8, I should add that Sorabji perspicuously writes also about that chapter: "Finally, in IX 8, 1050b7-8 and 20, the principle of plenitude is endorsed, but only in connexion with everlast-

that Aristotle could have done this by treating the statement that there can be a sea battle tomorrow, or that a particular cloak can be cut up, **as an elliptical statement about sea battles and cloaks in general**, that at least one sea battle will be fought, and at least one cloak cut, some time or other. I am not sure that I see convincing evidence that Aristotle intended this (Hintikka cites *An. Pr.* I 13, 32b4ff.). But at any rate the important thing is that such a use of the principle of plenitude would no longer mean that Aristotle was 'adopting...by implication anything like a deterministic doctrine' (*Time and Necessity* 201). So used, the principle would not authorize us to argue in deterministic fashion from the possibility that this cloak will be cut at noon tomorrow, or that a sea battle will take place then, to the conclusion that this cloak will then be cut, or that a sea battle will then take place. We could only argue in non-deterministic fashion to the conclusion that some time some cloak will be cut, and some sea battle will take place.[54]

Our concern in this book is not with the issues of determinism (which has different meanings for different scholars) or truth-values of future contingents. We can ignore, therefore, the last point in that regard, although Sorabji's conclusion is very sensible and one that I can accept. The crucial issue for us is the point about the Principle being elliptical for cloaks and sea battles *in general*, or as Hintikka and I would put it, for kinds (or sorts) of cloaks and kinds (or sorts) of sea battles. Later I will give additional evidence why Aristotle is speaking of "kinds" (of things) that can last eternally, which I trust provides the reader with the "convincing evidence," to use Sorabji's phrase, that Aristotle did intend to cover individuals that are not, in themselves, eternal but whose kind is eternal.

---

ing things" (p. 136). Because the Not to Fear Proof is only concerned with the "everlasting" universe, already we begin to see the soundness of the Proof in Aristotle's eyes.

54 Sorabji, *op. cit.*, 1980, pp. 132-3; his own italics but my bolding.

Statement 3

In summary: It is enough for Hintikka and Aristotle that one cloak be cut in infinite time to satisfy the Principle of Sortal (Genuine) Plenitude, and other cloaks having the same existential properties or results merely provides confirmation. Naturally, we must assume that the cloak is not made of some kind of "uncuttable" metal, e.g., "suits of armor" for knights. The "reach" of the Principle was never intended to apply to one thing for one particular time, like noon tomorrow. The Principle is more like a scientific law than a claim that any particular possibility for any particular object can be asserted for any particular (and restricted) time, even if in common parlance we say "It is possible that the game will begin late tomorrow." The game in this instance is being treated as an "accidental particular," not a member of a kind *per se*, or the sense of "possible" is not necessarily the ontological sense but one of the other senses discussed in list of six. Alternatively, we can add the notion of "accidental possibility" to that list and understand that, just as there is no science of accidents for Aristotle, the Principle of Plenitude is *not* intended to cover "accidental possibilities" that would ostensibly be realized during infinite time.

This concludes the excursus.

The adapted semantic model (dealing with truth) with which van Rijen concerns himself in the passage we started examining is therefore simply irrelevant in this context, being instead for him a matter of modal logic and modal possibility, or at least of semantics, and *not* ontological possibility. That the Principle of Sortal (Genuine) Plenitude may be restricted then to tenseless statements such as "Coats are cuttable," is perfectly what Aristotle had in mind for the "reach" of the Principle, to use van Rijen's term. The Principle is not saying, to reiterate, that if a coat has the possibility of being cut tomorrow at 14:00, then in infinite time it will be cut, for indexing the time to a particular moment makes the qualification after that time inherently absurd, especially if the coat is destroyed beforehand. Thus, van Rijen's worry about "how, in the adapted model, one [with the Principle] can account for the alleged necessity of temporally *definite*, true sentences" is completely irrelevant. This takes us to his next remark:

> For why should the sentence 'it is necessary that coat a̲ is cut at t_i,' be true if coat a̲ is cut at t_j, when other coats of the same kind are not cut at t_j so that it is possible for coat a̲ not to be cut at t_j according to the revised version of the *Principle of Plenitude* [what I myself have called the Principle of Sortal Plenitude]? **Since Hintikka did not raise this question, he did not answer it** [my boldfacing and comment in brackets].

First, Hintikka did not need to raise the question because on the assumption that necessity is omnitemporality, the question is absurd. No *particular* coat cutting for Aristotle could ever be necessary *in that sense*. Particular coat-cuttings are only finite and thus only contingent. If Aristotle ever speaks of the necessity of a coat-cutting at a particular time, say noon tomorrow, he must be using "necessity/necessary" in a different sense and with some unstated assumptions, either as "what cannot be otherwise" or in the sense of hypothetical necessity already discussed above, e.g., x is necessary if y is to achieve a certain goal or become a certain thing. Necessity cannot now mean omnitemporality, and truth is different from reality.

Finally, with respect to van Rijen's ending remark that Hintikka eventually proposed to treat Aristotle's modal theory "in terms of competing paradigms of which the statistical model is one": This means that Hintikka was wiser in renouncing the attempt to make all contexts subservient to the Principle of Plenitude. Hintikka restricted it to just a few arenas at most. However, this still allows him, as indicated, to be very successful in one of those arenas, at least dealing with ontology or metaphysics. Whether Hintikka achieved *complete* success even with respect to the more limited contexts, however, I do not, and need not, say. It is enough to give the evidence in the Greek corpus to show that in certain ontological contexts, for example, cosmology, the Principle was championed by Aristotle. Even van Rijen himself ultimately ap-

Statement 3

proves of those texts.[55]

In short, although van Rijen has revealed some flaws in Hintikka's attempt to make the Principle, and its temporal notion of the modalities, the one and only model in Aristotle's entire corpus, he has not undercut the claim that in some contexts Aristotle holds the Principle, nor has he shown the weakness of the Principle of *Sortal (Genuine)* Principle. As such, this formulation is extremely powerful, and arguably even intuitively correct, at least if Aristotelian metaphysics and the correct meaning of contingency are presupposed.

---

55   *Op. cit.*, pp. 70-1.

Broadie on the Principle of Plenitude

I now examine the position of Sarah Broadie. She argues that Aristotle accepted the Principle of Plenitude, which she calls A´ to exclude (modern) theological coloring. However, in her *Passage and Possibility*, she also argues that Hintikka improperly focusses on kinds when he should be focussing on modality as it applies to individuals or particulars. I am unable to determine with certainty from her deep, complex, and wide-ranging work, however, the exact scope of possibility in the Principle for her apart from the obvious things like planets that last eternally for Aristotle, but the scope appears to include at least organic substances that (as species) last forever. Broadie herself also does not recognize anything like the Not to Fear Proof, in spite of the other premises being very obvious ones in Aristotle's texts. However, like Hintikka, she acknowledges all of them, directly or indirectly, at one time or another. This in one way is unsurprising because in the 1990's she continued to try to interpret the Unmoved Mover in a way that resolves many of the perennial dilemmas, reflecting an admirable, if, in my view, overly optimistic, desire to protect the manuscripts as if they are all representative of Aristotle's mature thought.[56] She

---

56   Cf. Broadie, "What Does Aristotle's Prime Mover Do?", a paper presented to the Society of Ancient Greek Philosophy, Boston, Massachusetts, December 28, 1994, available at
http://orb.binghamton.edu/sagp/239/
with an alternative version published in French in *Revue Philosophique* 2, 1993, 375-411.

The "admirable...desire," however, needs one comment, and the arguments of this book give me the confidence to assert the following. We should strive to protect the complete manuscripts at all *reasonable* costs, and we should assume that they might have been Aristotle's view when he died. However, the qualification "all reasonable costs" is crucial. When the doctrine of the Unmoved Mover or anything else is so absurd or in conflict with so much else in the corpus, then in my opinion we must indeed question whether the doctrine was held always by Aristotle, as Jaeger wisely understood, and we must be willing to protect the integrity of his mature thought, even if

Statement 3

also follows Hintikka in focussing on intricate and difficult issues of truth, determinism, modal logic and the related Aristotelian metaphysics. Hintikka's sub-title of the crucial *Time and Necessity* (1973) is "Studies in Aristotle's Theory of Modality," and Broadie's sub-title of her own *Passage and Possibility* (1982) is "A Study of Aristotle's Modal Concepts." It is enough, though, in my view that these two scholars did extremely illuminating and ground-breaking work in those areas, for one person cannot solve all of the problems of Aristotle's logic and ontology in one, two or even five books. Without their contributions I would never have seen the Principle of (Genuine Sortal) Plenitude and how it is the key to the Not to Fear Proof.

In what follows, I primarily address Broadie's criticisms of Hintikka's use of "kinds" to substantiate the more plausible version of the Principle, namely the Principle of Sortal Plenitude.[57] However, subsequently, I take a slightly different approach to arrive at the same basic result that both she and Hintikka arrived at concerning the Principle and contend that Aristotle decidedly holds it in the most fleshed-out

---

some manuscripts (in this case at least part of *Metaphysics* Lambda) are thus shown to be earlier works that Aristotle disavowed. I cannot evaluate in this book where I disagree, and *agree*, with Broadie's SAGP Boston paper, because it is too complex and original to summarize easily here. Also, in private correspondence she informed me that she has changed her mind on some of the conclusions and is revising the paper, but that it is unfinished.

57   Broadie also informed me privately in 2017 that she has given up one of the basic tenets in *Passage and Possibility*, namely, that Aristotle had only one core notion of possibility (à la Hintikka, it appears, before he himself also decided that Aristotle had multiple paradigms). Thus, I need not address some of her views in *Passage and Possibility*, and assume that she, like Hintikka, can be essentially successful with respect to Aristotle holding A´, as long as the temporal notion of possibility holds in the relevant, ontological contexts. Because Broadie's work is highly respected and cited in this whole history, because others may not realize her position has evolved, and because they may follow her reasons in *Passage and Possibility* (as a search on the Internet shows has happened), I believe for their sakes it is important to clarify how Hintikka and myself could still advocate that the scope of the Principle is to kinds and to individuals but individuals *as members of a natural kind*.

form explained above. Before, though, explaining how artificial kinds like cloaks, which may not appear eternal for some readers, are also unproblematically in scope, I examine the relevant part of *On Interpretation* 9 that has exercised so many commentators.

Broadie questions Hintikka's claim that Aristotle accepts kinds of possibilities in the manner that Hintikka seemingly needs to accomplish his respective goals. In her own words:

> He [Hintikka] suggests that the possibility that this coat be cut up rests on the general possibility that such things should happen, which general possibility entails its own realization in some instance though not in any particular one. But this does not fit well with Hintikka's account of the basic confusion [that attributes the source of the Principle of Plenitude in Aristotle to the supposition that possibilities can be "realized only within this gradually unfolding progression of actual nows"], nor with the form that B′ ["If it is *always* the case that p, then it is *necessary* that p."] takes in *De Caelo*. For why should the alleged confusion operate on the generalized supposition 'Something coat-like is at some time physically divided' so as to generate automatically the corresponding assertion, but leave the singular one unaffected? And in any case, the text of *De Caelo* I.12 puts it beyond doubt that Aristotle is there concerned **with possibilities regarding individuals as such.** Thus his conclusion is not: 'If a type of situation S is always instantiated, then necessarily it is instantiated', where the antecedent does not entail that any one particular object is always or necessarily in the condition of realizing S. Rather it is: 'If it is always the case that **some particular object is** (or: is F), then it is necessarily the case that **that object is** (or: is F)'. And he equally clearly subscribes here to a proposition which entails a corresponding version of A′ ["If it is possible that p, then at some time it is the case that p," Broadie's version of the basic Principle of Plenitude], i.e.: 'If it is possible that an object is and is not, at different times, then *that*

object is and is not, at different times'.[58]

Broadie also addresses the issue of whether modality applies primarily to metaphysics or language for Hintikka, i.e.:

> ...is the possibility primarily relative to the *truth of a proposition* describing the actual situation, or to *the situation* itself...
> [and she adds]
> Professor Hintikka writes as if the difference of level [regarding metaphysics and language, in the context of the sea battle in *On Interpretation* 9] is immaterial.[59]

All of this enters, as mentioned, within her own discussion of various aspects of Hintikka's views with respect to future and past truth, contingency, possibility, necessity, and determinism, and she pinpoints arguable weaknesses, if not fatal flaws, in some of Hintikka's views regarding those various topics. She concludes in one regard:

> If change is unidirectional, and the Aristotelian modal asymmetry of past with future is a consequence of this; and if change is real and directional only *qua* caused; and if [as Broadie has convincingly argued is in the Aristotelian corpus] caused change is change in states of things in the world, not in truth-values of *logoi*: then Aristotelian modality *belongs primarily on the level of things and their states, and is restricted by the general conditions governing the changes of these*. If we look here for a further connection between "always" and "necessarily," "possibly" and "sometimes," we shall not be disappointed.[60]

I completely and emphatically agree with this last whole passage.

---

58   Broadie, *op. cit.*, pp. 55-6, *Passage and Possibility*; my boldfacing and comments in brackets.

59   Broadie, *op. cit.*, p. 117; my comment in brackets.

60   Broadie, *op. cit.*, p. 140; my italics and comments in brackets.

However, any confusion of Aristotle's views on Hintikka's part according to Broadie with respect to the Principle of Plenitude and its source and application is very complex. The alleged confusion involves, or pertains to, a theory of modality for Aristotle that minimally covers the arguments for the infinite existence of the universe in *De Caelo* and the application to future contingents in *On Interpretation* 9 (whether or not there will be a sea battle tomorrow and how one position seems to require determinism and to negate the result of deliberation). The confusion for Broadie also stems from the question whether modality is an "analytic" notion for Aristotle rather than a "synthetic" one (a notion that is relativized to time and the actual world). In other words, one question for Broadie, the last one quoted, is whether modality is primarily metaphysical or natural rather than logical. It would take us far beyond the scope of this work to summarize appropriately her book, including her discussion of whether the Principle of Plenitude is founded on, or is an expression of, logical or metaphysical principles (or both) and how and why Aristotle's views can be plausible (at least from his standpoint, leaving aside modern conceptions of logic and metaphysics). At the grave risk, then, of doing her own views an injustice—and in spite of my agreement with her on many positions—I focus here as much as possible only on her views on time and the modalities (possibility *qua* contingency, impossibility, and necessity) in the *ontological context*, which is all I need for the Principle of *Genuine Sortal* Plenitude and the ensuing Not to Fear Proof. No need surfaces in this very limited context to focus on truth, falsity or determinism (and, e.g., on the difficult views of *On Interpretation* 9 on, e.g., future contingents).[61] In other words, as mentioned, the terms "true,"

---

61 I give one example to show how complex the issues could be if we focus additionally on "truth" and "necessary truth." Broadie says about past events which are now true that on Hintikka's view: "The event itself is of course correctly classified as now necessary, **but only because the statement is necessarily true, not vice versa**. And if we were to tidy other cases into line with this, we should have to say that the necessity of the aether's everlasting motions is not primarily a feature of the cosmos or the aether or its motion, but derives from the fact that 'The aether is in motion' is

"false," and "determined" do not even occur in the Not to Fear proof and so will be left aside in this book.⁶² Nor are "dated future contin-

---

always, hence necessarily *true*. [This means, Broadie continues, that for Hintikka:] **Although truth itself depends on being, the *modality* of being depends on that of truth**" (p. 120, *Passage and Possibility;* my boldfacing).

If Broadie assesses Hintikka correctly, then indeed he is very unAristotelian, for truth is a property of categorical propositions, which for the Northern Greek are thought primarily and uttered secondarily. The reality, as we see throughout this book, for Aristotle does not depend on the thought; rather, the converse is the case, as even Hintikka also seems to emphasize at least in contexts apart from modal logic. How necessity depends on truth, which itself depends on reality, is mysterious indeed, if Hintikka holds such a view. Broadie attempts to illustrate what might be wrong with Hintikka's position in ways much too complex to summarize here. However, I would add that to disambiguate "necessary truth" in this immediate context, assuming the ontological sense of necessary (as that which exists always), we would have to discuss presumably whether a (true) sentence has to exist eternally in order for the truth to be necessary, given that for some sentences like "John is reading" the truth depends on the time at which the sentence is thought or uttered. This takes us into issues of timeless truths, like the Pythagorean Theorem and whether it was true before Pythagoras was born, when no one is thinking the proposition at any given moment in history. At any rate, Broadie claims that Hintikka's view flounders when Hintikka applies his sortal interpretation of the Principle of Plenitude to the future sea battle of *On Interpretation* 9: "it is hard to believe that Aristotle is not concerned above all to uphold the genuine contingency of particular future events *in all their particularity* [my italics]." If "all their particularity" means that Aristotle intended the Principle to apply to each and every unique, accidental event or thing, then I must part ways from Broadie (but that is a different issue from the matter of truth just described). If the phrase has another meaning, then I am simply not sure what it means and how to stand on the issue.

Broadie shows other, apparent problems with Hintikka seemingly identifying "necessity" with "always" or "omnitemporality," and "possibility" with "sometimes" (pp. 120-126). Whether Hintikka has a proper reply to any of these criticisms I leave for the future. I only emphasize that both authors stress (correctly in my view) in ontological discussions the connection between time and modality, even if they differ on some points.

62   A similar problem to the one that Broadie attributes to Hintikka regarding necessary *truth* is entailed by Alfred Tarski's approach, if we drop necessity and focus only on the relation between a true statement and the reality

gent" statements like "A sea battle will occur tomorrow" that are the

---

of the matter. For instance, Tarski claims that his approach to "truth" is Aristotelian in that:
> We should like our definition to do justice to the intuitions which adhere to the *classical Aristotelian conception of truth*... ("The Semantic Conception of Truth," *Philosophy and Phenomenological Research,* 4, 1944, pp. 341-376, p. 342).

However, Tarski gives what is in my view a very unAristotelian T-schema, which, *in effect*, is a definition of truth: "The sentence '*p*' is true if and only if *p*." (Strictly speaking, this for him is not a definition but gives the "material adequacy" of a definition, whatever that means precisely for him.) Yet Tarski is really Platonic in his metaphysics, mathematics, and logic, as the following example illustrates, given that for Aristotle truth is a property of categorical statements and is "to say of what is that it is," all of which entails that without a statement or proposition—which primarily is thought and secondarily uttered or written—no truth arises. Nevertheless, even without statements the reality holds. Take the example "All mature human beings are at least 1.234769877 inches tall." I am surely the first in history to utter this proposition (and if not I will simply add a few more digits onto the end randomly until I utter a distinctly new, never-before-constructed proposition). Yet surely the reality of that proposition held long before I uttered the (true) statement. Hence, truth cannot be the biconditional as Tarksi gives it while claiming to be Aristotelian. As any beginning student of the propositional calculus knows, the biconditional entails the *mutual* interdependence of the two sides of the biconditional. As we see from passages in other parts of this book, and as we already saw Brentano correctly emphasizing for Aristotle, the reality *p* never depends on there being an existing, "corresponding" statement "*p*," unless perhaps what we might call a second-order truth claim is made about another first-order sentence or the like. I do not suggest here that Plato-Tarski is wrong in absolute terms, for that would be another discussion, only that Tarski is *not* Aristotelian in the way he claims he is (although I would argue in another setting that Tarski's conception has gravely damaged sensible thinking about truth throughout the 20th century). Most relevant to this footnote is that Tarski correctly cites Aristotle's notions of truth—"to say of what is that is..."—but then rejects it with the vague complaint that it is not "sufficiently precise and clear" (1944, p. 343), ironically without giving, to use his own criteria, precise and clear reasons why Aristotle's notion is unsatisfactory! Likewise, Tarksi provides no "precise and clear" reason to reject Aristotle's very sensible formulation in "Truth and Proof," given as a Faculty Research Lecture at the University of California, Berkeley, on March 19, 1963, as well as the University of London, May 19, 1966, and included in various monographs.

subject of *On Interpretation* 9 relevant to this book. As just discussed with respect to van Rijen and Sorabji, The Principle of Genuine Sortal Plenitude and the Not to Fear Proof apply only to undated propositions. I will examine some of Hintikka's own words on the purported source of the Principle later because he explicitly admits that he is unsure why it came about for Aristotle and thus any confusion he attributes to Aristotle on the source of the Principle is qualified by his unwillingness to take a firm stance. I myself offer in this book at least one obvious option why Aristotle came to accept the Principle, insofar as it presupposes genuine sortals. It provides the lynchpin for the Not to Fear Proof and allows him to prove the eternality of the universe without the absurd doctrine of the Unmoved Mover of Pure Actuality. Needless to say, that is one very valuable reason.

At the worst for my account so far, Broadie is completely right, and Hintikka completely wrong concerning (the modality of) possibility and the Principle of Plenitude. However, she herself heartily defends the Principle, although with some caveats concerning at least time or relevant material conditions being required for any particular case. Her views on the temporal meaning of the modalities still allow us to arrive at the conclusions of the Not to Fear Proof. Let me explain.

Take a case similar to one we saw before, in *On Interpretation* 9:

> *It is possible that Eva's Milanese cloak with a red triangular wine-stain on the inside pocket is cut.*

Given normal states of the world, and the history of the universe so far, with cloaks not only being cuttable but having been cut many times, and with the Milanese cloak being constructed out of fabric similar to other cloaks, surely the possibility of the cloak being cut exists. Yet then the possibility should be realized in an eternity, given Broadie's A´ (again, the label she uses for the Principle of Plenitude). Yet sadly, the cloak gets destroyed tonight by burning or some other cause other than cutting. Here we have a possibility (of a very natural sort, like a sea battle) that does not get actualized ever, even in an eternity. Broadie would say—if I understand her correctly—that either temporal restrictions or historical states of affairs (or both) must be added to A´ to rule out of scope this particular case of the Milanese cloak being burnt before it is can be cut. Perhaps the cloak was never in its existence next to a sharp object (similar to Hintikka's distinction of the case as a mere partial possibility), but what those exact caveats are for the Principle I will not address, simply because I am not entirely sure of her current stance on these issues. However, I assume that the same caveats could be applied to the rest of the Not to Fear Proof to allow it to pass muster. Moreover, even that is not crucial. Because the universe with an infinite past and with an infinite future is a very different object from cloaks that go in and out of existence, Broadie's criticisms with respect to finite individuals does not impact the Principle of Plenitude insofar as the individual subject of the possibility, the universe, is eternal. *Everyone* agrees that for Aristotle, for eternal things, what may be will be. The Principle and thus the Not to Fear Proof very easily holds for eternal entities or eternal events, even if we have to exclude from the Principle's scope "particular" cloaks (like Eva's Milanese one with the red-wine stain). As both Broadie and Hintikka agree, insofar as any (individual) subject of A´ is eternal, any related possibility the subject has must be realized at some moment in time (as long as the time of the possibility is not inordinately restricted, like "next Monday at noon" but is left open). If the possibility is never realized then it could not have been a possibility (and *a fortiori* it could not be necessary *qua* omnitemporal). Rather it must have been, and be, an impossibility.

To switch now to finite subjects and to reveal further why Hintikka is not seemingly wounded with respect to the *Sortal* Principle by the criticism that Broadie makes, I break down her criticism into two points, and address them serially. The first point, again, is:

> He [Hintikka] suggests that the possibility that this coat
> be cut up rests on the general possibility that such things

should happen, which general possibility entails its own realization in some instance though not in any particular one. But this does not fit well with Hintikka's account of the basic confusion [that attributes the source of the Principle of Plenitude in Aristotle to the supposition that possibilities can be "realized only within this gradually unfolding progression of actual nows"[63]], nor with the form that B′ ["If it is always the case that p, then it is necessary that p."] takes in *De Caelo*. For why should the alleged confusion operate on the generalized supposition 'Something coat-like is at some time physically divided' so as to generate automatically the corresponding assertion, but leave the singular one unaffected?

First, regarding the "alleged confusion": Given that Hintikka says he is not sure why Aristotle proposed and accepted the Principle, his "basic confusion" appears to be recognized and acknowledged. I defer therefore this discussion for a few pages. How Aristotle arrived at the Principle—and whether it stemmed from a confusion, and what that confusion exactly is—is a different issue from him accepting it, which is all I need for the Not to Fear Proof. Without any doubt whatsoever, all three of us—Hintikka, Broadie and myself—emphasize that Aristotle held the Principle, with some unstated assumptions. *The only real issue is what those unstated assumptions are.*

Second, Broadie emphasizes the importance of the "unfolding pro-

---

63   The confusion that Broadie mentions may be the one she describes on p. 53: "Hintikka traces A′ … to a source in deep confusion affecting Aristotle's entire approach to modality. He focuses, in the first place, on Aristotle's method of deciding possibility by supposing-true-at-another-time. In Hintikka's view, Aristotle cannot see how to frame such a supposition without committing himself to the truth of what is supposed…" This seems to suggest that Hintikka is grounding ontology on truth, which itself is simply a property of some categorical sentences, strictly speaking, a topic just discussed in the previous footnotes. If that is correct, Broadie has indeed pinpointed a flaw in Hintikka's position, but, again, because the Not to Fear Proof does not involve truth *per se*, I leave aside this whole issue.

gression of *actual nows*" (my italics), couched in her terms as the uni-direction of time and actual events, which seems to suggest an emphasis on individual events (and their subjects) and not on kinds. The emphasis, she continues, in *De Caelo* is also on individuals, and not on kinds.

I see no evidence, however, that Hintikka would disagree with her on uni-directional time and on actual events in a way that influences this book (and I heartily embrace Broadie's claim, which means Aristotelians do not go backwards in time when it comes to causation). This all means, at least for me, that the crucial issue in this "first point" versus Hintikka pertains to her final question: "For why should the alleged confusion operate on the generalized supposition 'Something coat-like is at some time physically divided' so as to generate automatically the corresponding assertion, but leave the singular one unaffected?" However, if I understand Broadie correctly, the "something coat-like" (whether it be coat, clothing or fabric) is indeed still singular—it is "something" coat-like, not "somethings." Hintikka says (as I understand him) that the Principle of Genuine Sortal Plenitude is really an elliptical statement about kinds that have *individuals* as *members* (of the kind). He does not say that Aristotle would hold the relevant possibilities to apply to general, abstract categories (which may or may not be fictional) or to *groups* of individuals *qua* a group that has no relevant commonality among its members. I think this is all clearer if we go to Broadie's "second point"[64]:

---

64   I continue to this second point even though, e.g., van Rijen and Lindsay Judson ("Eternity and Necessity in *de Caelo* I. 12," *Oxford Studies in Ancient Philosophy*, 1983, Vol. 1, 217-55) have given arguments why Broadie should interpret *De Caelo* I 12 differently and Broadie seems to have accepted some of the replies (from private correspondence). Yet, the replies are different from the emphasis on individuals versus kinds, and even if they have entailments that support Aristotle dealing with kinds or not, nevertheless others may follow Broadie's *Passage and Possibility* without knowing, e.g., van Rijen's work. Thus, to make more precise what I alluded to above, it is worthwhile to handle Broadie's original objection to Hintikka that in *De Caelo* I 12

Statement 3

And in any case, the text of *De Caelo* I.12 puts it beyond doubt that Aristotle is there concerned with possibilities regarding individuals as such. Thus his conclusion is not: 'If a type of situation S is always instantiated, then necessarily it is instantiated', where the antecedent does not entail that any one particular object is always or necessarily in the condition of realizing S. Rather it is: 'If it is always the case that some particular object is (or: is F), then it is necessarily the case that that object is (or: is F)'. And he equally clearly subscribes here to a proposition which entails a corresponding version of A´, i.e.: 'If it is possible that an object is and is not, at different times, then *that* object is and is not, at different times'.

On Hintikka's account, as I understand it, infinitely existing *individual objects* (like the planets and perhaps the universe itself[65]) are, as individuals, already unproblematically within the scope of the Principle, and thus need not be considered as a type. I see no disagreement from Broadie on this precise claim. The cloak is dismissed for Hintikka because it itself does not exist for the infinite time needed to be relevant, at which point he needs to assume the scope is *individuals of the kind "cloak"* (which as a kind indeed could be considered to exist infinitely,

---

Aristotle is concerned only with possibilities concerning individuals, including, and this is the crucial point, individuals that do not last for infinite time.

65   In reply to private correspondence from a reader of earlier parts of this book: The universe as "The All" in a sense may be considered a (single) "subject," because Aristotle argues that there can only be one of them, especially in *De Caelo* II 6 (289a11-12), of which more below. For more on "The All" versus the *cosmos* and the *ouranus* ("heaven") for Aristotle, and how these can sometimes, but only sometimes, be synonymous, see M.R. Johnson, *op. cit.* An argument could be made that the universe *qua* "The All" is the only thing that is truly one of a kind (where the kind is taken to the most generic level). Anything else will always be an individual of a kind with other similar individuals, unless it is, e.g., simultaneously the first and last of a new invention, that is, of an *artificial* kind. However, for example, even the first invented computer was just another instance of a kind of calculating device or of a machine, and thus if we look at the higher generic level, it is not the first and only of a kind. More on artificial construction of kinds, and of higher-level kinds, later.

whether or not Hintikka himself provided the explicit argument for how artifacts can be an eternal kind for Aristotle). Hence, insofar as the discussion in *De Caelo* I 12 applies to individuals that exist in some sense eternally *via their membership in a kind*, that particular discussion, and those (finite) individuals, seemingly fall also within the scope of the Principle for Hintikka and should, as I aim now to show, fall within the scope for Broadie.

As a prefatory remark, though, I believe Broadie has hit upon a problem that I broached before. If indeed the scope of the Principle is only to infinitely existing individuals or to kinds of things (like kinds of cloaks), then it seems as if we cannot speak, in Aristotelian terms, of possibilities of individual, particular objects that do not last infinitely, which indeed seems counter-intuitive. We often speak of the possibility of an individual cloak, *this* one, being shortened (or cut), and *that* pair of shoes getting worn out through heavy walking (which is what Broadie appears to be ultimately stressing when she says "full particularity"), although we will have to balance this consideration with the prima facie implausibility that the Principle applies to every possibility concerning every individual thing at every time and in every circumstance, of which more shortly. For the moment, though, suffice it to say that, as I understand the matter, the Principle is not supposed to include individual cloaks being cut tomorrow at 11:27 a.m. Indeed, by indexing a possibility to a specific time, it becomes absurd to suggest the possibility would happen in an infinity, once that singular, precise time has passed. Aristotle simply could not have been so foolish as to suggest the contrary. Moreover, as we now discover further, even without an indexing, a statement about a particular individual *qua* accident will not be part of science for Aristotle nor will the particular *qua* particular be a candidate for the Principle. As succinctly put in the *Rhetoric*, "individual cases are so infinitely various that *no* knowledge of them is possible."[66]

---

[66]   *Rhetoric* I 2, 1356b32-3; my italics. Transl. by W. Rhys Roberts, in

Statement 3

What is it, then, that allows one finite individual to be in scope and another not? To help settle not only Broadie's claims about *De Caelo* I 12 but the scope of the Principle that Hintikka might have had, and that I myself will propound, we might make the distinction that I have been alluding to, between an individual (of a kind) and a "particular individual" that entails peculiar characteristics or "accidents" in standard Aristotelian terminology. "An accident is an attribute which can belong to a thing and also not belong [but obviously not at the same time and in the same respect]."[67] These peculiar characteristics (whether they involve a certain location or a certain relationship to other things or a certain quality, like being colored differently from all other similar individuals) give a uniqueness that is distinctive to an individual and make it, in effect, an accidental particular rather than a member of a kind, which has "similarities" to the other members, to use Hintikka's term. Essential characteristics such as "animate" and "rationative" hold for an individual as a member of the kind "human being"; blond hair and a scar on the right shoulder make him or her unique as an accidental particular.

To return to *De Caelo* I 12: Aristotle discusses whether anything that is ungenerated can be destroyed (which he denies) or whether anything generated can last forever (which, *contra* Plato, he also denies). He starts the chapter by saying "if certain things have the power both of being and of not being, an outside limit must be set to the time of their being and their not being...[and he adds] *We are speaking of being in all the categories—man, white, three-cubits-long and the*

The Complete Works of Aristotle. Ed. Jonathan Barnes, *op. cit.*

67   *Topics* IV 1, 120b35; my qualification in brackets. Transl. Pickard-Cambridge, in *The Complete Works of Aristotle*, ed. Barnes, as are all other translations of the *Topics* unless noted. My *caveat* is provided, perhaps unnecessarily, so no reader could possibly think that Aristotle would be denying his own Law on Non-Contradiction. An accident like "sore-footed" and its opposite could be held at one and the same time: the right foot might be sore but the left not. In this case, the respect is plainly different.

rest..." (281a29-34; my italics). He then always continues in the chapter while discussing "anything" or "a man" or the like, as if he is only concerned with individuals *of a kind,* even though admittedly on the surface, as Broadie emphasizes, they are typically discussed simply as individuals. The question is whether he ever intends the individual to be a "particular individual" (*qua* accident). Not once, though, in this whole chapter—and this is the crucial point for us—does Aristotle mention a "accidental particular" like Callias or an object with distinctive characteristics or accidents that would make it a particular accident-identified individual as opposed merely to an individual member of a species. It appears to me, then, that even though Aristotle focuses at times or always on "individuals as such," following Broadie, this really means individuals *presupposed* as members of a kind, and not some accidentally distinctive, one-of-a-kind individual, what perhaps Broadie means by an individual with "full particularity." Aristotle says things like "*Put generally*, the argument is this. Let A and B be attributes which can never inhere in the same thing..."[68] All of this seems evidence that the individuals are being thought of *in general*—as individuals of a kind or individuals in general (which was Sorabji's way of phrasing the matter), as opposed to an artificially constructed group (or team) in general with no important commonalities *and* as opposed to unique particulars with peculiar accidents. In other words, "an individual man" might best be taken sortally, as a member of a kind; "Callias" would be the particular individual considered as an absolutely unique singular, who is not a member of the kind "Callias" (even though it turns out there are other men named Callias, for reasons I deal with when taking up artificial kinds, which could comprise a team of men all called Callias).

Aristotle's approach is common, too, in English. Take the case of someone about to say:

---

68   *De Caelo* I 12, 282a14-15; my italics.

Statement 3

All men have 10 fingers.

Naturally, this can be read distributively or not. Are (all the) men sharing the only 10 fingers that exist in the whole world or does each man have 10 fingers (leaving aside the exceptions that prove the rule, like a notorious actress who in 2016 cut off one of her fingers in a boating accident)? Presumably, someone making the statement means that each man has 10 fingers, so a less ambiguous way of presenting the thought is:

A man has 10 fingers (or to be politically correct nowadays and to leave gender aside, ***An individual has 10 fingers***).

Given a certain setting, with the individual already being named, it may be the speaker means John or Kathy, but typically a speaker uttering such a claim means "*any* individual has 10 fingers." "An individual" means in effect "any individual," and is slightly shorter and easier to say, and the statement presents an account of the *general* case, or, to put it in terms of this context, conveys a claim about a species or kind, namely of *homo sapiens*.

Each member of *homo sapiens* has 10 fingers.

Thus, merely because a statement is couched using "an individual" as the subject, we should not assume automatically that generality or sortal nature is being excluded. The focus on individuals in *De Caelo* I 12 seemingly follows this habit. Aristotle indeed speaks at times of finite individuals, as Broadie properly stresses, but it is an individual in general, or one that is representative of a kind (unless, again, the individual exists infinitely in which case no problem exists for either Hintikka's *or* Broadie's view).

Let me put the matter in a different way. As is commonly known, an individual is sometimes considered by Aristotle in three ways. He, she or it can be an individual insofar it has numerical identity. The individual Yiwei is identical (numerically) only to Yiwei, born at a certain time and in a certain place to certain parents. However, an individual can also have "specific" (species-oriented) or generic identity for Aristotle. Thus, Yiwei is identical *as a member of the species* to other humans (in contrast to rabbits) or Yiwei is identical generically *as a member of the genus vertebrates* to rabbits (in contrast to reptiles or to rocks). Thus, truth-claims about an individual often depend upon how one conceives of that individual and the meaning of "same": Is Yiwei the same as a rabbit? If considered generically, yes, but not if considered numerically or specifically. Again, it seems to me that Aristotle in *De Caelo* I 12 focusses on individuals *qua* species.

Hence, Aristotle is not considering individuals insofar as they have numerical identity. They are not being considered as "accidental" individuals with peculiar accidental properties (unless the accident exists eternally, of which more later when I discuss "eternal accidents"). Instead, to underscore, the individual is a *single* member of a *species*. Likewise, the Principle of Plenitude presupposes the same outlook. Both Broadie and Hintikka are therefore correct. Aristotle focusses on individuals but in such a way as to imply claims about other individuals of the same kind (and here one might need to establish the correct kind, of which more soon).

All of this is analogous to Aristotle's doctrine of the causes, which include both individual causes and general causes. "Generic effects should be assigned to generic causes, particular effects to particular causes, e.g. statue to sculptor, *this* statue to *this* sculptor" (*Physics* II 3, 195b25). Notice that (the singular) "statue" and "sculptor" are listed as examples of *generic causes, not* "generic statue" and "generic sculptor," which means that Aristotle is quite happy at times to use a singular noun treated as if it were generic (or, *a fortiori*, "specific") rather than as an "accidental" or unique individual considered as a "this." The "this" (usually *tode ti*) is the particular individual, identified by accidents, "*this* statue."

Moreover, at the end of her book, Broadie seems to rely on sortal accounts, correctly and incisively arguing that for Aristotle any organic substance that is causally generated is always existent in some way, be it "specifically" or generically, and that causal continuity holds with no beginning, e.g.: "Thus to the extent to which causal continuity prevails, to that extent the coming to be of a new complex *kind* is impossible."[69] In my own words, there was always a chicken before an egg, and an egg before a chicken, in Aristotle's first philosophy and biology, *ad infinitum* to the past.[70]

To summarize the debate regarding *De Caelo*, as long as the individuals are being treated as members of the same kind (with the same essential or necessary characteristics), then the claim about the individual is a claim about a member of a kind. Conversely, kinds are only truly existent for a nominalist like Aristotle because of the individual substances that constitute them, or as he puts it: "...the species is synonymous with its individuals" (*Topics* VII 4, 154a18-9). The claim would only make sense were he considering the individuals to have the properties of the species, not considering their peculiar attributes. Those attributes are simply irrelevant.

---

69   Broadie, *op. cit.*, p. 152; my italics.

70   It may even be that for modern science and astronomy we could argue that there was always an *egg-like kind* before the *chicken-like kind*, and a chicken-like kind before the egg-like kind, *ad infinitum*, which handles even for us the chicken and egg paradox (as long as "-like" can be taken up to the proper level of generality, which would mean for us the basic types of life-forms). I discuss this issue more below, including life arising from non-life.

"Kind of Possibility" in *On Interpretation* 9

Like Aristotle, Broadie stresses continuity and discontinuity. What infinitely exists and is thus necessary has continual existence; what never exists and thus is impossible has continual non-existence; what has discontinuity is that which is contingent. Consider now again the case of the cloak being cut in *On Interpretation* 9. Aristotle says there, in a passage that most scholars cite without focussing on the penultimate sentence:

> ...in things that are *not always actual* [that is, that are intermittently or discontinuously actual and that therefore are not necessary[71]] there is *the possibility of being and of not being; here both possibilities are open, both being and not being, and consequently, both coming to be and not coming to be.* **Many things are obviously like this.** For example, **it is possible** for this cloak to be cut up, and yet it will not be cut up but will wear out first. *But equally, its **not** being cut up is also possible*, for it would not be the case that it wore out first unless its ***not*** being cut up were possible. *So it is the same **with all other events that are spoken of in terms of this kind of possibility**.* Clearly, therefore, **not everything is or happens of necessity**...[72]

---

[71] My bracketed comment. I do not claim that Aristotle always associates necessity with omnitemporality, only sometimes. The word "necessity" is ambiguous for him, as shown earlier, and some senses, like "hypothetical necessity," do not entail omnitemporality.

[72] *On Interpretation*, 19a9-19; my emphases and comments in brackets. Transl. J.L. Ackrill (*The Complete Works of Aristotle*, ed. Jonathan Barnes, Vol. 1, Princeton University Press/Bollingen Series LXXI, Princeton, NJ, 1984). Let me give but one example of an excellent scholar who essentially just reads over "*this kind* of possibility." Bäck deals with this passage in an enlightening article that presents in eighteen pages a number of the competing solutions to the various dilemmas pertaining to truth, necessity, determinism, and future contingent statements; he also presents his own solution (Allan Bäck, "Sailing through the Sea Battle," *Ancient Philosophy* 12, 1992, 133-51).

Statement 3

He restates the passage saying "Aristotle then gives his own view... He says that all events that come to be by chance have *this kind of potentiality*, of happening or not happening [my italics; p. 139]." However, immediately thereafter, Bäck says "Once he [Aristotle] has noted that certain events are contingent, he immediately concludes (19a17-22) that chance is saved. Thus he has made a strong connection between future statements and possibility (p. 139)." Notice how Bäck drops the "kind of" in the further account, although perhaps it is assumed (and notice how he uses "potentiality" rather than "possibility," which shows how these terms can function the same for Aristotle and how difficult at times it is to choose one translation or the other). Whether or not dropping "kind of" would make a difference to his ultimate conclusions is too difficult to say easily, and I note it here only as an example of how the "kind of" is not stressed. As I show throughout this book, this is a common practice in English and in ancient Greek. This is similar to the actions like patricide in the *Dramatics* that Aristotle claims individuals (like Oedipus) can do *again*, as I discussed when explaining "possibility" as believability. Ignoring that Aristotle presupposes "kind of" makes that passage ridiculous, suggesting that Oedipus (or anyone) could re-kill his father. Thus, presupposing "kinds," as Bäck seemingly does, is exactly what Aristotle could be presupposing when dealing with individuals in *De Caelo*, as just discussed in showing how both Broadie and Hintikka could both be right on individuals.

On a related matter: Bäck insightfully adds one remark and then cryptically adds another: "Hintikka also thinks that Aristotle makes a strong connection between temporal and modal operators; e.g., if p is necessary it is **true** always, and *vice-versa*... My view provides a way to explain how a particular event can be taken to be contingent, as a particular and not merely as a member of a class of similar events. I would say that appeal to **classes of events** is relevant for determining whether the event in question **is contingent or necessary**, but not to the contingency **or necessity of the event itself** (p. 146; his italics but my boldings)." For once, I wish Bäck had explained more, unless I misunderstand his remark. That is, ignoring truth, if necessity in this context has Hintikka's sense of omnitemporality and the class of events in question are cloaks being cut at some times but not at others, then the *occasional* existence of cutting requires that *any* instance of the kind of coat-cutting is contingent. How is then that "the event itself," say, one particular cutting, could be "necessary," unless "necessary" now takes on a different sense or unless the event were itself eternal (like the circular motion of the outer heavens)? Surely, unlike the necessary movement of the outer heavens (which are necessary because continuously omnitemporal), any particular coat-cutting is intermittent and hence contingent. The only way a coat-cutting could be necessary in the relevant, current sense is if the coat were infinite

This passage is typically discussed—minus the penultimate sentence and its focus on "kind of possibility"—in relation to future contingent statements, truth, determinism and to the famous case of a future sea-battle, which occurs in the same chapter. Clearly, with respect to the final conclusion, not everything happens of necessity for Aristotle. However, the relevance of the passage and especially of the penultimate sentence for our concerns is Aristotle saying *"this kind of possibility."* The implication is that there could be different kinds of possibility other than the kind just noted, because otherwise there would be no need to say anything more than "possibility,"—"this kind of" would be obviously redundant. It is unclear to me, however, whether Aristotle suggests by "this kind of possibility" the kind of obvious contingent possibility like cutting and not cutting, with a positive and negative side both "open" (two possibilities total), or whether he means perhaps "this (complex) kind of possibility," as described fully right before the claim, meaning something which actually has at least three or four options (and, as discussed, I assume "worn out" means destruction like "burned up"). Let us examine the various scenarios.

Scenario 1
"This kind of possibility" involves two options, to be cut or not (or to be worn out or not). These are the two "open" options, to use the phrase of the translator. However, one might argue that this scenario does not really allow Aristotle to get to his conclusion that not everything happens of necessity, because *either* side of the contingency might have happened because of necessity. Depending on the state of affairs for the item to be cut, it was necessary that it got cut (by the scissors that were closing in on it and did not stop, given laws of mechanics) or not (because the cloak had been locked in a drawer, which itself was covered by lava from an erupting volcano and no one and no cutting device were anywhere near the cloak for centuries, until it

---

and the cutting kept going on and on. However, Aristotle rejects infinite bodies. The focus on "truth" has seemingly muddied the waters, again.

finally dissolved).

Scenario 2
"This kind of possibility" refers to two contingencies, each of which is open in two ways, for four total options.
(i) The cloak is worn out.
(ii) The cloak is not worn out.
(iii) The cloak is cut.
(iv) The cloak is not cut.

Like in Scenario 1, though, it is not clear how this would entitle Aristotle to arrive at his conclusion that not all things or events are necessary, because a clever determinist might say that the laws of nature and the material conditions *determined* which of the four options got realized. The determinist need not deny that we can *formulate* contingencies; the determinist arguably only needs to claim that the option which gets realized is realized necessarily, by natural laws and material conditions and as determined by the exact history of the universe.

Scenario 3
"This kind of possibility" refers to a complex, *serial* type of possibility, with four total options.
(i) The cloak is not worn out *and* is cut.
(ii) The cloak is worn out *and* thus not cut.
(iii) The cloak is cut *and* thus not worn out.
(iv) The cloak is not cut *and* thus worn out.

Nevertheless, like Scenario 1 and 2, it is not clear how this entitles Aristotle to arrive at his conclusion that *not* all things or events *are necessary*. Again, the clever determinist might continue to argue that whichever serial option occurs in any given case follows from the necessary, antecedent laws and conditions.

It is absolutely clear, though, that Aristotle gives the "kind of possibility" as a *reason* for the conclusion that not all things or happenings are necessary. Somehow he believes he is giving a counter-example to necessity and as long as the counter-example is a real contingency, then the (ontological) determinist must accept that some things (or happenings) are not necessary. As the Northern Greek says: "Many things are *obviously* like this [in having contingency]."

Scenario 4

Curiously, Aristotle argues at the end the following, suggesting that all of the statements before were him exploring *aporiai* (puzzles) and that they were not necessarily his views.
1) A cloak is possibly cut.
2) The cloak wears out first, so is not cut.
3) But the cloak "equally" has the possibility of "not being cut" or else it would not have worn out first.

How does this, though, give the grounds for the final conclusion that necessity does not always hold? That is, how does this *prove* a possibility *actually* exists rather than exists merely conceptually (which the determinist need not deny)? Does Aristotle go beyond merely asserting that *real* or *ontological* contingency (to be or not to be) *actually* exists?

The answer is quite simple, once one ignores for the moment issues of truth, future contingent statements and related issues like choice. Aristotle appeals to the notion of necessity and contingency as found in Theta 8. Necessity is equated with omnitemporality, namely, with something that is "always actual," as the matter is phrased at the beginning of the passage above (from *On Interpretation* 9). Impossibility (which need not, and does not, come into play in this passage or in the rest of Chapter 9) is equated with the lack of existence throughout *all* time; and possibility *qua* contingency, which definitely does come into play, is equated with *some intermittent existence*. Clearly, since some things, like cloaks or cloak-cuttings are discontinuous and intermittent (because no cloak is infinite and no cutting of a cloak could therefore go on for an infinite time), we have an immediate counter-example and immediate *proof* of things or happenings that are not necessary. That is, "some cloaks are cut" is a suppressed premise that everyone would acknowledge so easily that Aristotle simply does not state it. The mere physical happening of just one case (of a cutting or a wearing out) is proof in and of itself of a *real* contingency, and indeed that is Aristotle's suggestion at the very end. Recognizing that intermittent *contingent* events happen at times but not at other times is obvious evidence that not all things are necessary, i.e. omnitemporal. *This* is why Aristotle gives Scenario 4. It shows the opponent that no matter which path you take, you are led to the conclusion that two alternatives (in a pair) exist intermittently and at least one happens in front of us, sometimes repeatedly, in our lives.

If the determinist still objects that we need further proof, Aristotle has compelling answers available, which we observed and will observe more in different contexts. Just as we do not, and cannot, ask for proofs for axioms, so we do not try to prove that nature exists. Nor do we ask for proof that cloaks get cut or worn out when everyone knows they do from experience. Ontological contingency is therefore indubitable, just as the nature of the difference between necessity and contingency is. Simply look at a common case of coats getting cut or not, and getting worn out or not. Nothing further need be given to "prove" the existence of the contingency. Determinists might try to change the meaning of "necessity," which is what appears to happen, for instance, in Scenarios 1-3 above, where "necessary" suggests "in line with natural law (given any physical condition at any moment)." However, once someone (like a determinist) starts using the terms differently or once, e.g., "contingency" has merely a conceptual sense (as could be implied in Scenarios 1-3), then "necessity" has a merely conceptual sense, too. Yet mere conceptual necessity would pose no worry in the context of Chapter 9. The underlying concern is not whether people actually say or conceive something, but whether reality is determinate or not. If (real) contingency exists, then not everything is (ontologically) necessary, and if not necessary, then not (really) deterministic (in the relevant senses of the terms). Thus, the worry of the determinist's position in *this* context simply dissipates. (I leave aside other issues of truth, psychological or epistemic determinism, and future contingent statements because they are different matters, even if a few of the ambiguous *concepts* overlap with my concerns.)[73]

What is very clear in this passage is that Aristotle argues that one of two sides of a *kind* of possibility, whichever this refers to, Scenario 1, 2, 3 or 4, does not *always* happen (it sometimes is one way and sometimes the other). If one side always happened, it would be omnitemporal, necessary and deterministic. Hence, if *even one* contingency is real, *not everything is necessary* (nor would everything be impossible but this is so implausible as to be ignored in the current debate). I have suggested that Scenario 4 is intended, giving an obvious case that no one would deny, of a contingency existing, but either of the other scenarios would work also, as long as one realizes that Aristotle is insisting in the penultimate statements that a *pair* of "to be or not to be" options are the focus, with each side sometimes (but only *sometimes*) happening, as common experience shows. This obviously (and correctly) entails in his view that necessity does not reign supreme over everything,—his conclusion and goal of the whole passage.

What is important now is that, however we interpret *On Interpretation* 9 with respect to traditional debates, it is illuminating in a crucial way for our concerns. It helps answer the question that Hintikka once posed: What does the Principle apply to, events or things or some-

---

[73] For what it is worth, I favor the view that the future contingents are indeterminate until the event occurs or not, and thus that at times Aristotle has trivalence with respect to truth for reasons given earlier in this book: true and non-true are the strict opposites, the latter of which includes "false" and "indeterminate." However, we have no need while discussing the Not to Fear Proof to examine the competing interpretations, and therefore I leave this matter only as a personal preference, given the attention that has been paid to this topic by previous specialists.

Statement 3

thing else? Aristotle indirectly gives the answer by indicating in the passage above from *On Interpretation* that *events* or *kinds of events* are within the scope. As he says: "So it is the same *with all other events* that are spoken of in terms of this *kind of possibility*." Because events require substances that actively or passively are an agent of the event, then obviously "things" too are covered. As Aristotle concludes: not everything **is or happens** of necessity. By extension, what "is or happens" is relevant to the kinds of possibility employed in the Principle.

To summarize the discussion from *On Interpretation* 9 and to offer some final thoughts: If anyone insists on the simplest version of the Principle for each and every ("accidental") particular or every accidental event (like the Milanese cloak that gets burned tonight before it gets cut tomorrow on the seamstress's previously scheduled plan), the principle is clearly false. In fact, it is so absurd that Aristotle could not have intended it, and both Hintikka and even Broadie herself suggest exactly this point. You might as well imagine Aristotle being the driver who obeys the "No Stopping" sign on the freeway while driving at 70 miles per hour, when cars 100 yards ahead are completely stationary, and who tells the police on the way to the hospital (if he survives) "Well, the sign ordered me not to stop."

Whether Broadie herself is able to maintain a "particular" reading, one which allows accidental individuals or events to be in scope of the Principle, or whether she only intends her A′ to apply to accidental individuals or events but with temporal and historical restrictions that *function* the same way as kinds for Hintikka and that protect the Principle, again, I cannot determine. Is it because she, at least at one stage of her thought, temporally relativizes (real) possibilities and because the temporal and existential, historical state of affairs do not allow a particular cloak to exist or to be cut at the required moment? Perhaps no possibility arises because of the historical "actual nows" for the cloak to be subsequently cut. That is, maybe the particular cloak will never be in a situation that involves a sharp object being near enough to cut it or anything of the sort (as alluded to, this would be similar to Hintikka's "partial possibility" recounted by van Rijen). Thus, because the "immediately realizable" conditions (that are crucial for a particular cutting) never exist and could never exist once the cloak dissolves, then strictly speaking there never was, or is, a possibility *per se* of the cloak being cut, nor will there be one (although readers might complain and say that possibility is now being used in a different sense, as "immediately realizable" and not as mere contingency). As fortune had and now has it, the possibility of being cut could not occur, before the cloak goes out of existence. However, then we apparently revert to the case above, where temporal restrictions and material conditions need additionally to be presupposed for the Principle (just as, in a similar way, temporal restrictions are arguably presupposed by the "No Stopping" sign on the highway, that is, "No Stopping, except *during those times* when injury or damage would result if one does not stop"). Maybe Broadie or anyone following her would say "sortals" and "genuine" are not the two preconditions of the Principle; rather, temporal indexing and requiring proper material conditions are.

I have already discussed, though, the problems with temporal indexing of a claim, and nothing Aristotle says, as far I can see, suggests that the cloak in *On Interpretation* 9 required material conditions. That is, nothing Aristotle says suggests it lived a very protective life, as it were, distant from all sharp objects in the same way that the princess in *Sleeping Beauty* was kept away from all needles so that the curse of the wicked fairy would not get realized (until the wicked fairy smuggled a needle into Aurora's 16th birthday party). In other words, in *On Interpretation* 9 the Northern Greek seemingly ignores on the surface the conditions of "immediate realizability," as a more precise notion of contingency, although on at least one analysis of the complex scenario above, that indeed was suggested. *Not being burnt up* might be considered a pre-condition to being cut and, thus, mere contingency may not be the only notion of possibility in the whole passage.

Broadie might require, therefore, the importance of historical factors and immediately realizable conditions as one resolution of the current problem (of how to allow individuals *qua* particulars and not *qua* members of kinds to be in scope of the Principle). We will see later, though, that in the argument of Theta 8 or in the Not to Fear Proof, Aristotle does not need "immediate realizability" to push through his argument. Moreover, Scenario 4 appears to be a logical argument that sticks the opponent on the two horns of a dilemma (forcing them to accept that both sides of an ontological contingency do indeed hold, as *empirical experience* proves in and of itself) rather than an appeal to material conditions *per se* for one side of a contingency. Thus, for the purposes of this book I leave aside this tentative solution on behalf of Broadie, in part because I am unsure if even she herself would now try to champion such a solution.

Be all of this as it may, the phrase just quoted from the passage in *On Interpretation* 9—"this kind of possibility"—shows irrefutably yet again (recall the *Dramatics* for the first case) that "kind of possibility" is a legitimate and not uncommon phrase for Aristotle. This surely grounds the Sortal Principle of Plenitude's "kind of possibility." Moreover, Aristotle's conclusion applies to not only the complex example of the cloak-cutting or cloak-burning but to *"all other events that are spoken of in terms of this kind of possibility,"* in his own words, and later we will see this confirmed in *De Caelo*. Thus, the guidelines elucidated apply universally when "contingency" is the sense of possibility, and we have now answered Hintikka's questions about whether the scope was to things or events. The scope could be to either, and so even in *On Interpretation* 9, a treatise that functions as a foundation for logic, *de re* possibility and *de re* necessity are primary.

Let us conclude this section. More than ample evidence has been adduced already, I believe, for why the Principle of Plenitude presuppos-

es sortals or *kinds of individuals*[74] (unless the individual is eternal):
- Our own way of speaking, similar to the Greek practice, in which we drop "kind of" for simplicity, one example in the *Dramatics* about patricide being a possible action because of Oedipus's killing, all of which only makes sense if the (individual) action is elliptical for "kind of action";
- Aristotle's claims in the *Topics* VII 4 that the species is synony-

---

74 Given that for Aristotle all natural kinds have many members each (even infinitely many over the duration of infinite time, notwithstanding that a finite number exists at any given moment), "one of a kind" or "sui generis" is a figure of speech within Aristotelian metaphysics or pertains to artificial kinds. To continue the discussion from a previous footnote: The exception regarding natural kinds would be of the universe *qua* "The All." "One of a kind" that is *sui generis* seemingly means (apart from "The All") "one of an artificially constructed kind," in contrast to an artificial kind itself, e.g., "creations after 500 BCE," which could include members as disparate as a trireme and the theory of alchemy. Any "one of a kind" is a human invention with a first incarnation that is also the last, e.g., "my one-of-a-kind invention of a 1/3 helicopter-1/3 plane-1/3 submarine with Java 7 as the computer language running the software." Obviously, this kind is artificial but, more crucially, it is *also* a kind of artifact. Because artifacts are natural kinds, these sorts of examples (of artificial kinds and sub-kinds) in no way impact negatively the conclusions of this book, as I demonstrate in the next section.

I should now handle another possible objection that if one member of a species achieves something, all others in the species could also do it because of the strictures of similarity between members of a kind that I have emphasized. Does my view not require that others of the same species can run as fast as, say, an Olympic champion runner? The answer is no. It is not necessary that anyone else ever achieve the world record to maintain Aristotle's Principle of Plenitude, if the scope of the Principle is to either eternally existing objects or to natural kinds. The amazingly fast running can be treated like the Java 7 vehicle, as a particular "accidental" action rather than as an essential characteristic of the species. Running *per se* is a derivable necessary condition of the species as a whole, subject to caveats for exceptions that prove the rule. Setting a world record is different and is accidental. Alternatively, setting a world record can also be properly described as being the maximum in an activity, which indeed has, and will always continue to have, many parallels in human activity insofar as humans breathe. It is crucial how one describes an event or possibility at times, and we examined possibility *qua* maxima in the list of six major senses of possibility.

mous with its individuals;
- Aristotle's distinction between generic versus individual causes and using examples of individuals (sculptor and statue) to explain the generic causes;
- Aristotle's seeming presupposition of an individual as an individual of a kind rather than as an "accidental particular" or a "this" in *De Caelo* (reconciling Broadie's emphasis on individuals with Hintikka's emphasis on kinds);
- Aristotle's very clear understanding in *On Interpretation* 9 that there will be individual possibilities (of a natural and not wildly fictional type) that never get realized in an eternity, which, as Hintikka, Sorabji and others intuited, must mean Aristotle is thinking of a member of a kind rather than an "accidental particular" when he advocates the Principle of Plenitude; and
- Broadie's own reliance and emphasis on "kinds" at various stages of her book.

Obviously, with infinitely existing objects, some alleged possibilities are conceptual only (like going out of existence), because in virtue of one alternative being continuously infinite, its negation will never be fulfilled and thus does not truly exist (as a real possibility). That is, no *contingent* possibility actually exists in that case. This is simply the nature of contingency for Aristotle—it is incompatible with something that has (continuous) infinite existence and that is therefore (temporally) necessary. It need hardly be repeated that contingency is incompatible, too, with something that is (temporally) impossible and thus that *never* occurs in an infinity.

I believe we have seen by now why Hintikka was perfectly right in questioning the scope of the Principle of Plenitude, given Aristotle's own seeming counterexample of the cloak that dissolves before it is cut. Objects like a particular (accidental) cloak are ruled out for Hintikka and are not "genuine," because they go out of existence, in contrast to eternally existing planets or to *sorts* of things (like cloaks).

However, this all leads to the question: What if the *sortal* does not last forever? Is the kind "cloak" eternal like a Platonic Form, and if not, does that not exclude cloaks from the Principle of Genuine Sortal Plenitude? Can textual evidence be given to show that cloaks are eternal kinds for Aristotle and thus that the possibilities function similarly for them, or at least for artifacts in general, in the same way that possibilities function for planets and eternal organic species? Hintikka, like Broadie, recognizes, e.g., that the human species for Aristotle is infinite.[75] However, neither thinker seems to affirm (or deny) that works of art and craft, like cloaks, are also eternal as a kind, which I will argue is entailed by Aristotle's explicit views (using art in a broad sense that includes crafts and that can include cloaks or all production by humanity). Broadie and Hintikka, therefore, may be right with respect to the basics, but if I can give an account of possibility that covers other cases, this strikes me as better, in being wider ranging concerning the scope of the Principle of (Genuine Sortal) Plenitude. I do this not to present additional evidence that the Not to Fear Proof goes through, because given that the Principle undoubtedly applies if its scope is to infinitely existing individuals, like planets or stars or the universe as a whole, surely (we will see) the Not to Fear Proof holds insofar as its subject is the eternal universe. Rather a secondary goal of this book is to demonstrate that Aristotle holds the Principle with respect to kinds that function as infinitely existing individuals and to be clear on which sorts of finite things are in scope.

---

75 Hintikka, 1979, p. 113.

Statement 3

Why Artifacts like Cloaks are within Scope

Aristotle would reject a Platonic Form of "cloak" that exists forever, just as he rejects the Forms in general. It is not clear whether Hintikka thinks the kind "cloak" is eternal for the Northern Greek, and Hintikka, like anyone else nowadays, might think that they are not because they are "man-made" or "artificial" and because probably they only began long after a Big Bang. Here, then, I give reasons why cloaks, which are not normally thought of as "natural" kinds, nevertheless function like natural kinds or are, depending on the senses of the terms, indeed natural kinds *for Aristotle*. Hence, insofar as individual cloaks are members of a natural kind in a legitimate sense of "natural," they properly fall within the scope of the Principle of Genuine Sortal Plenitude, even though the temporal existence of any particular member is obviously finite.

I demonstrate all of this by first giving the meteorological texts that suggest (but only suggest) that for Aristotle what is eternal are only the planets, living organisms, and four elements (fire, earth, air and water) before going on to show that texts like the *Dramatics* prove that the former texts are not expressing the Northern Greek's complete thoughts on this whole issue.

Let us start with Johnson, who says:
> The lower *kosmos* is continuous with the upper *kosmos*, and the things that happen in the lower *kosmos* are effects of the cause operating in the upper *kosmos*. In a sense the expression "the upper *kosmos*" refers to a *kosmos*, the one which consists exclusively of eternal aetherial bodies in constant circular motion, and which is not itself limited in its motion with respect to place, in distinction from "the lower *kosmos*," which is limited both below and above, consisting of the four elemental bodies that are constantly moved by the upper *kosmos*, **thus generating and de-**

stroying living substances.[76]

One source that Johnson gives is the *Meteorology*, part of which states:

> The whole world surrounding the earth, the affections of which are our subject, is made up of these bodies [i.e., fire, air, water, and earth]. This world necessarily has a certain continuity with the upper motions; *consequently all its power is derived from them.* (**For the originating principle of all motion must be deemed the first cause. Besides, that element is eternal**...) So we must treat fire and earth and the elements like them as the material cause of the events in this world (meaning by material what is subject and is affected), but **must assign causality in the sense of the originating principle of motion to the power of the eternally moving bodies.**[77]

Keeping in mind for the discussion in Part 2 that the "first mover" in this passage is not the Unmoved Mover but the eternal moving bodies, we should continue with texts that suggest only planets, living organisms and the four elements are eternal. I start with a preface before addressing passages that I anticipated in speaking of the "kinds of possibility" in *On Interpretation* 9 that Aristotle says are applicable to all events:

> For *everything is capable* of acting or being acted upon, of **being or not being**, either for an infinite, or for a definitely limited space of time... (*De Caelo* I 12, 283a6-8; my emphases)

Presumably ruling out wild figments of Greek imaginations that in no way could exist and be part of "everything [that is] capable of acting or being acted upon," Aristotle adds later:

---

76 Johnson, *op. cit.*, p. 104; my bold italics.

77 *Meteorology* 1.2, 339a19-32; my emphases. Transl. E.W. Webster, *The Complete Works of Aristotle*, ed. Barnes; all translations from the *Meteorology* are his.

> ...things that we call natural are either substances or functions and attributes of substances. *As substances I class the simple bodies—fire, earth, and the other terms of the series—and all things composed of them*; for example, the heaven as a whole and its parts, *animals, again, and plants and their parts*. By attributes and functions I mean the movements of these and of *all other things in which they have power* in themselves to cause movement, and also their alterations and reciprocal transformations (*De Caelo* III 1, 298a26-b1; my italics).

"Everything is capable" and "all other things" in the two passages suggests no restriction to the kinds of real, *natural* things that have capability, but especially the *cosmoi*, the four elements, and the living things. Capability and power often go hand in hand with possibility, as we see throughout this book, especially in Theta 8. I should add immediately that Aristotle allows with these statements the possibilities pertaining to thought but as an *attribute* of a living organism. Thus, when I think of Hamlet, the thought *itself* clearly exists as a natural mental phenomenon, even though Hamlet *per se* is a fictional prince.

Indubitably, Aristotle maintained that the species "human" is eternal even if individuals are each finite, and, I show now, the same principle applies for him to artifacts like cloaks even if he does not mention directly artifacts in the passages above. Artifacts in a very proper way are derivative from the eternal organic species, which themselves depend on the eternal planets for Aristotle. Thus, we need not restrict the scope of the Principle of Plenitude to *organic* eternal kinds, although at times we may have to give the proper level of generality for the sortal, be it 3-vested suit, suit, clothing or fabric. That is, there are sortals of sortals, or kinds of kinds, just as there are not only species but genera for Aristotle. As a result, cloaks, raincoats, and the like may be subsumed under clothing that itself is subsumed under fabric (which can be used for sheets as much as for clothing). Once the correct level is articulated, this "higher level" is equivalent to a sortal, and the sortal possibility may be at the generic level rather than the "specific" (species-oriented) level, just as a root directory in a computer is a directory in the same sense as one of its sub-directories, with the root directory functioning as a genus. Similarly, Aristotle articulates "general causes" and "general effects" (in *Physics* II), so "general possibilities" are equally legitimate and "possibilities" on occasion may simply be elliptical for him.

Take, now, the typical distinction between natural and artificial kinds, as, for instance, "not made by human beings" and "made by humans," respectively. What if the individuals who create are not human? When beavers make dams and birds construct nests we tend not to say that the animals' products are artifacts but that they are part of the natural world. Clearly, then, both the capacity of human beings to produce artifacts like houses, strictly or loosely speaking (as with bird nests), and the need for the creation to follow scientific laws are also natural, in the sense of "following laws of nature." In creating arts and crafts, that is artifacts (and in this context we need not distinguish arts from crafts), sculptors, pottery-makers and architects do not cause water to stop boiling at 212 degrees Fahrenheit nor cause wood to lose its natural properties. Artifact as a rubric for all production is still part of the natural world in the sense that the production must follow natural laws, and when Aristotle at one moment compares art and nature he does not make such an exclusive division as the terms "natural" and "artificial" for us sometimes suggest:

> If a house, e.g., had been a thing made by nature, it would have been made in the same way as it is now by art; and if things made by nature were made not only by nature but also by art, they would come to be in the same way as by nature... *Generally art in some cases completes what nature cannot bring to a finish, and in others imitates nature.* If, therefore, artificial products are for the sake of an end, so clearly also are natural products. The relation of the later to the earlier items is the same in both. This is most obvious in the animals other than man: they make

> things neither by art nor after inquiry or deliberation. That is why people wonder whether it is by intelligence or by some other faculty that these creatures work,—spiders, ants, and the like.[78]

Hence, just as spiders make webs and birds nests, so men make houses, even if the latter is a result of craft or deliberation. Since art sometimes finishes what nature does not complete, the process must moreover be equally "natural" (in the sense of following natural law). However, just because in some contexts we distinguish art from other practices, perhaps because deliberation is involved in art in the strict sense of the word (and Aristotle says in the *Nicomachean Ethics* VI 3 and 4, especially 1140a20-1, that art is making according to "right reason"), we do not thereby make art "unnatural" *in the sense that it does not follow laws of nature*. As William Burroughs once quipped "The only unnatural act is the one that cannot be performed."

The typical and sometimes important distinction "made by nature" and "made by humans" is consequently not the only distinction between natural and artificial, and being artistic or creating artifacts is a natural capability for human beings. "Natural" and "artificial" are sometimes compatible, not contrary, terms, with artificial kinds simply being a different subclass from "natural kinds" as used in one of its senses, *with both sub-classes falling within nature*. Thus, artifacts, according to Aristotle, merely have the principles of production outside of themselves.[79] It is not as if they are outside of nature. The animate types of natural objects have the principles of *reproduction* in themselves.[80]

---

78   *Physics* II 8, 199a19-24; my italics. Transl. by R.P. Hardie and R.K. Gaye, *The Complete Works of Aristotle*, ed. Barnes, *op. cit.*

79   *Physics* II 1, 192b29-30.

80   We need not discuss the case of robots being created that themselves create other robots. Aristotle does not care about robots. Still he might say, were he alive today, that if and when that happens, the robots will not be reproducing biologically or as animate objects. Moreover, the original source of

Cloaks are therefore implicitly considered by Aristotle to be artifacts not only in our typical sense of the word but as natural kinds—equivalent to spider webs and beaver dams—and, like the species, **they exist eternally** (as an *artificial natural kind*). Thus, it is perfectly proper for him to hold that if no cloak whatsoever considered as clothing (or as fabric or as an an artifact) is ever cut in an eternity, no possibility of being cut exists. Furthermore, it is also perfectly proper for him to treat the cloak as an example of the whole kind, similar to what Hintikka wishes to do and similar to what I believe Broadie is committed to, whether she intended it or not, when she discusses the impossibility of creating new complex (but organic) kinds for Aristotle. To take another, related example: If no cloak (in typical relevant earth-like conditions, and not being part of some unique and science experiment) merely in being folded ever causes a nuclear explosion in all eternity, then it would be proper on Aristotle's view (and on ours, too) to say that "It is not (genuinely) possible that merely folding a cloak causes a nuclear explosion."

Confirmation of the eternality of cloaks or at least of clothing or of fabric for Aristotle comes, again, not from a scientific treatise appealing to laws of physics (although at heart that is also at issue here, underneath the surface) but from the *Dramatics*, this time Chapter 4. Eternal or infinite art (as a practice) is in effect guaranteed because making and acting are said to be natural to man. Hence, so as long as the species is eternal, artistic forms, including mimesis (which was just noted in the passage from the *Physics*), and similarly products such as cloaks will be eternal. Aristotle says in *Dramatics* 4 that *mimēsis* (impersonation or representation) is natural, as are dancing (*rhuthmos*) and music (*harmonia*).[81] It follows that, *by nature,* for

---

production will still have been the human creators.

81   *Dramatics* 4, 1448b4-6; b21-22. For why *rhuthmos* should be translated as "dance" following Plato's explanation of *rhuthmos* as "ordered body movement" in *Laws* II 665a rather than as "rhythm," cf. Scott, *Aristotle on Dramatic Musical Composition*, 2018, pp. 28-105 and 144ff. However, one

Statement 3

Aristotle the rational creatures sing and dance, which means those practices are as eternal as the species and as walking or breathing. Infinite art is also confirmed by the Stagirite's views on knowledge, of which there are three types: theoretical, practical, and *productive*. For Aristotle, rational creatures, eternally existing, would have all three forms, including the knowledge of how to make body coverings, to greater or lesser extent. Thus, cloaks always exist in some form or another—as clothing or artifacts—for him, and obviously they do not have to be the ancient Greek equivalent of Armani or Issey Miyake. The cloaks or clothing and the related actions and possibilities such as cutting (or not cutting) will exist throughout all time as contingencies, even though a certain, individual cloak considered as an individual "accident"—Plato's favorite green wool cloak with a food stain on the side—may not be cut. The situation is no different for Aristotle, with respect to possibility, from humanity as a species existing as a natural kind (versus any particular human being), although, to reiterate, the organic animate species by their nature propagate themselves whereas the artificial ones do not. Thus, natural kinds (as following laws of nature) are not only organic but inorganic and, at times, artificial.

To emphasize: If no cloak or fabric considered as a natural artificial kind was ever cut in infinite time, it would not be really possible to cut cloaks (or clothing) on Aristotle's view. Yet the fact that many cloaks were cut before his time and surely known by him to be cut (as surely as he knew pigs ate food, even if he never states this exactly in *On Interpretation* 9), shows that the possibility must continue to exist, given the statement above from the *Dramatics*. In fact, the possibility continues to exist even if all cloaks go temporarily out of existence, for were the first "born again" cloak to reappear after five years (because fabric or animal skins continued to exist), it would then be capable of being cut because of its natural constitution, similar to the earlier

---

could accept the misleading traditional translation. Still, Aristotle is claiming that certain artistic capabilities and actualities are natural to mankind and thus by implication must last as long as the species lasts.

ones.

The final evidence showing that for Aristotle possibility entails realizability in time for any particular cloak *qua member of a kind* follows, whether or not the realizability stems from the capacities of the essential conditions of the subject, strictly speaking, or more "remotely," from derived but necessary conditions that themselves can be deduced from the essential conditions. Take the example from the *Dramatics*, of an individual particular action of patricide versus the *kind* of (individual) action of patricide, to build on what was said before.

Aristotle indicates that things which have happened are obviously possible (*Dramatics* 9.1451b17-8). As we also saw, however, this statement, like the elliptical Principle of Plenitude, cannot be taken too literally. Otherwise, to continue the famous example, it would follow that a real Oedipus who had committed patricide (something which "has happened") could commit the action again. The action is "obviously possible." Yet, to emphasize one last time, this is absurd, because he could have had only one biological father and because he had already killed that father. Now, obviously Aristotle is not suggesting Oedipus has a stepfather. Leaving aside eternal recurrence, as favored by Stoics, killing one's father twice is contradicted not only by common sense but by *Generation and Corruption* II 11, 338b12ff, where Aristotle rules out that events could be repeated "numerically." He allows that they can be repeated only "specifically" (that is, pertaining to the species). Thus, the emphasis in this context of the *Dramatics*, on *an action* being possible *because it happened*, must be assumed to be within the context of the species or of the kind. The action cannot be numerically repeated, even though particular individuals act or are acted upon and commit patricide or are killed by children. It is because the species has the capability of patricide—because the nature of the kind allows it, and because one's ancestors, including, in the case of Oedipus, King Laius, had it—that the individual has it. Indubitably, King Laius's father also had the capability,

Statement 3

whether he exercised it or not by killing Oedipus's grandfather. Again, this is not to assert that the species has any particular, accidental capability just because a peculiar individual has it. Otherwise we run into the dilemma (footnoted before) that if someone high-jumps seven feet, other individuals can high-jump the same exact height. Rather, it is only to assert that Aristotle can hold both doctrines, namely, that individual, concrete "accidental" possibilities exist just as sortal possibilities do. Yet the best, most explicit formulation of the Principle of (Genuine Sortal) Plenitude only applies ultimately to the latter, sortal possibilities (of natural kinds, including artificial kinds that are also natural).

Aristotle reasonably assumes, then, that the reader of the *Dramatics* would presuppose that a numerically-identical event cannot be repeated, given the uni-direction of time, and thus for the sake of brevity leaves off reference to the *kind* of event. He mentions only the action itself. Recall the discussion of individuals in *De Caelo* that I argued are not accidental individuals but individuals as members of a kind. Therefore, Aristotle, in saying that things or events that have happened are obviously possible must mean that a *similar* patricide could be committed by someone else (because, as we saw, possibility does not apply to the past). Indeed, he adds later in the *Dramatics*:

> ...for there is nothing to prevent some of the things that have happened from being the *sort* of things that may happen, according to probability, i.e., that are possible.
> ...*tōn gar genomenōn enia ouden kōluei toiauta einai hoia an eikos genesthai [kai dunata genesthai]* (1451b31-33, Janko tr. but my italics)

In brief, anyone who is willing to accept the formulations given in the *Dramatics*, knowing that certain commonsensical assumptions must underlie them, should be willing to accept the Principle of Plenitude with its own commonsensical assumptions. Thus, the passages from the *Generation and Corruption, On Interpretation, De Caelo* and *Dramatics* suffice, I contend, to ground the suggestion that statements about possibilities concerning cloaks, which suggest possibilities of individuals, are really elliptical claims about the possibilities of *kinds* of cloaks and that these kinds, as *natural* products of the biological species, are eternal.

To conclude this sub-section pertaining to the scope of the Principle: It is clear given the example of the cloak not being cut or not being worn out that we have to take the Principle as applicable to less than the domain of all individual things or particular events in the universe *qua* particular accidental individual things and events. Given my explanation, it appears that the Principle should apply, though, to more than just infinite things like planets, especially because of Aristotle's often casual formulation of the Principle and his desire usually to be in touch with common speech. The Principle seems for him to apply very broadly, and indirect evidence for this was given above when the "kind of possibility" referred to in *On Interpretation* 9 (meaning contingency) was said to be applicable to *all other events* for which contingency applies in the context of coats being cut or worn out.

It is an advantage of my interpretation that Aristotle's theory appears to be more in line with common ways of speaking—often a very important consideration for him—if the scope of the Principle of (Genuine Sortal) Plenitude is as I describe it. We do speak very sensibly about possibilities of (genuine) things that do not exist yet (and so here I differ from Hintikka) but which we plan will exist, even if for some unexpected reason the things do not come into existence. Again, "genuine" for me means "allowed by nature" or the like, versus "merely imaginative" (which may be impossible). This is slightly different from Hintikka's use of the term even if there is some overlap. Two parents say things like "Our upcoming child (which we are still trying to conceive) might go to the University of Toronto" and they often engage in action to accommodate that possibility, for example, starting a savings account for tuition before the child exists even as an embryo. On Hintikka's account, the non-existent thing seemingly should not have a possibility; as I understand him, the thing is not "genuine." Yet everyone understands what we mean. Another option is that, before the child is conceived, this is not a case of contingency but of the mere conceptual possibility or believability that is consistent with natural possibility—of other children having received a good education and having gotten accepted into the school or one of the equivalents around the world. This (merely) believable possibility then subtly morphs into contingency once the child is conceived. The morphing is simply not acknowledged or may not even be recognized cognitively. A third option is that the subject is a "possible subject" and any predicate is a "possible event (or state)," so we have two possibilities embedded in one sentence. This is similar to Aristotle speaking in *On Interpretation* 7, 17a37-b16, of one sentence having two universals, namely a universal subject that has a universal predication, whether or not he allows that *that* particular example can be true.

In any event, the Principle is not intended to apply to our own child as a particular child but only as a member of a kind that already has been actualized in an infinity,—in fact actualized millions of times at least. Insofar as our planned child, then, is considered a member of a natural kind, and insofar as a member of that natural kind has or can expect the two contingent possibilities to be satisfied in an infinity, then whether or not *our* planned child gets accepted into a particular university (or even gets conceived and born), one of the others has been or will get accepted and the Principle arguably holds with respect to (the kind of) possible acceptance or rejection. To stress, though, we might need to be careful whether one sense of possibility morphs into another sense at any stage of discussions that continue over time regarding the one and the same (planned) child.

Statement 3 in the Not to Fear Proof, the Principle of Genuine Sortal Plenitude, is therefore truly Aristotelian. It should be acknowledged immediately, however, that some of the claims above are couched in terms of an infinity of time, which is how the Principle is also couched, whereas the conclusion of the Proof is couched in terms of eternity. An infinity of time (like the past) will probably be considered by some to be less than an eternity of time, and thus it is necessary to argue that an infinity and an eternity function equivalently in the Proof for Aristotle in an appropriate sense of "equivalent." Alternatively, we can see that such a comparison is inappropriate. I discuss this whole matter later, when covering Premise 9, even though the astute reader can quickly guess what the explanation will be, given the previous discussion of Philoponus.

4) Therefore, every sort of genuine possibility has already been actualized.

Assuming Statements 1-3 are correct, (4) easily follows. Myles Burnyeat, unwittingly given the conclusions of this book and how they are at odds with his own preferences, provides ironic support for the statement. As he says:

> Any instance of being potentially such-and-such is preceded by an instance of something else being actually such-and-such (*Met.* Θ 8, 1049b10-50a3). More simply, *there is nothing new under the Sun*—nor, of course, above the Sun, given the unchanging circulation of the stars in the Aristotelian universe.[1]

---

[1] Myles F. Burnyeat, *Aristotle's Divine Intellect* (Milwaukee: Marquette University Press, 2008) p. 36; my italics. In his book, Burnyeat accepts the legitimacy of the Intellect of the Unmoved Mover of Lambda. Obviously, if I am right, and Aristotle renounced that particular kind of Unmoved Mover (as opposed to ones with matter), the whole issue of how the rest of Aristotle's more empirical corpus can be reconciled with a Pure Actuality and a divine intellect need not exercise scholars anymore. Either the notorious passages in, e.g., *De Anima* III 4-5 were "juvenile indiscretions" or they were interpolated later by other editors. For an up-to-date synopsis of how the issues of a separate divine intellect that requires no body impacts current exegesis, see Iakovos Vasiliou, "Theoretical *Nous* and its Objects in Aristotle," in *Proceedings of the Boston Area Colloquium in Ancient Philosophy*, Vol. XXVIII, 2012, pp. 161-86. As to be expected, Vasiliou subsequently continues the tradition of trying to offer a solution to a perennial dilemma, which in my view may or may not be correct, but if it is correct is from the youthful Aristotle, assuming Aristotle was indeed the author of all of the passages.

Finally, Vasiliou not only refers to the discordant treatments of separate intelligence (without bodies or matter) in the *De Anima* and *Metaphysics* Lambda but in the *Nicomachean Ethics*. However, David Sedley has given powerful evidence that Aristotle's concern for being "godlike" in the *Ethics* stems from Plato ("The Ideal of Godlikeness," in *Plato 2: Ethics, Politics, Religion and the Soul*, ed. by Gail Fine, Oxford: Oxford University Press, 2000, 309-28, esp. pp. 324-7). From my perspective, Sedley's conclusions mean that this part of the *Ethics* is relatively early or at the latest mid-life. All of this, I believe, also helps confirm the "juvenile" stage of the Unmoved Mover. We must also always bear in mind that even if Aristotle had an earlier

Playing Devil's Advocate, we might say in reply to Burnyeat that the iPhone 8 or the Google Kitty Hawk (flying) car are new and in terms of some features, they are. However, in support again of Burnyeat's statement, as a kind they are not, and they are certainly not *completely* new. In this respect Burnyeat and, for instance, Broadie and I, agree. Burnyeat simply uses an elliptical expression "nothing new under the sun," rather than "no kind (of thing) new under the sun," just as Hintikka deduces that Aristotle uses the Principle of Plenitude elliptically for Genuine Sortal Plenitude. Readers might complain that by considering the phone or flying car under more general kinds, rather than assuming that a new kind has been created when either innovation materialized, we will of course have to agree that nothing completely new ever gets actualized. However, three retorts immediately come to mind.

First, what is wrong with the claim that nothing *completely* new ever gets created? The claim seems utterly innocuous and correct. Where is any counter-example? Second, we can grant that a new *artificial* sub-kind was created with respect to the iPhone (and the same principles will apply to the flying car), but if we take the object to a higher level *as a natural kind* as explained above, obviously the iPhone is not the first telephone, nor as a "smartphone" is it the first communication device or human product. Third, our concern in the Not to Fear Proof is ultimately with the universe as a whole, and not with some part that can change in accidental ways, that is, in ways that we saw above are excluded from the Principle of (Genuine Sortal) Plenitude, pertaining to "particulars." No matter how many new (sub-)types of the iPhone or anything else that inventors create, their arrival and use in no way

---

view that he renounced, he could have left it in the manuscript as a hortatory remark, for students who might need a "god" in their lives or who need to be gently pushed to perfect themselves in all the legitimate ways. Finally, we examine more later the absurdity of a "god" with intellectual capabilities like foresight when the god has no body, when examining Cicero's report of Aristotle's deity.

impacts the *fundamental* principles concerning human products. Artificial products in one sense of "unnatural" (because they are man-made or do not reproduce themselves) might be new (although never *completely* new). Artificial products in the sense of products that humans naturally make (according to laws of nature) can also be new, but only in accidental ways (and the "accident" now applies to a group of similar products), not in terms of their necessary characteristics of being a human product. We saw above that the latter always exists for Aristotle. Natural (as "not man-made") happenings that *seem* new are clearly not a new kind of event, because given the infinite past and all of the permutations that have happened, something specifically or generically identical to the so-called "new" thing or event had (for the Northern Greek) to have happened somewhere, at some point.

5) The universe (still) exists.

Need I even say that this premise is self-evident? I myself do not care to argue with anyone who claims the opposite, or who claims the universe is a mere dream, or a grandiose computer simulation,[2] or anything similar. In any event, that simulation would be the universe and the Not to Fear Proof arguably would still hold, because programming, simulations and "divine" super-computers are also subject to natural laws.

---

[2] A number of scientists and computer technologists, including Elon Musk, the founder of Tesla, apparently are now claiming, or at least suggesting, this. In one way it is a variation of George Berkeley's idealist hypothesis that reality is just in the mind of God. However, for Musk and others, God is not the programmer; other more advanced beings are. As Philip Ball says:
> Musk and other like-minded folk are suggesting that we are entirely simulated beings. *We could be nothing more* than strings of information manipulated in some gigantic computer, like the characters in a video game. Even our brains are simulated, and are responding to simulated sensory inputs [from "We might live in a computer program, but it may not matter," September 5, 2016, as published on the web: http://www.bbc.com/earth/story/20160901-we-might-live-in-a-computer-program-but-it-may-not-matter; my italics].

Hence, the tradition continues of considering anything imaginable as if it *could* be the case, and I only hope Tesla's engineering teams invest as many computer bits (that is, 0's and 1's) in figuring out the various ways in which his self-driving cars might fail—what are called "exceptions" in the Java programming language—to anticipate the relevant potential problems before the cars become common on the road.

6) Thus, there has never been the sort of genuine possibility that would cause the universe to not exist.

This intermediate conclusion follows from Statements 1-5. Any possibility that the universe might not exist is merely of the conceivable type that is as fantastical as any supernatural or utterly fictional imagining. The possibility is no better than Hume's billiard balls causing a nuclear explosion when one strikes another under normal conditions.

7) The universe could not simply disappear into nothing.

Aristotle holds this position in *Physics* III 6, 206a10 and VIII 1, 251b29-252a6.[3] A related consideration is that possibility or contingency when further qualified as "immediate realizability" applies both ways, not only to fulfillment but to non-fulfillment. Destruction could be characterized under either heading. No (contingent) possibility of creation (say of a baby or of an event) exists unless the pre-conditions are there (sperm and egg in the case of the baby or runners entering the stadium and getting prepared in the case of an Olympic race). Yet similarly no possibility of destruction exists unless the pre-conditions are immediately available before the destructive event. No boat (or tree) can be blown up by explosives unless the boat (or tree) and the explosives are suitably juxtaposed. Thus, the universe, meaning "The All" rather than just our solar system or our galaxy, could not have been, or cannot be, destroyed unless the suitable cause of the destruction was, or is, also existent and, as it were, properly positioned, or "immediately realizable." The suitable cause need not be external; it could be internal, like a virus in a body. Yet how could it be external? If it existed, it would have to be part of "The All." At any rate, how could anything be properly positioned in this case or what could have that awesome power? Aristotle describes the difficulties with determining a suitable cause in *De Caelo*, and the same difficulties holds for us, be it with theories either of entropy (which themselves only show at most that everything gets equally distributed, not that the universe vanishes into complete nothingness) or of anything else. Even now, cosmogonical theories involving something always existing to the past (Big Bang from a singularity, Steady State, or brane) are infinitely

---

3   As we have seen, Aristotle says: "No eternal thing exists potentially." (*Metaphysics* IX 8, 1050b7) and "No capacity relates to being in the past, but always being in the present or future" (*De Caelo* I 12, 283b12-13). For something eternal, with no potential there is no potential of going out of existence.

more plausible (pun intended) than a theory like Big Bang *ex nihilo*.[4] This last theory reflects scientific views that are more indebted to imaginative conceivability than to empirical evidence.

---

[4] We can reconsider, if only as a lark, the issue of how life on earth came about and whether life resulted necessarily from completely inanimate components. Even if we (rightfully) reject Aristotle's view that the species are eternal, still we might argue that a chicken-like thing comes from a previous chicken-like thing or, if we climb the sortal tree, an organic thing comes from an organic thing *ad infinitum*. This may be false if we discover that life came from some combination of inorganic materials, but even now the issue has not been settled for scientists. As recent findings show, it may be that life on earth came from pyrophosphate, which arrived via meteorites. If pyrophosphate could arrive via interstellar transport, why not some very basic organic compounds, in which case our evolutionary life forms stemmed from other life around the universe? This would mean, again, that organic things came from organic things, all of which arguably could still satisfy the appeal to (the most generic) natural kinds and to individuals of a kind having the same, natural behavior. If an organic kind can be shown to arise from inorganic matter, then these speculations may be irrelevant, but, nevertheless, theoretically the animate "seeds" might have been introduced by a meteor-type structure to our earth *before* animate life was created from inanimate components. I merely offer these speculations and take no stance one way or the other.

8) Nor could the universe come from nothing.

Aristotle states this at *Metaphysics* VII 7, 1032b30, and *De Caelo* I 10, 280a24-28. No additional argument needs to be given for him in this regard, even if modern scientists use experiments showing that a sub-atomic particle can disappear and then reappear in another location, *seemingly* from nothing, to argue that the Big Bang came *ex nihilo*. Along with what was said before against this claim, a host of other explanations are more palatable than claiming that something arises from pure nothingness, even on modern scientific grounds. No scientist in history has ever detected (apart from the new dubious case of sub-atomic particles) something verifiably coming from *nothing*. Induction or past human history is not a guarantee, as stock brokers like to say, "of future performance," but neither induction nor history should be dismissed too lightly.

9) Regarding (sorts of genuine) possibilities occurring, temporal infinity is the same as eternity.

Aristotle indubitably thinks that, in the case of eternal things, what may be will be. He says so in a number of places, including *Physics* III. However, the Principle of Plenitude (and Broadie's A´) are couched in terms of infinity whereas some of the premises and the conclusion of the Not to Fear Proof are couched in terms of eternity. How can we be sure that Aristotle wishes to sustain the Principle if eternity and infinity differ in an important way, like in magnitude? I am not aware of any passage in the entire corpus in which Aristotle explicitly discusses the relation of infinity to eternity, although they might be identified in a passage mentioned already, at *De Caelo* I 9, 279a27, with the *kai* of "that is," namely, *to ton panta chronon kai tēn apeirian*: "all time, that is, infinity." Broadie for one supports the view that infinity and eternity for Aristotle are equivalent, at least in a loose sense of "equivalent" and not in a sense that necessitates mathematical equality (which is not to say that Hintikka disagrees, but I know of no discussion on his part of this precise issue). She notes that Aristotle takes the phrase "'for an infinite time' as tantamount to 'always'."[1] This is because, she says, "in *De Cael* I 12 he equates being always F with being F for an infinite time"[2] and she supports this claim by citing 281a33-282a4, "where the proof of imperishability and ingenerability is mainly conducted with the phrase 'for an infinite time', while the conclusions are drawn at 281b25 and 282a3 in terms of 'always'."[3] Sorabji confirms

---

[1] p. 65, *Passage and Possibility*.

[2] p. 69, *Passage and Possibility*.

[3] p. 69, *Passage and Possibility*. Admittedly, Broadie notes in a discussion too complicated to summarize here that there is actually a passage in *Physics* III 6 which suggests that infinity and eternity are not synonymous (pp. 76-77). However, she offers a resolution to this apparent inconsistency and says "hence, 'for an infinite time' may stand in for 'always' even if taken in the sense

Broadie's view in at least one place, assuming that "the whole of time" means "all time." Without citing a passage, he writes "the suns and stars last for the whole of time, and for Aristotle the whole of time is an infinite amount of time."[4] (Here is a case where the infinite is called a "whole," but surely as a figure of speech. Otherwise, as discussed, it implies that the infinite is like a box and is finite.)

One might object and say that Sorabji's view does not commit him (or Aristotle) to symmetry. That is, it does not follow from the claim that the whole of time is infinite that an infinite amount of time is the whole of time. To put the issue differently, as we did much earlier vis-à-vis Philoponus, the claim that infinity and eternity are equal in terms of length may strike one as simply wrong. It seems as if the past to Socrates's time is shorter than the past to 1950 CE, or better yet, since this case was already covered in dealing with Philoponus, that the past is shorter than the *whole* "past, present and future." Thus, the whole of time (which is to say, all time or eternity as "the past/present/future") has more possibilities, one of which might be for the universe to disappear completely.

For three reasons, this objection fails to undercut Statement 9.

First, the infinite past has been actual for Aristotle and, insofar as it is the past, necessary; the future is always potential. Thus, if "always" is equivalent to what has been *actual in the fullest way*, then the past plus the merely potential future (which is never fully actual insofar as it is still the future) is effectively no different—in terms of full actuality—than the past. The present is a boundary but because the boundary, as an instant of time, is analogous to a point and thus has no duration *per se*, the present adds nothing in terms of length to the past insofar as we are dealing with full actuality. At least it gives no

---

of *Physics* III" (p. 78). Sorabji addresses some of these issues (1983, p. 279).

4 Sorabji, 1980, p. 128.

Statement 9

full actuality to the future. The past (with the present as the boundary) plus potential future is always like a quantity 1 plus a potential 0, which is still actually 1. Thus, do not count any part of the future as being a positive *additional* full actuality on par with the past, even if, insofar as the future is *potential*, it is actual *in a certain sense* (as explained throughout Theta).

The next reply to the claim that eternity is longer than infinity pertains to *Metaphysics* II 2, 994b27, where Aristotle says that "the notion of infinity is not infinite." This apparently means that a finite mind cannot completely comprehend or truly grasp an infinity (or an eternity), and implies that by making the notion finite our minds inevitably distort the reality. To offer an example somewhat (but only somewhat) comparable to Plato's Allegory of the Cave in the *Republic*, it is like trying, if I may construct the example in spatial terms rather than temporal ones, to view and thus understand even a finite universe while always confined to a room that one was transported to far beyond the Milky Way. The shape of the room is indeterminable and the "prisoner" can only see the outside universe through one tiny window, which cannot swivel. All of this entails that the viewer cannot even see what is right below the window or what is around the first outside "corner" of the wall, if a wall truly exists. How, then, could the confined viewer ever sensibly compare what is fully *outside, above and below* the window with what is *outside and around the "corner"*? He might be able to compare two "slivers" of reality, like two sounds coming from *somewhere* outside, but that is a far cry from a full comparison. Moreover, how would he know that "around the corner" is not the void or is not anti-matter at the edge of the universe? The same considerations would apply to cases of infinite time (="above and below the window") and eternity (="above and below the window *and* "around the corner"). Who would dare accept that the eternity has, e.g., greater potentials for enmattered things when it might be the region of anti-matter?

Third, if the previous solutions are not satisfying, then the best way of resolving these issues is to return to the passage at *De Caelo* I 6, 274a8, which is repeated at I 7, 225a13, discussed already with respect to Philoponus. As Aristotle says and as Averroes recognized: "...a ratio...exists between a shorter and longer time when they are finite" and "There is no ratio in the relation of the infinite to the infinite (*Physics* VIII 1, 252a12-13)."

It follows, then, that even an infinity like the past cannot be said for Aristotle to be longer or shorter *or even equal*, strictly speaking, to eternity. Neither is finite. Eternity for Aristotle is therefore no longer than infinity; nor of course is it shorter; nor, strictly speaking, is it even "equal," which is a predicate for finite numerical quantities, as we saw amply when discussing Statement 2. Any attempt to compare (with respect to number or magnitude) infinities of whatever type leads to absurdity, and saying that they are "equal" is simply a figure of speech. To try therefore to compare two infinities with respect to the number of possibilities, even if the infinities share one aspect, is to open the door for all of the paradoxes given above vis-a-vis Philoponus. Thus, it follows for Aristotle that we must simply stay away from such comparisons, at least when speaking strictly.

Because both infinity and eternity are non-finite, one "contains" or "allows" no more possibilities than the other, and hence it is not the case that eternity as "past/present/future" has a possibility for the universe disappearing that the infinite past did not. For other reasons amply discussed, completely new possibilities moreover could not simply appear, as if by magic.

Premise 9 must therefore hold for Aristotle. The terms infinite and eternal are interchangeable in the context of the Not to Fear Proof.

10) Therefore, "the sun and the stars and the whole heaven are *ever active*, and there is no fear that they may sometime stand still, as the natural philosophers fear they may."

As we saw, this is stated at *Metaphysics* IX 8, 1050b22-24.[1] Aristotle thought that the upper celestial bodies and the infinite rotatory movement as described in *Physics* VII and VIII and in the *Meteorology*, and by consequence the lower cosmos and earth, are eternal. In order to get the modern impact that the conclusion had for him, Conclusion (10) might be transposed in our minds to matter and energy *always* persisting because of the laws of the Conservation of Mass and Energy.

I emphasize that we could omit "sort(s)" in the premises and still arrive at *this* conclusion (which obviously does not contain "sort"). Not only is the simplest version of the Principle of Plenitude—**for infinite things,** *what may be, will be*—unquestionably held by Aristotle, but the initial premises demonstrate that the heavens are truly infinite for him.

---

[1] Transl. W.D. Ross.

(11) What is necessary is "that which cannot be otherwise," and since what is *ever active* (that is, eternal) cannot be otherwise, what is *ever active* is necessary.

As explained in the preliminary remarks, Aristotle gives "what cannot be otherwise" as the most important of the different senses of "necessary," from which the others are derived (*Metaphysics* V 5, 1015a20-1015b16 and especially 1015a34-1015b1). We will see in Part 2 how this follows Plato's emphasis on using eternal things and truths as the primary objects and the truths for scientific knowledge, notwithstanding the Northern Greek's disagreement with Plato on issues such as the Forms. Most crucially, though, Aristotle equates eternality and necessity in Theta 8. If something is omnitemporal, it has no possibility *qua* contingency to be the opposite and so can be neither impossible nor possible. It must be necessary.

12) Hence, eternal motion of the universe exists *necessarily*, which entails that the universe is not contingent, obviating the Unmoved Mover of Pure Actuality.

This follows from the previous statements, especially given Aristotle's association of omnitemporality with necessity in this context, and given the equivalences (T, T*, T**, and T***) of the Principle of Plenitude when formulated either using possibility, impossibility or necessity, as Hintikka demonstrated. If something is omnitemporal, then for Aristotle it must be necessary and no contingent possibility exists for the opposite (even if we concoct a *conceptual possibility* claiming that the opposite could occur). Because the motivation for the Unmoved Mover in Lambda was to guarantee eternal motion of the *contingent* eternal universe, the more mature Not to Fear Proof and its final conclusion removes any need for that (merely conceptual) Entity. Because the universe and its motion are necessary *in and of themselves*, no additional reason needs to be given to ensure that the motion never stops.

Aristotle's "Not to Fear" Proof

Leibniz on the Principle of Plenitude

In closing the textual support for the Not to Fear Proof, let us examine two other views of the Principle, one by Gottfried Leibniz (1646-1716) and another by Jonathan Barnes, the highly respected contemporary British philosopher who contests Hintikka's claims. Although I cover historical reasons and figures later in Part 2 for why the Not to Fear Proof, and the Principle, was not seen for Aristotle, it is appropriate to cover these two thinkers now, because Barnes, like van Rijen, reacted to Hintikka and because Barnes also introduces Leibniz's related views.

The relevance of the Principle for Leibniz results ironically from an argument *for* the Unmoved Mover, the so-called "cosmological proof," which Leibniz devised and (part of) which started this book. The following summary is provided by Comte-Sponville, who was worried enough by the cosmological proof that he was willing to accept not only that contingency is absurd but that we should accept the absurdity rather than a (more absurd) supernatural god:

> It [the cosmological proof] is an *a posteriori* rather than an *a priori* proof. Its starting point is an experiential fact, namely the existence of the universe. Like all facts, it must have an explanation, ...what Leibniz calls the principle of sufficient reason, i.e., nothing exists or is true without a cause or a reason. Now, **the universe is incapable of explaining itself: Its existence is not necessary but contingent (it could have *not* existed)**. Thus, it must have a cause or a "sufficient reason" other than itself. What could that be? Were the cause itself contingent, it would need to be explained by another cause, which would in turn need to be explained by a third, and so on and so forth; this would end up leaving the entire series of contingent phenomena, thus the existence of the universe, unexplained. To satisfy the principle of sufficient reason, it is necessary, as Aristotle already pointed out, to stop somewhere... **We can escape from the endless**

regression only by positing as a sufficient reason for the universe the existence of a being that does not itself need another reason—one that, as Leibniz puts it, carries "its own reason for existing with it." **In a word, the set of contingent things (the universe) can be explained only by an absolutely necessary being located outside of itself; and that being, or "ultimate reason for things," is what is known as God.**[1]

Barnes deserves credit for recalling what Leibniz additionally says, which ties all of the above directly to the main thesis of this book:

> The principle [of plenitude] aroused Leibniz' wrath: "I do not believe that a more dangerous proposition than this could be formulated. For if matter takes on, successively, **all possible forms**, it follows that **nothing can be imagined** so absurd, so bizarre, so contrary to what we call justice, that it would not have happened and will not some day happen... In my opinion, this is the 'first falsehood' and the basis of atheistic philosophy."[2]

Clearly, Leibniz associates possibility with imagination. Worse, he never recognizes the Principle of *Genuine Sortal* Plenitude and thus the rest of the Not to Fear Proof, which entails that the universe is inherently necessary and *not* contingent. The cosmological proof is therefore obviated for Leibniz or for anyone else. Just as "God" explains itself for Leibniz, so the universe "explains" itself, once we understand the Not to Fear Proof. Moreover, the "more dangerous proposition" is arguably bifurcated: Leibniz's own conception of possibility as that which is (merely) "distinctly conceivable" and the arbitrariness of allowing God to explain itself, as if by definition. In another book,[3] I argue that this conception of possibility, as opposed to Aristotle's con-

---

1   Comte-Sponville, *op. cit.*, 2007, p. 81; his italics but my bolding.
2   Jonathan Barnes, "The principle of plenitude," in *Method and Metaphysics: Essays in Ancient Philosophy I*, ed. by Maddalena Bonelli (Oxford: Clarendon Press) 2011, pp. 364-70; my emphases.
3   *The Meanings of Life*, in progress.

ception of genuine possibility as even used in the *Dramatics*, has done more damage to philosophy and to Western culture than any other conception or falsehood. Mere conceivability allows doctrines of witches and werewolves and of religions that try to subjugate all others in the name of a deity that cannot be proven or objectively experienced.

Perhaps mere conceivability is also responsible for other ontological doctrines, like Platonic Forms, which involve the empirical world being only secondarily real (and the object of, say, "true belief") with the primary world of reality (and of knowledge *per se*) being beyond sense perception and only graspable through thought or faith. A devoted Platonist, though, may well argue that solid grounds exist for at least devising the doctrine and that the Forms are not *merely* conceivable. Leaving aside that Aristotle rebuts the Forms with the Third Man Argument, we would need to go too far from our important concerns here to determine whether the Forms are *merely* conceivable or whether they are *mostly* conceivable with *some* evidence motivating the whole doctrine. All of this is grist for another mill. The point here is that Leibniz not only missed Aristotle's view that the universe is *necessarily eternal* but gave the Principle of Plenitude an undeserved interpretation and evaluation.

Barnes on Hintikka and the Principle of Plenitude

Barnes's citation of the passage from Leibniz comes from Barnes's book review of Hintikka's *Time and Necessity* of 1973, to which itself I have appealed frequently. Barnes's review was published in 1977 and recently re-published as a chapter in his *Method and Metaphysics* (2011). The review needs addressing because of Barnes's reputation and because throughout the whole review Barnes doubts whether Hintikka is right about Aristotle accepting the Principle of Plenitude, which Barnes abbreviates as "(PP)". The most Barnes is willing to concede is that "if Aristotle did not argue for (PP), he did produce an excellently bright argument for a *related* thesis (p. 370; my italics)." Let us start with his basics and see that the "bright argument for a related thesis" is probably the Principle of *Sortal Genuine* Plenitude. Barnes says:

> The evidence for ascribing the Principle of Plenitude to Aristotle is not vast: indeed, Hintikka produces no passage which explicitly states (PP). Perhaps there are other passages waiting to be produced; or perhaps (PP) regulated Aristotle's thought from the deep caverns of his mind. *At any event, we may legitimately doubt that the Principle of Plenitude had any large part to play in Aristotle's conscious philosophizing* (p. 368).

If Barnes is right, something is gravely wrong with my arguments. In what follows, then, I wish to dissipate Barnes's legitimate doubt. First, Barnes does not avail himself, even in the recent re-publication, of Hintikka's 1979 work, which I believe demonstrates conclusively that the four forms of the Principle noted at the beginning of this book (T, T*, T**, and T***) are held by Aristotle and are equivalent. As Hintikka powerfully argued, accepting one means accepting the rest, but he published that related work after Barnes's review. Unless Hintikka is wrong with respect to his equivalences, then one and only one statement establishes the ground for the Principle (by giving the equivalent form in terms of necessity):

> For **what is of necessity coincides with what is always**, since **that which must be cannot not be**. Hence a thing is eternal if it is of necessity; and if it is eternal, it is of necessity (*Generation and Corruption* 337b35-a2; my bolding).

Moreover, Barnes to my knowledge never considers Broadie's *Passage and Possibility*, and she also gives powerful grounds for Aristotle being committed to the Principle. Finally, although Barnes proceeds admirably, systematically going through the passages of Aristotle that Hintikka used in 1973 to attribute the Principle to the Northern Greek, and although Barnes properly rejects or questions some of the Greek texts, he allows (on p. 367) that three passages might ground the Principle: *Metaphysics* E 1026b27-37 (which "identifies what is or happens always with what is or happens 'from necessity'"); *Generation and Corruption* B 11, 337b36: "what holds from necessity and what holds always go together" (which I just noted seems to be sufficient in and of itself, given Hintikka's "equivalences"); and *De Caelo* A 12, which has been discussed amply above. Furthermore, in my view, Barnes is not right to reject as evidence Aristotle's statement that "If what we have described is the possible or a consequence of the possible, evidently it cannot be true to say 'this is capable of being but will not be'" (*Metaphysics* IX 4, 1047b3-6). Barnes does not give the exact reasons why he rejects Aristotle's statement there as evidence for (PP), saying only that "...despite Hintikka's ingenious commentary, I am unconvinced that the Principle is to be discerned in the thickets of *Met* Θ 4, 1047b3-6." Readers can decide for themselves now whether this passage at Theta 4 is sufficient in and of itself for Aristotle holding the Principle or whether it is merely additional evidence. However, even if not completely sufficient by itself, I think that given the rest of this book, the passage of IX 4 provides still more evidence that Aristotle accepted the Principle. In any event, I address Theta more later.

Barnes rejects, too, that the arguments of the passages around one of the conclusions of the Not to Fear Proof in *Metaphysics* IX 8 are true evidence for (PP), saying:

> *Met* Θ 1050b6-24 is said by Hintikka to "sketch arguments that relate some of the variants of the Principle to each other"; but (PP) is present in the passage, if at all, only in the identification of eternal items or *ta aidia* with *ta aphtharta*, and there too *aphthartos* may mean "such as not to be destroyed."

In reply to Barnes: Aristotle makes it clear in that passage that anything potential is a potential too for the opposite, showing a tight connection between potentiality and possibility *qua* contingency (which, again, is always a possibility to be *or not to be*). To repeat part of the passage we saw before, Aristotle says: "that which is capable of not being may possibly not be; and that which may possibly not be is perishable (1050b12-13)." This establishes, at least in this context, a linkage between capability (or potentiality) and possibility, and between possibility and perishability, and thus transitively between possibility and time (which, along with motion, is clearly presupposed by perishing for Aristotle). We also saw before that in the *Prior Analytics*, in the passage that Ross and Patterson found mysterious, Aristotle assigns possibility three senses, one of which was potentiality. Thus, possibility and potentiality at times are synonyms. Aristotle adds in Theta 8 "nor can anything which is of *necessity* be potential" (1050b28), the underlying reason being that that which is eternal cannot be potential (because then, by the definition of contingent possibility, and likewise by extension to contingent potentiality, it could be also its opposite), which would contradict the hypothesis that it is eternal.

I explained already how possibility *qua* contingency in Aristotle's sense makes it improper to say "It is possible that animals die" (because animals must die and if used as contingency then it is possible that animals will not die). As we have seen to some extent and will see indubitably later, the necessity in Theta 8 must be omnitemporality. The sense of possibility then cannot be homonymous with necessity here. For this sense of necessity, "not necessary" must mean either "possible" or "not possible" (or we could sub-divide the whole category into "impossible"/ "not impossible" but the result would be the same). "Not possible," then, on this schema must entail no occurrence ever, and possible *qua* contingent must entail some occurrence *intermittently or at least once*, as van Rijen properly summarized (because if the possibility was realized always, it would have to be necessary). If Barnes appeals at least implicitly to the notion of an eternal accident, that is, a possibility that exists eternally but never gets actualized, then he unadvisedly follows the view that I discuss in depth at the beginning of Part 2.

Once we recognize the proper, temporal use of necessity by Aristotle in *this* context, its meaning is quite simple, if technical, and we do not need to resort to the very sophisticated logical analysis that Barnes develops to analyze the issues. As Barnes himself acknowledges, Aristotle in this context speaks about that which can exist *and perish*, all of which I have argued means that Aristotle does not care about wild fictions that do not obey natural laws and thus that never exist in the first place (because, obviously, if they never exist, the matter of perishing is *a fortiori* irrelevant). This, then, rules out the cases that Barnes lists in his review/chapter, such as "the first daffodils of autumn will appear when the leaves fall upwards to the trees" (p.365). Even less here than in the *Dramatics*, Aristotle simply does not care about such wild, contrary-to-natural-law fantasies, which ignore gravitation. Barnes implies that possibility for Aristotle is mere conceivability.

Still more arguments surface against Barnes's "legitimate doubt." I believe it can be shown that Barnes does not consider sufficiently the reason that Hintikka makes use of sortals in order to evade the problem with a particular accidental cloak not being cut before it wears out. Hintikka seems committed, at least implicitly, to a Principle of *Genuine Sortal* Plenitude. As good as Barnes's arguments are against the most elliptical version of the Principle of Plenitude, which even Hintikka and I would not accept unless the scope is only of eternally existing individuals, Barnes's arguments do not touch the more reasonable, completely fleshed out version of the Principle.[4]

---

4   Ignoring the difference between the Principle of Plenitude *per se* and the Principle of Genuine Sortal Plenitude is also something that Lear does in *Aristotelian Infinity, op. cit.*, in spite of Lear's effective assessment concerning Kant on the infinite past, as discussed earlier. Lear says further:
> Hintikka has argued that, for Aristotle, every genuine possibility is at some time actualized. Aristotle's theory of the infinite seems to provide a counterexample, *since it appears that the infinite has merely potential existence and is never actualized...* in Hintikka's interpretation, the infinite does not constitute a counterexample to the principle that every possibility is at some time actual. Though some variant of Hintikka's interpretation is commonly accepted, I do not think that it can be correct (1980, *op. cit.*, pp. 189-90; my italics).

Lear asserts immediately afterwards (and correctly) that Aristotle accounts with his doctrines of infinity for three distinct phenomena: the infinite divisibility of magnitudes, the infinity of numbers and of time. However, Lear states that Hintikka's view does not provide the adequate solution for them all.

In reply to Lear, his claim that "infinite has merely potential existence and is never actualized" *in the domain of historical events (or time)* is simply wrong. As we have seen and as discussed more below when showing how Aristotle drops certain aspects of the Unmoved Mover of Pure Actuality, in *Metaphysics* IX 8 the eternal entities can have no potential *qua* contingency in terms of existence. Yet they are actual more than any other kind of substance (or they have substantial actuality with only the accidental potential for whither and whence). What is infinite is *always* actual, and not just intermittently actual. Certainly, the eternal actuality has no *substantial* potentiality or possibility (*qua* contingency) for Aristotle. Thus, temporal "infinity" in this case, *contra* Lear, has been actualized and continues to be actualized, forever. The outermost spheres may be finite in size but their motion is infinite. As a predicate or subject of a proposition, "infinite" is (or has been) actual in a legitimate sense for Aristotle. As we saw before, he says: "We say that the infinite is in the sense in which we say it is day or it is the games, *existing* the way the day or Games *are actual*" (*Physics* 3.6). In short, the eternal universe excludes the proper notion of *contingency* as something applicable to itself. Strictly speaking, no possibility exists to get actualized (essentially) for that

If the above is not conclusive enough to remove entirely Barnes's "legitimate doubt," then, to return to his remark that "perhaps there are other passages to be produced," I would appeal to the primary meaning of "necessary" as discussed above, which proves that for Aristotle the word has multiple senses; likewise for an opposite, "possible" (with "impossible" being another opposite). Again, in *Metaphysics* V 5 (1015a20-1015b16), Aristotle says that the most important sense of necessary from which the others are derived, is "what cannot be otherwise." If something can be otherwise, it cannot be necessary. If not necessary, then either it must be possible or impossible, as just explained, in which case possibility not only *allows* but also *requires* intermittent existence, or at least requires one instance of existence. Finally, we could drop the focus on finite things and simply repeat the unequivocal passage from *Physics* III 4: "In the case of eternal things, what may be, is."

In short, what seems to have muddied the exegetical waters for everyone, including Barnes, is that not all senses of "necessary" for Aristotle are associated tightly with temporality, and the word, like possibility, is a rich word for the Northern Greek, with multiple senses. Although I think Barnes recognizes this to some extent, he seems to interpret Aristotle too many times as if the term is univocal or has more limited senses that it really has. I believe, therefore, that Barnes, adroit as he usually is, for once slipped on some very treacherous ice, and I myself must follow Hintikka on the matter of whether Aristotle consciously held the Principle of (Sortal Genuine) Principle. Not only did Aristotle consciously hold it, it was crucial for him renouncing the Unmoved Mover of Pure Actuality.

---

particular case. This may be the only case in which actuality never comes from a possibility but simply always exists and never has a "becoming" (from something different). In the *different* sense of possible *qua* "allowable by nature," of course, the ongoing, future universe *is* possible (or potential), but then the universe *continually gets actualized at every successive moment*, so with this meaning of "possible" the Principle is still also upheld.

Aristotle's "Not to Fear" Proof

PART 2

Aristotle's "Not to Fear" Proof

Introduction to Part 2

In Part 1, I defended the thesis that Aristotle consciously held, and importantly used, the Not to Fear Proof, including the Principle of (Sortal Genuine) Plenitude. In what follows, I cover in order these related matters:

- an objection that Platonists or anyone else might make pertaining to "eternal accidents";

- whether Aristotle championed the Principle of Plenitude, which as we have seen is the secret key to the Not to Fear Proof, for other reasons, too;

- what the Not to Fear Proof reveals about the arguments for the eternality of the world that is different from the *De Caelo*, *Metaphysics* XII and *Physics*;

- what doctrines caused commentators to ignore the Proof;

- other reasons the Proof was not seen historically;

- and, finally, how the Proof helps explain the unsolved puzzle why not only the Peripatetics immediately after Aristotle but even schools like the Stoics and Epicureans did not debate the Unmoved Mover of Pure Actuality.

Aristotle's "Not to Fear" Proof

Aristotle and Eternal Accidents

How would Aristotle handle an objection that the universe could be an "eternal accident," with the implication that the universe could go out of existence at any time, just as an "accident" of hair-color or specific weight could change at any time during the existence of a subject but never does?[1] That is, if the universe is eternal by accident, or by luck, then the universe is not necessary *in and of itself*, which of course contradicts the conclusion of the Not to Fear Proof, opening the door again for the Unmoved Mover. As emphasized, the Mover is supposed to guarantee the existence of a *contingent* eternal universe. Two Aristotelian replies to "eternal accidents" exist in the corpus, the first utterly repudiating them and the second allowing them but in a manner that in no way undercuts the Not to Fear Proof.

The first reply is that the Proof completely excludes any (genuine) possibility for the universe going out of existence, whether accidentally or not. There simply is no possibility (apart from some wild imagination) of this phenomenon, or it would have happened already in infinite time and we would not be here. This is supported by what Aristotle says, as we saw already: "An accident is an attribute which *can belong* to a thing and also *not belong*" (*Topics* IV 1, 120b35; my italics). In this sense, accident is clearly contingent. It can be or not. As such, it is the opposite of necessity and thus the necessary eternal universe excludes it. This is confirmed by what Aristotle states in a different treatise:

> "Accident" means that which applies to something and is truly stated, but *neither necessarily nor usually*; as if, for

---

[1] I am grateful to Francisco Gonzalez, a specialist of Plato, for encouraging me to cover a question that other readers might have. Indeed, Beere, as discussed below, offers an objection along this line, suggesting that Plato's God *could* will an infinite universe out of existence, even if It never does. This option might be easily interpreted as entailing that existence is an eternal accident. As a result, the universe would still be contingent.

> example, while digging a hole for a plant one found a treasure (*Metaphysics* V 30, 1025a14-17; my italics)."

This reveals why the existence itself of the universe cannot be an "eternal accident," in the sense that "existence" is an accident that *happens* to exist for an infinity. Accidents do not even exist *usually* much less *necessarily,* and the universe, we have shown for Aristotle, is necessary always in and of itself. From an Aristotelian perspective, to be necessary (or eternal) is utterly inconsistent with being "accidental." In other words, "eternal accident" is an oxymoron given the current meaning of "accident." Indeed, the passage just given reflects that at times accidents for Aristotle are like chance, which can happen when one is not expecting them, like meeting someone in the marketplace "by chance" even though one went there to shop:

> Nothing that is by chance can be indestructible or ungenerated, since *the products of chance* and fortune *are opposed to what is*, or comes to be, *always or for the most part*... But in things of that character the contradictory states proceed from one and the same capacity, the matter of the thing being the cause equally of its existence and of its non-existence. Hence opposites would be present together in actuality [if chance were indestructible or ungenerated] (*De Caelo* I 12, 283a31-283b5; my italics and my comment in brackets).

In short, neither chance nor accidents *in the current sense* are compatible with eternal existence. As Aristotle says, they are "opposed," meaning surely that the eternal existence could not just "chance" upon non-existence. However, Aristotle adds immediately in the explanation of "accident" in the *Metaphysics*:

> "Accident" has also *another sense*, namely, whatever belongs to each thing in virtue of itself, *but is not in its essence*; e.g., as having the sum of its angles equal to two right angles belongs to the triangle. *Accidents of this kind may be eternal, but none of the former kind can be* [my italics] (*Metaphysics* V 30, 1025a30-34).

Aristotle is now allowing that there could be "eternal accidents" but only because the meaning of "accident" has changed. In *this* sense, an accident could be something that belongs to the subject necessarily *but not in its essence* (typically given by the definition or formula of that kind of thing). The difference between essential and necessary is a subtle distinction for Aristotle (one finds the distinction in the definition of tragedy in the *Dramatics*, as the essential conditions *per se* and then as the "mere" necessary conditions that from the essential conditions get developed in the rest of Chapter 6; for Aristotle those would be "accidents" *in the second sense*[2]).

The difference might be considered in this way: Essence is expressed by the definition (*Topics* VII 3, 153a15). One can derive the necessary characteristics from the essential but not vice-versa. So, to continue Aristotle's example of the triangle, "having 180 degrees total," the sum of two right angles, is a necessary feature or "accident (in the second sense above)" of a triangle even though (or better yet because) it is *not* in the definition as "three-sided geometrical figure." Nevertheless, all triangles, forever, will each have 180 degrees total. Yet, the reverse does not hold. 180 degrees is also the angle of a straight line, so, from that one feature, one cannot deduce that the geometric element is a triangle as opposed to a line. Clearly, on this second meaning of accident, the subject in question, triangle, has the accident *necessarily*, and must have it as long as the subject exists. Because the universe exists eternally, a derived (necessary) "accident" of the universe will exist at all times, too, but in no manner that suggests the universe then could simply disappear. *There is no accident in the second sense like "complete self destruction" derivable from the essence of the (eternal) universe.* The only "accidents (in the second sense)" of the universe are derivable properties such as time, assuming that time is derived from, or is a measure of, motion, and assuming that motion is indeed

---

2   See my Ch. 2 of *Aristotle on Dramatic Musical Composition*, 2018, espec. pp. 138ff.

part of the essential nature of the eternal universe. "Nature is a principle of motion and change."[3] "Non-existence" or "complete self-destruction," is, therefore, no accident in the relevant sense. Later, when discussing Theta 8, we see that eternally-existing spheres have an "accidental" eternal motion in one and only prescribed way.

To conclude this section: Aristotle rules out that the possibility of the universe completely disappearing exists even at one moment in time. Much less could the possibility exist during some interval of time or during a multitude of intermittent intervals. *A fortiori,* he would not allow that the possibility exists throughout a continuous infinity of time,—an accident merely waiting always to happen "by chance" but simply never happening. This kind of "possibility" regarding eternally existing things can happen only in supernatural religious thinking or in the kind of conceivable possibility *qua* fiction that goes against natural law, like a 90-year old man almost expired on his deathbed with stage 4 cancer jumping up and defeating the healthy world champion miler by ten seconds in a mile race that sets a new world record. As we have seen, this kind of fiction often occurs not only in film-making but in philosophy (e.g., Hume's billiard balls). However, a philosopher imagining the fantastical event, even one as capable as Hume, does not increase its plausibility.

---

3   *Physics* III 1, 200b12. This, arguably, is Aristotle's tip of the hat, but *only* a tip of the hat, to Heraclitus and to the doctrine of flux. Aristotle certainly never becomes a Heraclitean *per se.*

Why Did Aristotle Champion the Principle of Plenitude?

Hintikka asks why Aristotle adopted the Principle, and after offering some inconclusive thoughts on the matter, says "I suspect that the Stagirite had further reasons for adopting the principle of plenitude. However, as I have emphasized, they are rather elusive."[1] As alluded to, Barnes questioned Hintikka's three major (but tentative) reasons for why Aristotle adopted the Principle and, after a series of very precise and very difficult-to-summarize deductions, concluded (as we saw) that "if Aristotle did not argue for (PP), he did produce an excellently bright argument for a related thesis."[2] I now offer some reasons for Aristotle's motivation, in part because Barnes seemingly takes up only one of the senses of "possibility" of the many I gave at the beginning of the examination of Statement 3 (given his example of possibility as leaves floating upwards and re-attaching themselves to twigs.)

Hintikka may have come upon one of the reasons earlier, without realizing it. As is known by all specialists of Plato and Aristotle, the Athenian believed that only what existed always—viz., the Forms—could be known truly. Aristotle rejects the Forms, which would include any Form "Cloak." Yet, Hintikka himself notes how much Plato's focus on the eternal still could have influenced Aristotle's thought, without Hintikka precisely naming Plato:

> ...Aristotle argues for his doctrine that we have knowledge in the full sense of the word only of what is eternal or forever unchangeable:
>
>> Now what scientific knowledge (*epistēmē*) is, if we are to speak exactly and not follow mere similarities, is plain from what follows. *We all suppose that what we know **is not even capable** of being otherwise*; of things capable of being otherwise we

---

1   *Time and Necessity*, p. 107.
2   Barnes, "The principle of plenitude," p. 370.

do not know, when they have passed outside our observation, whether they exist or not. Therefore *the object of scientific knowledge is **of necessity***. Therefore ***it is eternal***... (*Eth Nic*, VI 3, 1139b18-23).

It is worthwhile noticing Aristotle's locution "We all suppose." It shows that Aristotle thought that what he was saying was not a peculiarity of his but rather a commonplace among the Greeks.³

The Principle of Plenitude is just a variation of the stricture that, as Hintikka and Broadie have both shown and as we saw at the beginning with Hintikka's four equivalences, indicates "in an infinite time, what necessarily is always is." Therefore, this "necessarily is" and "always is" must be the object of scientific knowledge. Aristotle also says in the *Metaphysics*, part of which I emphasized before:

"...actuality is prior [to potentiality] in a higher sense also; for eternal things are prior in substance to perishable things, and *no eternal thing exists potentially* (1050b6-7)... Nor can anything which is of necessity be potential; yet these things are primary; *for if these did not exist, nothing would exist* [my italics] (*Metaphysics* IX 8, 1050b18-19).

Note also *Metaphysics* XI, and its further agreement with Plato:

For in pursuing the truth one must start from the things that are always in the same state and suffer no change. **Such are the heavenly bodies**; for these do not appear to be now of one nature and again of another, but are *manifestly always the same and share in no change* (*Metaphysics* XI 7, 1063a13-16; my italics and bolding).

Aristotle must mean that the heavenly bodies share in no *substantial* change because, as we see soon in detail, he specifies in Theta 8 that they have one potential: They eternally move in a certain circle, only

---

3   *Time and Necessity*, p. 75; my emphases.

having the possibility of going from "here to there." This is an eternal accident (in the second sense of accident that we examined). Yet, to emphasize, the heavenly bodies have no potentiality "for opposites," e.g., to stop or reverse course or to disappear. In effect, eternal heavenly bodies in some important ways *function* like the Platonic Forms, although, of course, unlike the Forms, they are physical. Aristotle also states, as we saw once before:

> "...of necessary things, some have an external cause of their necessity, and others have not, but it is through them [those whose necessity is internal] that other things are of necessity what they are" (*Metaphysics* V 5, 1015b9-12)... [and] "therefore if there are certain things which are eternal and immutable, there is nothing in them which is compulsory *or which violates their nature* (*Metaphysics* V 5, 1015b15-16; my italics).

The last phrase is crucial. It is *the nature* of the eternal heavenly bodies to move always. No other explanation is needed, confirmation of which we see later.

Aristotle may have stumbled then upon the Principle because of his reflections on Plato's epistemic principles or because of the importance of eternality and necessity, or both, as just noted in the passages from the *Ethics* and the *Metaphysics*. Once Aristotle accepted in some contexts that possibility (*qua* contingency) meant intermittent existence (in nature versus in thought) for both the "to be" and "not to be" sides of the contingency; that necessity involved omnitemporality (and vice-versa) in some ontological contexts; and that impossibility meant no occurrence ever, it is an easy insight to recognize that any kind of (real) possibility will occur at least once in infinite time. It is virtually a matter of definition once one leaves aside preposterous fictions. I venture to say that Aristotle's empiricism is so often contrasted with Plato's idealism that their commonality with respect to the importance of eternal phenomena is too often under-appreciated.

The Principle could also have arisen during Aristotle's logical reflections, although for both Broadie and Hintikka arguably no great distinction holds between Aristotle's logic and his metaphysics with respect to the modalities, at least in terms of fundamentals, given what both scholars say at one stage of their thought. I have reported some of those views, although I noted that both scholars subsequently changed their initial position that the temporal notion of the modalities is the one and only notion across all domains for Aristotle. We also saw that they focussed at times on whether modality was analytic or synthetic. Hintikka asserts that "there was no sharp distinction in Aristotle between logical and natural possibility."[4] On a closely related issue, though, Hintikka lays down a seeming paradox, writing:

> Another consequence of the principle of plenitude is that if there *can* be exceptions to a temporally unrestricted generalization, there *will in fact* be such exceptions. **In other word, the only *true* unrestricted generalizations will be the necessary ones**... The outcome of our analysis is almost paradoxical. The very difference between assertoric and apodeictic generalizations seems to disappear for Aristotle. This is paradoxical, for Aristotle was the founder of modal logic...[5]

First, a preliminary remark, which is to say, a rhetorical question: Why would Hintikka find it odd that "the only *true* unrestricted generalizations will be the necessary ones," given his own citation (as shown a few paragraphs above) from the *Nicomachean Ethics* that "Therefore *the object of scientific knowledge is of necessity*"? Aristotle seems perfectly consistent. In any event, in what follows, I aim to show that the difference between assertoric and apodeictic generalizations disappears at least at times for Aristotle and *should* disappear given his metaphysics and semantics. He did not think he had two different kinds of logic, with modal logic somehow being distinctively different from assertoric logic.

---

4   *Time and Necessity*, p. 107.
5   1973, pp. 112-3; my bolding but his own italics.

Why did Aristotle Champion the Principle of Plenitude?

Logic for him has modal aspects but this is not modal logic in the modern sense. He certainly does not think, for instance, that the differences in validity between some particular propositions and some universal ones involve two difference kinds of logic: universal logic and particular logic. Why should we therefore attribute to him two different logics just because assertoric statements are discussed with their peculiarities at some times and apodeictic ones are discussed at other times with their own peculiarities? It is wrong in my opinion to view him anachronistically through our lens of modern logic.[6] Much better is to take the approach that Patterson champions in trying to understand Aristotle's logic, using the concepts, approaches and principles that Aristotle himself used, as much as we can determine, whether or not Patterson is right on each and every point (and I make no claim on that issue). It is open for debate, then, whether Aristotle merging assertoric and apodeictic generalizations is paradoxical concerning modal logic, and it also depends on how one defines "modal logic." However, I only offer some basic thoughts and need not settle completely this particular issue here, leaving it to those specialists working on *On Interpretation* and the *Prior Analytics* (and I emphasize the first treatise also, because, however one defines logic, whether as the study of valid forms of argumentation or of valid deductions or the like, clearly the preliminary definitions and aspects like negations of sentences are part of the foundation of logic and those are covered in *On Interpretation*).

Suffice it to say now that Aristotle makes modal claims with assertoric sentences, where "necessary" is used at times as a copula (in the form "need be" or "must") and at other times as a predicate, and thus in a way the assertoric and apodeictic generalizations can indeed collapse into one system, whether or not other concerns with validity or with the formal properties of implication or deduction or with *de dicto*

---

6   This is not an uncommon practice among current ancient Greek specialists who were first trained in modern (modal) logic and then who look at Aristotle through that prism.

properties of sentences rather than *de re* claims about the real world cause a shift in the meaning of any of the modal terms. I pursue all of this here further only as a step toward giving some evidence that the Principle of Plenitude seemingly was not inspired by logical considerations for Aristotle (at least on the surface), although the evidence I adduce hardly rigorously proves that particular point. Still, Aristotle never emphasizes the Principle in the logical treatises, even though he does, e.g., explain possibility *qua* contingency in *On Interpretation* 9 and then in other ways in *Prior Analytics*. We might, therefore, more fruitfully consider the epistemological domain, as just discussed, or the upcoming metaphysical-theological domain as being the most likely source of the Principle (and in some ways the latter domain overlaps with the epistemic concerns already noted).

The *prima facie* evidence that Aristotle does not make a hard distinction, as moderns tend to do, between assertoric ("to be") and apodeictic ("necessary" and "possible") logic is seen in four ways:

1) As alluded to, he uses the term "necessary" (or "possible") as a copula and at other times a predicate in assertoric generalizations (which immediately collapses or combines the assertoric and the apodeictic);
2) "what belongs," "what must belong," and "what may belong" are all at the same level and treated by him throughout the two logical treatises (*On Interpretation* and *Prior Analytics*) as being part of *one* enterprise;
3) deductions are claimed by him to be the same for necessary and for "merely assertoric" propositions, in spite of minor (and admittedly important and complicated) differences;
4) negation is covered for both "modes" (assertoric or apodeictic) in a few chapters of one treatise, as if they belong to one system, notwithstanding that the modes have differences.

Let us cover some preliminaries before going systematically through the four points, although I cover (4) in the prefatory remarks because

Why did Aristotle Champion the Principle of Plenitude?

that issue is covered in *On Interpretation* whereas the rest are covered in the *Prior Analytics*, and the latter presupposes and extends the former.

Language is invented for Aristotle (*On Interpretation* 2 & 4) in the sense that it is conventional, even if the capability of making sounds, mapping the sound to an object in the world to give it meaning, and communicating are natural. As emphasized repeatedly in this book, truth does not make reality but vice-versa, for truth is a property of categorical sentences (*On Interpretation* 4, 17a3-6; 9, 19a33). Also, "...it is not because of the affirming or denying that it [a state of affairs] will be or will not be the case..." (*On Interpretation* 9, 18b38-39). (Categorical) sentences, which we are concerned with in logic and which are holders of truth, falsity and indeterminacy, as opposed to interrogatives or commands, are made in the simplest cases by conjoining a subject and verb, *the latter of which conveys the time*. As the Northern Greek says:

> A verb is what...signifies time" (*On Interpretation* 3, 16b6) ... [and] "Every statement-making sentence [which are the only candidates of truth and falsity, unlike, say, a prayer] *must contain a verb or an inflexion of a verb. For even the definition of man is not yet a statement-making sentence—unless "is" or "will be" or "was" or something of this sort is added* [my italics] (*On Interpretation* 5, 17a7-9).

This means that a thought, or a corresponding utterance (which expresses the thought), or a written proposition like "My mother Catherine walks" is true or not depending on the time it is uttered, unless the statement is always true (or always false); cf. Theta 10, 1051b6-17. In that latter type of "timeless" case, as I once suggested, obviously we do not need to add the time but only because the temporal qualification is redundant, not because time is irrelevant (which, again, means that these truths are timeless not in the sense that they are "out of time" but because they are *always in time*). Additionally, and more to the crux of the matter in the passage just quoted, in no way is the present tense or merely assertoric "is"/"to be" given more priority by Aristotle than, say, the future or past tense, or the kind of modality like "must be" that is surely covered under the qualifying phrase "something of this sort."

Aristotle then indicates that we can add a predicate to a simple subject-verb, of which more later, but the important consideration for the moment is that *because of the verb*, temporality is built into Aristotle's notion of truth, which itself is a precondition of his logic (for syllogistic and validity cannot be formulated without using the notion of truth). It does not matter whether the statements in a syllogism are formulated with the verb "is," "must be," or "can be."

As the final bit of background, Aristotle covers negation in *On Interpretation,* my point (4) above. After covering negations of "to be"-type of sentences, he adds at the beginning of Chapter 12 that because of unique problems we need to handle negations and implications also concerning the possible (*dunaton*), which could be synonymous for the potential; the admissible (*endechomenon*), which could be synonymous for the possible; the impossible (which obviously, then, is not just the opposite of possible), and the necessary. That "impossible" is not simply a shortened form of "not possible," as it often is for modern thinkers, is shown at the end of Chapter 12, before he proceeds to the implications of various statements within this group: "We must take the opposite expressions to be these: possible—not possible; admissible—not admissible; impossible—not impossible; necessary—not necessary; true—not true" (*On Interpretation* 12, 22a10-12). The crucial point now is that the "unique problems" with statements involving necessity ("must be") and possibility ("may be") are merely an extension of the previous discussion, not a whole separate field of logic.

Let us now cover the other three points noted above, again, showing that Aristotle has one logic, not two.

Why did Aristotle Champion the Principle of Plenitude?

1) Aristotle uses "necessary" (and sometimes "possible") as a copula and at other times a predicate in assertoric generalizations (which immediately collapses or combines the assertoric and the apodeictic).

It is often assumed nowadays that necessity, like possibility, is a fundamental property of some sentences (like laws of logic, e.g., "X cannot be both y and not-y at the same time and same respect" or "It is necessary that X is not both y and not-y..."), especially when *de dicto* and *de re* senses are distinguished, with *de dicto* being naturally applied to sentences. Modern logicians typically assume that Aristotle not only follows suit but holds the same fundamental divisions in his work. However, necessity and possibility are for Aristotle more fundamentally properties of, say, events, such as "the necessary (or possible) event." In this way, possibility is no different from a predicate like straight, or red, or good, and could be used in the same way logically or metaphysically that these other predicates are used.[7] As Aristotle says in *On Interpretation* 12:

> For as in the previous examples "to be" and "not to be" are *additions*, while the actual things that are subjects are white and man, so here "to be" serves as subject, *while "to be possible" and "to be admissible" are additions*—these determining the possible and not possible in the case of "to be," just as in the previous cases "to be" and "not to be" determine the true (my italics; 21b26-32).

Thus, I might say in discussing animals wanting to live: "Oxygen is necessary." As we see throughout this book, Aristotle uses "necessary" and "possible" as predicates in various claims, e.g., "Eternal motion is necessary." The claims are emphatically "modal," in that they use terms like "necessary," and yet ontological in that they are direct claims about existence. Moreover, they are part of assertoric formulations. Are they therefore assertoric or apodeictic claims? Presumably both,

---

[7] Hintikka himself provides elegant graphs and explanations of Aristotle's modal logic (especially Ch 2 of *Time and Necessity*, pp. 27-40), at least from one perspective.

if by "apodeictic" we simply mean "clearly demonstrated" or "necessarily true" or the like, because by various (assertoric) arguments that we see throughout this book Aristotle will demonstrate that what is eternal is necessary (and if "apodeictic" requires a full syllogism for the reader, then it is odd that Hintikka speaks of an "apodeictic generalization," which would be merely one proposition). Even basic valid syllogisms like bArbArA with "is" as the copula are demonstrated by Aristotle to be *necessary*, so arguably the assertoric forms of validity are, by definition, apodeictic.

Moreover, as just suggested, Aristotle treats the modals at other times not as predicates or "additions" but as verbal copulas (e.g., "must be" in lieu of the equivalent "necessary"), which takes us to our next point.

> 2) "what belongs," "what must belong," and "what may belong" are all at the same level and treated throughout the two "logical" treatises (*On Interpretation* and *Prior Analytics*);

Following the remark that the verb gives the time, with the examples being "is," "will be" and "was," along with the other options noted, Aristotle suggests that no important fundamental difference exists between the modals and the "to be"-type of sentences. He asserts "Every proposition states that something either *belongs* or *must belong* or *may belong*..." (*Prior Analytics* I 2, 25a1-2; my italics). He does not indicate that the different sentences belong to two different systems of logic. He also says at *Prior Analytics* I 13, 32b2, that "possibility" is in the "same rank" as "to be," and he notes at the beginning of I 8:

> Since there is a difference according as something *belongs*, *necessarily belongs*, or *may belong* (for many things belong, but not necessarily, others neither necessarily nor indeed at all, but it is possible for them to belong), it is clear that *there will be different deductions for each of these*, and deductions with differently related terms, one concluding from what is necessary, another from what is, a third from what is possible (*Prior Analytics* I 8, 29b29-35; my italics).

Why did Aristotle Champion the Principle of Plenitude?

Again, the differences in deduction are for the Northern Greek part of the current examination, and not a new field or different type of logic. Notice the "a third from what is possible." Does this mean that there is a third type of logic, of "possibility logic" that is distinct from assertoric and "modal (*qua* necessary) logic"? No one to my knowledge ever claims this, but they should if they consider modal logic regarding necessity to be different from assertoric. This take us to our final point.

> 3) deductions are claimed by him in effect to be the same for necessary and "merely assertoric" propositions;

This point is made immediately by Aristotle after (2) above. He adds:

> In the case of what is necessary, things are pretty much the same as in the case of what belongs; for when the terms are put in the same way, then, whether something *belongs* or *necessarily belongs* (or does not belong), *a deduction will or will not result alike in both cases*, the only difference being the addition of the expression "necessarily" to the terms (I 8, 29b35-30a1; my italics).

This entails that the following deduction—to take but one example—is valid and is similar to bArbArA (which itself normally has "is" as the copula). In other words, the deduction is similar to the case in which something "belongs" (as opposed to "necessarily belongs"):

All men must be animate (things).
All animate things must be mortal (things).
Thus, all men must be mortal (things).

Again, this is the valid figure bArbArA as typically conceived when "are" historically has been used instead of "must be." However, there are not two logics, assertoric and apodeictic (even if other, various combinations of "must" statements, or of "must" and "is" statements, are different in terms of validity from the combinations of only "is" statements). Again, the apodeictic is merely part and parcel of one overall system of reasoning *and of deduction*, the main focus of logic. If not, again, we would have actually three logics, with the one pertaining to possibility separate from the others pertaining to statements involving "something belongs" or "something necessarily belongs." Yet, to emphasize, no one to my knowledge maintains that Aristotle has three logical systems, nor should anyone make such a declaration.

Thus, for Aristotle not only can we make assertoric claims and use assertoric logic but we make deductions about the world while using modal terms. Is this assertoric logic, then, or apodeictic? Again, it seems to be both.

A word of caution and I believe a source of historical dilemmas: Aristotle acknowledges (as we saw above) in *Prior Analytics* I 13 that "possibility" can be used in two ways, which complicates his deductions and conversions, as he explicitly admits. He proceeds with an analysis that takes this into account, and the analysis becomes extremely complicated, especially when he tries to determine the implications or deductions that hold validly or not between "what belongs," "what need belong," and *"what may belong,"* as the many who have worked on his *Prior Analytics* over the centuries can attest (and van Rijen gives a short but illuminating summary in the work cited). However, again, as Patterson and others have emphasized, it will not do to apply our modern divisions of logic or our modern principles to Aristotle. To emphasize, not only does Aristotle make apodeictic generalizations with assertoric forms (and this is not something Patterson says, to my knowledge, although my knowledge may be lacking here) but the Northern Greek examines "to be," "must be," and "may be" throughout the same book, as if they are all part of one system, distinguished because of the meanings that each has, *with possibility being especially ambiguous and requiring extra analysis.* (As we saw when he evaluated van Rijen's work, Patterson discusses various deductions with mixed premises, and whether a necessary conclusion can follow from two premises when only one is necessary, so what I mean is that

Why did Aristotle Champion the Principle of Plenitude?

I am not sure about Patterson's view on how Aristotle conceives of the general relation between assertoric and apodeictic logics and whether there are two logics or only one).

We should not be surprised, therefore, that, in Hintikka's words, "the very difference between assertoric and apodeictic generalizations seems to disappear for Aristotle." Again, whether paradox raises its ugly head concerning related, more advanced issues in what moderns consider modal logic, I leave to the specialists like himself, Patterson and van Rijen. In his own mind, Aristotle may not have completed his full system and what we have may be his first attempts to get the very complex, very detailed, and lengthy matters right, as an in-depth look at the extremely technical *Prior Analytics* shows in and of itself. Alternatively, and this is only one other option, logicians may not have fully realized the subtle difficulties because possibility has (at least) two senses for Aristotle and two possible outcomes in any deduction (recall how the truth of "Animals may die" differs depending on whether "may" has the sense of contingency or has one of the other senses of "may"). Hintikka is an exception and those wishing to pursue how two different senses of possibility (contingency versus possibility that is homonymous with necessity) affect deductions in the *Prior Analytics* will find him introducing the topic in 1979 (pp. 118-24, espec. 119).

To conclude, necessity and other modals can be at times:
1) considered as properties of the world and of its objects, and thus the associated reasoning regarding validity can be reduced at least in some ways to (assertoric) syllogistic;[8]

---

[8] See Hintikka, p. 112-118, *Time and Necessity* on this topic. My just-finished account helps explain the paradox Hintikka believes we are stuck with on his p. 113: "Indeed we have a contrary problem in our hands..." See also his pp. 136ff, on the apodeictic-assertoric confusion. Lastly, note there how for Hintikka using techniques of modern logic do not capture Aristotle's thought processes, being "ahistorical," whereas reducing to the syllogistic, which Hintikka ultimately agrees Aristotle does, appears to be perfectly consistent with what Aristotle could have done initially before he applies "ne-

2) used by Aristotle via his semantics (of, e.g., truth and affirmation) to tie his whole system of logic to his fullest ontology in an analogous way that assertoric syllogistic is tied to a sub-domain of ontology (represented by "is" statements). By this I mean that, although syllogistic validity is purely formal—allowing us to insert any terms into the propositions that make up syllogisms, such as "All A's are (or must be) B's,"—nevertheless, what grounds validity of the modals are deductions or proofs from the real world, including the eternal universe, using truth and real-life cases, with eternal truths suggesting necessity or "must be" claims.

This brings us to the ramifications for this book. Even though contingency is used very clearly in *On Interpretation* 9 as *one* of the senses of "possibility," the Principle of Plenitude is never emphasized anywhere in the logical treatises. Does this mean Aristotle had not already formulated it? No, not necessarily. Why would he mention it? What would it give him in the logical treatises, which are part of the so-called *Organon*? It is very hard to see how the Principle would contribute to the goals of logic, so no judgment can be made, at least as far as I can determine, on whether logical considerations motivated Aristotle to accept the Principle. Conversely, though, his not explicitly using it to explain a logical principle has no apparent bearing on whether it was already accepted by him or not.

In summary with respect to modal logic: Aristotle could have developed his views on modalities, and by extension, the Principle of Plenitude in many ways. It is plausible that the easiest or most fitting way was to first use the modalities as predicates, that is, as ontological properties *of objects or events in the world*, like "red," in conjunction with the (assertoric) syllogism. Only later did he extend the scope

---

cessity" and "possibility" to three-part sentences as an *additional*, perhaps *de dicto*, component.

Why did Aristotle Champion the Principle of Plenitude?

from ontology to sentences that themselves refer to reality (or not), all of which complicates the whole matter. That is, he could have developed first the syllogistic with "possible" and "necessary" as mere attributes of a subject or as a "middle term" in a deduction, or as a copula "must," *expressing merely a different aspect of time*. Then, in formulating his thoughts in *On Interpretation* and *Prior Analytics*, or working them out in preliminary ways, perhaps with diagrams, he may have arrived at *de dicto* insights and at the Principle (whether or not in line with Plato's principle that the best knowledge is of what exists always). Because "necessity" is first used as a predicate or as a copula, and especially in the latter case—*since the verb gives the time*—Aristotle could then have drawn out the temporal associations that the modal terms have, with "necessary" or "must" being associated with "always." In short, *de re* necessity trumps *de dicto* necessity not only from the perspective of the current issues but from the perspective of the chronology of Aristotle's discoveries (which is not to deny that there may be situations in which *de dicto* necessity is more important).

While on the topic of chronology: Before leaving the topic of assertoric versus apodeictic generalizations (and alleged multiple "logics"), I finish with one observation, starting with the relevant question: Is syllogistic primary when it uses present-tensed verbs like "is" or infinitives such as "to be" or when it uses modal notions like "must be"? On the surface, it may seem as if (mere) assertorical statements using "is" are primary. Is this Aristotle's deeper view, though?

In *On Interpretation*, Aristotle proceeds systematically from the simplest to the more complex, starting with the atomic elements of a statement (name/subject, verb, and predicate), then negation, then combination, then the options of combining with negation, including the differences when negating a particular subject like Socrates or a universal ("which is by its nature predicated of a number of things…. man, for instance is a universal, Callias a particular" [*On Interpreta-*

tion 7, 17a38-17b1]). He then in *On Interpretation* 10-11 explores systematically affirmation (or negation) and its opposite using "is" with respect to universals and particulars. Afterwards, at the beginning of *On Interpretation* 12 (21a34-37), he states, as I alluded to:

> *Having cleared up these points*, we must consider how negations and affirmations of the *possible to be* and the *not possible* are related to one another, and of the *admissible* and *not admissible*, and about the *impossible and the necessary*. For there are some puzzles here (my italics).

It seems, then, as if "is" or "to be" is more fundamental than, or prior to, the modalities of possible, admissible and necessary, because the discussion of "is" is "cleared up" first.

Yet, Aristotle may have proceeded in this manner in *On Interpretation* simply for heuristic purposes. When dealing with syllogisms, Aristotle presumably worked out first the laws of syllogistic with basic categorical sentences (with a subject, verb, and predicate), because those cases seem simpler than adding "It is necessary that" (or "It is possible that") to a categorical sentence. Basic syllogisms take three elements maximum whereas adding "it is necessary that" to a categorical sentence adds another element, and creates many more permutations. That Aristotle is well aware of what complications ensue when adding more elements is shown by his discussion of *On Interpretation* 10, when he mentions that adding a third element, a predicate, to a subject and verb increases the number of cases we must cover with respect to negation. Once sentences, rather than the *de re* realities with which the basic sentences concern themselves, become the target of the modalities, the whole system becomes more complex.

Still, this should not cause us to ignore insights when sentences are used with only three elements, but with, for instance, "must be" as the copula instead of "is." In this case, comparing kiwis with kiwis, we can see that the seeming priority in *On Interpretation* and *Prior Ana-*

lytics of "is" or "to be" and the related syllogistic may be simply from the standpoint of explanation or of teaching, not from the standpoint of ontology (recall how the three-dimensional object for Aristotle is actually more fundamental ontologically than the mere point or line, even if the latter two concepts might be explained first in geometry).

The following statements suggest that for Aristotle necessity is really prior in logic, at least in the sense of most important. At the end of *On Interpretation* 13, Aristotle suggests that necessity is more fundamental than mere existence (typically captured by "to be" or "is") or than non-eternal existence:

> Perhaps, indeed, *the necessary and not necessary are first principles of everything's either being or not being, and one should look at the others as following from these.* It is evident from what has been said that what is of necessity is in actuality; so that, if the things which are eternal are prior, then also actuality is prior to capability (*On Interpretation* 13 23a19-23; my italics).

"Necessity" or "must be" is therefore ultimately prior to every other type of being. "Is" or "to be" may be prior (or not) to "capability" (i.e., "may" or "is possible"), and both may be prior to "impossibility," but I leave aside these secondary issues (e.g., of whether impossibility is prior to possibility or vice-versa). This captures the views of Theta 8 and of the Northern Greek's theory of scientific knowledge, which is of the eternal or of the necessary, and which cannot be otherwise, all of which suggests, to emphasize, that propositions using "is," "to be" and "may be" are secondary. It also repeats the emphasis on necessity *qua* actuality and how it is prior to potentiality (or possibility), the latter of which, we saw, gets linked with intermittent existence throughout an infinity, as discussed in almost identical terms in *Metaphysics* IX 8. Thus the same doctrine extends across *On Interpretation, Nicomachean Ethics*, and the *Metaphysics*, which attests to Aristotle holding it for long periods or throughout his career.

To return to the question of how Aristotle came upon the Principle of Plenitude: After the insights connecting necessity with omnitemporality, it would have been a tiny step for Aristotle to arrive at the following equivalences, which Hintikka showed, although the order of realization may have occurred as follows:

First, (T*) that which is always, is by necessity (because of the primary meaning of necessity as "that which cannot be otherwise" and because of the other reasons given above);

Second, (T***) that which never is, is impossible (this is the other, simple extreme, suggested by the just-mentioned "*necessary and not necessary are first principles*");

Third, (T) each possibility *qua* contingency must be realized at some moment of time (this is the only option left, because if neither omnitemporality nor "never-in-all-time" applies, then temporary duration is the only remaining choice); and

Fourth, (T**) nothing eternal is contingent (which we can deduce from T* and from the definition of contingency, which itself *requires* that something *be and not be intermittently*; if something is eternal, its negative intermittent option is forever excluded).

Whether or not this was Aristotle's exact sequence of discovery, again, the Principle of Plenitude is not at all apparent anywhere in *On Interpretation* or *Prior Analytics*. Thus, even though at least the groundwork is seemingly laid in these treatises for holding the Principle, including recognizing possibility as contingency, or even if the Principle had been understood already—in which case Aristotle thought it was irrelevant for the themes in the two treatises—it appears that he had some other motivation for recognizing the Principle. Alternatively, he became aware of the Principle after he wrote the treatises.

Why did Aristotle Champion the Principle of Plenitude?

Before continuing with the other options for how or why Aristotle first articulated and championed the Principle, we need to return to the different versions of the Principle to be clear that we need only search for Aristotle's motivation, or at least source, of the Principle of *Genuine Sortal* Plenitude. In the four equivalences above, the subjects could all be eternal things and without question Aristotle had formulated the most basic version of the Principle by the time he wrote *Physics* III 4, 203b30. As we saw, he avers there that "In the case of eternal things, what may be is." This passage, and its context, follows the advice given by Plato, to start first with what always exists for the best knowledge before advancing to other areas.

Hintikka himself says that "the most explicit argument, or approximation to an argument [for the Principle], is found in *De Caelo* I 12.281a28-282a5," which is intriguing because in that passage Aristotle deals not merely with possibility *qua* contingency (which even an eternal subject like a planet can have concerning, say, motion at a particular moment) but with "things capable of being and not being." That is, he now in *De Caelo* appears to have recognized that the Principle could apply to *finite* things or, at least given my arguments regarding Broadie, finite things *qua* members of sortals. This is confirmed by him immediately adding "this is true in every category..a man or white..." Because this chapter deals with the ingenerability and indestructibility of the universe, the application of the Principle follows the suggestion above. The eternal things are primary, as they were with Plato, and the other knowledge results secondarily. Hence, arguably by *De Caelo* I 12, Aristotle had recognized, or started to realize, the Principle of Genuine Sortal Plenitude.

There is a good chance, then, that the Principle arose in the context of physics or ontological metaphysics and then inspired the Not to Fear Proof, which was invoked to replace the Anaxagorean-influenced Unmoved Mover, of which more in the next section. Perhaps, though, the Principle arose instead in the context of epistemology and then was applied to first philosophy (or any combination of these options).

This takes us to the final option. Aristotle may simply have intuited the Principle at any stage of his thought, for we may ask the same question about how, why and when he devised the Law of Non-Contradiction or the syllogism or any other analytical tool that we attribute to him. He typically does not say what drove him to accept, or devise, a doctrine and probably the answer is the same as for most other ancient and modern thinkers. One intuits something new or imagines a solution to a problem. Examining the various texts to see if and when other passages presuppose the Principle, and thus what the chronology is for the source of the Principle, might be a very difficulty undertaking.

In summary, we cannot easily say for certain given the extant texts when and why Aristotle first accepted the Principle of Genuine Sortal Plenitude, although I have suggested that the natural progression for him was to accept the basic Principle for eternal things (in the *Physics*) and then to adapt it to the finite things (in the *De Caelo*). I recount the most obvious choices for the source of the Principle:

1) Aristotle in his epistemology and science follows Plato's emphasis that true knowledge is of what exists always and that what exists always is necessary. Thus Aristotle comes to accept that science is of "the necessary," and his other theory, with the other modals, develops accordingly.

2) Aristotle fleshes out the meanings of necessity and possibility over time, in the same way he fleshes out the meaning of other words in his lexicon (later when discussing Theophrastus I give another example of this same phenomenon in discussing how "unity" acquires a new meaning in his later doctrines). This led to him recognizing the Principle. We will see an apparent example of the result of this richer and more sophisticated understanding of the modals when examining how and why Aristotle gives up certain claims in Lambda 6 about Pure Ac-

tuality to arrive at his most mature Not to Fear Proof.

3) Because Aristotle indicates that the verb expresses the time, he realized in the logical treatises that "must," "is" and "may be" have different temporal implications, with "must" meaning "always," "is" meaning "currently" (or at the time implied by the speaker), and "may be" meaning at least some (but only some) future existence not coinciding with the "must" or "is." This led to the four different "equivalences" of the Principle, as Hintikka had articulated them.

4) Aristotle simply intuited the Principle at any stage of his career, probably from about mid-life onward when he was at the Academy, notably because of the discussion in the *Phaedrus* that is similar to the unmoved mover and the heavens not stopping that I will reproduce and examine in the next section.

Whatever the origin of the Principle, Part 1 of this book reveals that it is the key to the Not to Fear Proof, with substantial parts of the Proof being in *Metaphysics* IX 8 (a text that is universally granted to be from the later years of Aristotle's life). All of the other statements of the Proof are easily found in the Aristotelian corpus, and without question the Proof then obviates any need for the Unmoved Mover of Pure Actuality. Given the importance of "first philosophy" for Aristotle and how he actually agrees with Plato on the importance of eternal things for truth and for the existence of anything else, his professional reflection on the related issues of eternality must have started early in his days as a student in the Academy. It would not be surprising that this reflection caused the realization of the Principle of (Genuine Sortal) Plenitude, which then was appropriately applied first (and by a happy coincidence) to "first philosophy" or to metaphysics-ontology-meteorology, or to epistemology and science, and then later, if at all, to other arenas like logic. The combinations, though, are numerous, and let us leave the matter as is. Without question, how Aristotle first recognized the Principle is different from him accepting and applying it, and Part 1 has amply shown an extremely important, if not the most important, way in which Aristotle applied it.

Ramifications for *De Caelo*, the Unmoved Mover of Lambda, and *Physics*

De Caelo

We see now that the Not to Fear Proof goes beyond anything that Aristotle says in *De Caelo* to insure the *necessary* eternality of the universe, despite Hintikka mentioning that the closest formulation of the Principle of Plenitude comes in this book. Broadie herself stresses "the continuity of nature," and (correctly) accepts the position in *De Caelo* I 12 that the universe will always exist, although whether it always exists *necessarily* in and of itself is not at all clear from *De Caelo* or from her own account. Nor is it clear from van Rijen, who replies to some of Broadie's arguments pertaining to the sense of possibility in *De Caelo*, especially with respect to maxima. Aristotle advances the claim in *De Caelo* I 10, especially 280a29-31, that if the heaven is ungenerated, it cannot be destroyed (and vice-versa, that if it can be destroyed, it must have been generated, *contra* Plato, who in the *Timaeus* thought that the universe, or at least the heavens, could be created and yet be never destroyed). However, what grounds the protasis—the "if" clause—in the argument for the ingenerability of the heaven? Aristotle cannot simply assert "if p, then q." He must give the evidence that p is true, for q to follow demonstrably. One place, seemingly the primary and maybe only place, where he clearly argues for the protasis is *De Caelo* I 3, where he highlights the infinite circular motion of the primary body to support the claim that the heaven is ungenerated:

> The *mere evidence of the senses* is enough to convince us of this, at least with human certainty. For in the whole range of time past *so far as our inherited records reach*, no change appears to have taken place either in the whole scheme of the outermost heaven or in any of its proper parts (270b12-16; my italics).

Any reflection, however, by Aristotle or his critics on this assertion, especially given the views of Zeno and others who suggest that perception cannot detect minute changes (one example being the millet seed falling and striking the ground, the noise of which is too soft to detect), would or should have forced Aristotle to understand that the changes in the outermost heaven might have been too subtle to detect. The inherited records might simply be too short to show the true reality.[1]

The heavens could have been imperceptibly altering or diminishing and thus at some point in the very distant future, they would perish (which meant that they had to have been generated also, but at some instant long before the "inherited records" began). The arguments in the *De Caelo*, therefore, are not as powerful as the Not to Fear Proof. Even if Aristotle has a slew of arguments for ingenerability and indestructibility, the universe might be *contingently* eternal for him, with this type of universe still fulfilling the arguments of the *De Caelo*. I myself have never read anyone claim that the ingenerability and the indestructibility are *necessary*.[2] It is very difficult to determine from the texts whether the doctrine of *De Caelo* absolutely prevents The All from having at least the possibility of being destroyed in the sense of contingency that Aristotle invokes in Lambda, even if the destructive side of the contingency never occurs.[3] As shown above, though, the

---

1   In the "Unmoved Mover" folder of the Gregory Vlastos Collection at the Harry Ransom Center, University of Texas, Austin, Vlastos writes in his notes that Aristotle knew of the history of written records going back 600,000 years for the Egyptians and almost 1.5 million years for the Babylonians. Vlastos does not cite any passage, nor does he state where he acquired this information, and it would be interesting to discover what the general view of the Peripatetics or classical Greeks were regarding this matter. Plato in the *Timaeus* 23e suggests only 8,000-9,000 years. Still, whatever the time period, it is finite, and the problem of deducing an infinite result from finite unaided visual perception remains.

2   Broadie for one seems to accept that *De Caelo* is compatible with the *contingent* eternal motion of Lambda, or at least, to my knowledge, does not point out that *De Caelo* entails *necessary* eternal motion. In this respect, as far as I know, she is like all other commentators.

3   Beere's "will of God," as I discuss below, might be invoked in this re-

Not to Fear Proof with possibility *qua* contingency is impervious to, for example, the objection of "eternal accidents" and is also more concise than the difficult arguments of *De Caelo*.

In summary, the Not to Fear Proof takes us beyond the arguments of the *De Caelo* I, even if it shares much with them and even if the *De Caelo* provides additional direct support for the Principle of Plenitude and therefore indirect support for the Proof. The Proof insures the inherent necessity of the eternal universe, which then has no proper possibility to disappear whatsoever, at any time. The Stagirite has no need to rely on historical records anymore, although they can provide some *secondary* support for his theory and need not be omitted, even were he to rely primarily on the Not to Fear Proof.

Additional confirmation for all of this comes from *De Caelo* II 1 (283b27-31). Aristotle writes:

> That the heaven as a whole neither came into being nor admits of destruction, as some assert, but is one and eternal, with no end or beginning of its total duration, containing and embracing in itself the infinity of time, we may convince ourselves not only by the arguments already set forth but also by a consideration of the views of those who differ from us in providing for its generation.

It *appears* that Aristotle presents the conclusion here of the Not to Fear Proof, but notice that "necessarily" is not stated. Moreover, that he has to argue for six more chapters for his conclusions suggests lingering doubt on his part for the previous conclusions or least not complete confidence that his previous arguments would persuade a neutral audience. That is, after the six chapters, at the end of II 6 he adds "that there is one heaven, then, only, and that it is ungenerated and eternal, and further that its movement is regular, has now been sufficiently explained" (289a11-12). He is not, it seems, speaking therefore of The All (*to pan*), which is the focus of the Not to Fear Proof, and

---

spect.

which is sometimes but only sometimes synonymous with the heaven. This is confirmed by him immediately afterwards in II 7 saying "We have next to speak of the stars..." (289a13). Given that the conclusion of II 6 does not apply to the stars, but only to the one heaven, much less does that conclusion apply (directly and explicitly) to the whole universe. All of this shows another difference between the Not to Fear Proof and the arguments from *De Caelo*. The Proof not only is much more compact and decisive but applies to The All. The Proof shows both that The All always exists and that it *necessarily* always exists. Whether Aristotle initially formulated the notion of heaven "embracing in itself the infinity of time," in effect the claim that the heaven inherently always moves, and then applied the insight to The All[4] once the Principle of Plenitude was clearly articulated, or vice-versa, is impossible for me to say, and is something I leave to others more sharp-sighted than myself to ascertain. As we shall see, though, this "embracing in itself the infinity of time" is the position that Theophrastus, Aristotle's successor as head of the Lyceum, advocated regarding The All.

More textual evidence can be adduced for why the Not to Fear Proof is stronger than the arguments in *De Caelo* for the *necessary* eternality of the universe. Aristotle acknowledges cataclysms that destroy most of the civilizations (even if mere traces are left), as Hintikka himself recognizes in a fascinating way (1973, p. 112), pertaining to a ramification of Aristotle accepting the Principle of Plenitude in Lambda:

> Our forefathers in the most remote ages have handed down to us...a tradition, in the form of a myth, that these substances [the planets or spheres that move through heaven, just discussed in Lambda 8] are gods and that the divine encloses the whole of nature. ... We must regard

---

4   Recall that in *Metaphysics* IX 8 Aristotle says "Hence the sun and stars and the whole visible heaven are always active...," and I presume The All is made of the sun, stars and the whole heaven, which for Aristotle sometimes contains the earth and living creatures; cf. Johnson, *op. cit.*, 2019.

> this as an inspired utterance, *and reflect that while probably each art and each science has often been developed as far as possible and has again perished*, those opinions, with others, have been preserved until the present like **relics of the ancient treasure**.[5]

For Hintikka, this passage and others are important because:

> The principle of plenitude gave Aristotle an important theoretical reason for his peculiar relation to his predecessors. If no possibility can remain unactualized for an infinity of time, every possible truth must presumably have been thought of some time or other. *Hence a sufficiently comprehensive survey of the opinions of earlier thinkers will comprise each desired truth within its scope.* The central problem thus lies in the sifting of the true opinions from the false ones *rather than in the difficulty of discovering the truths in the first place*; and, of course, also in collecting a large enough sample of well-established earlier opinions (1973, p. 111; my italics).

This is profoundly insightful in helping explain Aristotle's frequent reliance on the history of previous thinkers when the Northern Greek begins discussing topics throughout his corpus. Usually readers, including myself, have simply assumed that Aristotle treats the history as an efficient cause to provide the fullest explanation (the more "be-causes" the better), following, e.g., *Posterior Analytics* II 11 (94a35ff), where Aristotle uses "the Athenians raiding Sardis" as the efficient cause of the Persian war. The comment about the ramifications of every possible truth having been recognized previously

---

5   *Metaphysics* Lambda 8, 1074b1-b12; Hintikka's italics but my bolding. Hintikka also notes *Politics* VII 10, 1329b25-35, in which Aristotle seems to accept that the previous institutions were infinite. This is all similar to the infinite artificial kinds made by humanity that, I argued, stem from infinite species, so the evidence for the infinite institutions supports my claim that clothing and other artifacts, at least as kinds, are eternal for Aristotle also. For more on cataclysms destroying civilizations for both Plato and Aristotle, see Anton-Hermann Chroust, "The 'Great Deluge' in Aristotle's *On Philosophy*," *L'Antiquité Classique,* 1973, 42-1, 113-22.

is additionally fascinating (although in my view the mature Aristotle would have constrained the truths to the eternal objects or to kinds, excluding "accidental particulars"). However, what Hintikka misses is the ramification of Aristotle relying on "opinions" that are analogous to evidence like "ancient relics." This is similar to the problem we saw before in *De Caelo*, in which the reason to justify the protasis "*if* the heaven is ungenerated..." was that all records of the previous generations indicate the heaven is the same. This reliance on previous records invited the blistering retort that the changes were so imperceptible that the generations of men simply did not notice them or that the correct records had long ago disappeared, meaning the heavens could have originally been different and thus generated. Here again, in Lambda 8, Aristotle is relying on the "opinions" as if they are like "relics of ancient treasure." Yet, again, it would not take even a Theophrastus to complain that these myths are hardly demonstrative proof for the infinite past or, better yet, the *necessary* eternality of The All. What, however, I believe this all shows is that the doctrine from Lambda emphasizing previous myths is roughly at the same stage chronologically as Aristotle's doctrine in *De Caelo* when he also relied on previous records.

Metaphysics Lambda

A similar comparison can be made between the Not of Fear Proof and the arguments of *Metaphysics* XII 6-7, in which Aristotle acknowledges eternal motion but considers it contingent, forcing a need for the Unmoved Mover. That is, the Unmoved Mover of Pure Actuality is posited by Aristotle to protect a universe that is contingent even though it is acknowledged by him to be temporally infinite. The Not to Fear Proof, for further reasons I give in detail when discussing Gerson, is again more powerful although perhaps not simpler. Suffice it to re-iterate that because the universe is inherently necessary and not contingent, no need arises to posit the Unmoved Mover, which brings

De Caelo, Metaphysics Lambda, and Physics

with it the absurd theoretical baggage that has been debated for hundreds and hundreds of years (but only starting with Alexander of Aphrodisias, who flourished around 200 CE and who was thus reviving some texts that had not been commented on for almost 500 years, if ever).

To be more precise, Aristotle has simply enriched his understanding of the modalities (necessity and possibility) and of the relation of substance to potentiality. Regarding the modalities, they become more sophisticated if more polysemic, similar to his use of unity (or "oneness"). In his earlier work, Aristotle had four senses of unity: numerical, specific (as "species-oriented"), generic (as "genus-oriented"), and analogical. In his later work, he adds "focal point" unity, but he does not renounce the other four notions (I cover this more when discussing later the relation of Theophrastus' metaphysics to Aristotle's). His empiricism forces him to realize that oneness is used in this additional way and that he can, and should, follow suit. Similarly, Aristotle develops his notion of necessity, and correspondingly of possibility, in the ways I have articulated, and he realizes that he can keep the other senses of the modal terms in other arenas, along with *almost* all of his doctrine of Lambda and *De Caelo*. The eternal spheres move eternally, but now he has the way of explaining with the Not to Fear Proof and Theta 8, and the ontological sense of the modalities, how their essence allows them to move eternally *and necessarily,* in virtue of their very nature, despite not having the power of stopping, reversing course, or going out of existence. Rather, they only have the power (the "distinctive matter") of changing place in their perpetual, unique circular routes, to go along with their essential actuality, of which more later.

Regarding substance and potentiality, the "distinctive matter" is the second doctrine that Aristotle welcomes in Theta 8, *contra* Lambda, which itself we saw in the Introduction. I repeat most of the argument:

> Since there were three kinds of substance, two of them
> natural and one unmovable, regarding the latter we must

assert that it is necessary that there should be an **eternal unmovable substance**. For substances are the first of existing things, and if they are all destructible, all things are destructible... [Thus] even if it [a mover] acts, this will not be enough, ***if its substance is potentiality***; for there will not be *eternal* movement; **for that which *is* potentially [such as anything with matter] may possibly not be**. There must, then, be such a principle, whose **very substance is actuality**. Further, then, **these substances must be without matter;** for they must be eternal, at least if anything else is eternal.

Let us start from the top and leave aside the way in which Aristotle describes at the end the eternal unmovable substances in the plural. Assuming that the text is as he wrote it, we can consider this for the moment a figure of speech (for how could pure actualities without matter be differentiated and be multiple?). Given the Not to Fear Proof, or maybe as a cause of his realizing it, Aristotle must have understood after he wrote Lambda that to have the third kind of unmovable substance (Pure Actuality) is pointless when the sun, stars, and whole heaven (and by implication the whole universe, The All[6]) are completely necessary inherently. For reasons that follow, Aristotle must have realized more precisely that the *substance* of those eternally existing things (like the stars or The All) is *not* potentiality. Rather

---

6   It was objected in private correspondence that Aristotle is speaking of The All as a *collection* of substances, with the implication that the argument here in XII 6 would not apply to the whole universe considered as *a* (single) substance. However, Aristotle often speaks of things as substances that are collections, like a *polis*, which would have many citizens, and we saw before him equating not only species and the corresponding individuals as "synonymous," but speaking of the "one heaven" as if it were a substance: "...that there is one heaven, then, only, and that it is ungenerated and eternal, and further that its movement is regular, has now been sufficiently explained" (*De Caelo* II 6, 289a11-12). "Divine beings and the parts of these" are also given as examples (*Metaphysics* V 8, 1017b12). The one heaven has many individual planets but similarly an individual has many parts (arms, legs, etc.). Hence, if even as the *subject of predication*, one of the meanings of "substance" in the *Metaphysics*, The All is therefore a substance.

only one, *secondary* aspect is potentiality, whereas the primary aspect is (eternal) actuality, despite the eternal movers (and by implication The All) being enmattered,—as he says right before one of the conclusions of the Not to Fear Proof in IX 8:

> N*or does eternal movement, if there be such, exist potentially*; and, if there is an eternal mover, **it is *not* potentially in motion (*except in respect of 'whence' and 'whither'; there is nothing to prevent its having matter for this*)**. Therefore the sun and the stars and the whole heaven are ever active, and there is no fear that they may sometime stand still, as the natural philosophers fear they may. Nor do they tire in this activity; for movement does ***not*** imply for them [the eternally moving things like the sun and stars and the whole heaven], **as it does for perishable things, *the potentiality for opposites***, so the continuity of the movement should be laborious; for it is ***that kind* of substance which is matter and potentiality** [and which is *not* eternal, namely, the perishable substances], not actuality, that causes this [being laborious] [my boldfacing, square brackets and inserted comments].

Therefore, Aristotle in Theta 8 and in the Not to Fear Proof renounces the claim of Lambda 6 that "**these substances *must be without matter*; for they must be eternal**." Contrary to Lambda 6, he allows eternal movers like the sun, stars and whole heaven, to have *some* potential for movement and thus some matter, immediately on the heels of his claim that eternal movement does not exist potentially! (Recall the passage also from *Meteorology* in which the outer heavens are said to be the "first movers.") Aristotle has come to realize that potentiality is not the *substance* of any eternal mover that is enmattered, his worry in Lambda 6. The reason he gives in Theta 8 is that anything which is eternal has no potential, with one important qualification: Contrary to the movement of perishable things, which have the potentiality *for the opposite* (presumably, not to move at all or to reverse direction or to perish), the uniqueness of an eternal mover or by implication The All entails that its potentiality is not the potentiality for *essential* opposites (such as non-movement or non-existence). Rather, the only potential for a sun or star is for movement in a certain respect regarding the same circular pattern *and only* regarding whence and whither. That is, the only potential the eternal movers have is when and where they go, on their *unique* eternally circumscribed circular path, again, of which more soon. For the moment, it is sufficient to grasp that this type of potentiality is not a *substantial potentiality* (the worry of XII 6), but a potentiality *as a property* (of an eternally actual substance) that nevertheless itself even as a property always exists (call it an eternal accident in the second sense of "accidents" discussed above).

To underscore, the eternal movers like the heaven, sun, and stars, and by implication The All, are the only substances with matter that nevertheless have no potential to disappear, unlike perishable substances like men and trees. Why are the eternal substances different from everything else in this way? The answer is the same as the one to an interlocutor who asks why dogs are different from human beings or from trees: Their nature is at bottom different. We can examine zoological differences with the other mammals, because we have close access to them, unlike the outer heavens, but the basic answer will ultimately be the same.[7] Diversity has always existed in nature, and

---

[7] A disputant might complain, saying that to rely on nature as the answer is tautological and explains nothing. Maybe that kind of disputant would say a better answer is that the DNA in dogs is different from our DNA. Yet, this merely pushes the problem back one step: *Why* is the DNA for dogs different from that of *homo sapiens*? Either, then, we set up an infinite regress or we ultimately say that nature is such that different elements and different objects have different powers because of an inherent diversity. That diversity has always existed in the universe for Aristotle and, although we might get more insights into the nature of each particular sort of being, we will never explain why the universe has the diversity it has, no more and no less. We could, perhaps, accept an anthropomorphic god who determines the diversity but that means simply not having the courage to know our limitations and accept them, because the same question could be asked with respect to this type of

always will exist, and Parmenides was wrong to think the true reality was completely the same everywhere (for a number of very well-known reasons that Aristotle gives in various places). How the diversity happens *in detail*, when explainable and in contexts that Aristotle believes he can describe, is offered in various texts, including, for example, *Meteorology*, when at its beginning Aristotle says:

> We have already discussed the first causes of nature, and all natural motion, also the stars ordered in the motion of the heavens, and the corporeal elements—enumerating and specifying them and showing how they change into one another—and becoming and perishing in general... *When the inquiry into these matters is concluded let us consider what account we can give, in accordance with the method we have followed, of animals and plants, both generally and in detail. When that has been done we may say that the whole of our original undertaking will have been carried out* (338a20-339a9; my italics).

In short, the reason eternal planets have the qualities they have, and dogs and humans the qualities they have, is grounded in natural diversity, and if that is too unhelpful or simplistic an answer, then explore

---

god. Why does it not have angels with wings intermingling with us and why did it choose the diversity it chose? Alternatively, one might say that the diversity came from random intermingling of elements and forces, along with, say, natural selection (which is no selection at all, of course, but a result of the random factors that allow the unplanned survival of the fittest). How, though, is this any better than saying that the nature of the different things are fundamentally the reason they are different? If it is better, then let us agree to accept that answer, but then the Aristotelian type of modern reply is that chance made the "fifth element" of the outermost heavens with the nature they have. Actually, the better reply, since chance could not have made something eternal for Aristotle, is to say that explanations like DNA are modern discoveries, and in this book we are addressing Aristotle's views with the options and frameworks that he could conceive. For Aristotle, the diversity was fundamentally a result of the outer heavens and the manner in which earth, air, fire and water could interact and transform. The more precise manner in which this diversity occurs is explained in detail in, e.g., *Generation and Corruption*, at the end of *De Caelo,* and in *Meteorology*, of which more in a moment.

the treatises, including the *Meteorology* and the biological and zoological ones suggested at the end of the passage, for the more precise explanations. Because fundamentally we are animals for Aristotle, additionally all of the books like *De Anima, On Memory, On Sleep*, and on how we think, act and produce, be it ethics, politics, art, rhetoric and other types of theory, would also contribute to understanding the universe and reality in the fullest possible, *reasonable* way.

To begin finishing this discussion of the difference between the Not to Fear Proof and Lambda: Aristotle does not come to his conclusion of Theta 8 in his middle or old age out of the blue. Almost the whole doctrine of the Not to Fear Proof is similar to what he had previously advocated. He has simply finessed his theory. He had even stated in Lambda 2 that:

> ...all things that change have matter, but different matter; and **of eternal things those which are not generable but are movable in space have matter—not matter for generation, however, but for motion from one place to another** (1069b25-7; my bolding).

It should be clear now that Aristotle renounces the following (italicized) protasis of the conditional from Lambda 6: "...even if it [a mover] acts, this will not be enough, *if its substance is potentiality.*" The claim itself as a mere hypothetical, we can accept, assuming we can even make reasonable sense of something whose substance is potentiality (most commentators, I believe, assume that this means the substance is matter).

There are four options for Aristotle in this whole matter. The explicit worry that we need not accept, and that I assert Aristotle rejected upon reflection, is that (i) an eternal mover has *substantial potentiality*, perhaps what we could call "pure potentiality" (with *no* actuality). Another way of interpreting "substance is potentiality" is that (ii) the mover is *primarily potentiality* with some "accidental" actuality, whatever this might mean and whether this is even really possible (for it may be merely a string of words). As we have begun to see, Aristotle rejects both of these two choices in favor of a third or fourth choice: Either (iii) the mover is pure actuality (the Unmoved Mover) with *no* potentiality or (iv) the mover is *primarily actuality* with some potentiality entailed accidentally *but not substantially*. Even though Aristotle accepts (iii) in Lambda, in Theta 8 he settles on (iv). The *substance* of an eternal enmattered mover (and by implication The All) in Theta 8 is not potentiality, but *actuality* (which is either necessary because omnitemporal or omnitemporal because necessary or both), although one aspect of this actuality *does* entail an accidental potentiality, namely, motion in respect of whence and whither. *This* kind of motion and *this* kind of eternal mover necessarily presupposes matter, as confirmed by Aristotle's claim in Theta 8 that "there is nothing to prevent its [the eternal mover] having matter for this" and as doubly confirmed in Lambda 2. The *ungenerated* eternal substances, which are "movable in space," have the relevant matter.

Physics

Having established what Aristotle abandoned with respect to the Unmoved Mover of Lambda, we can now easily see what he relinquished, too, concerning the similar doctrine in the *Physics*. This has usually been taken by scholars to be also his life-long doctrine, with the exception of those like Jaeger. Aristotle states there:

> *Anaxagoras is right* when he says that Mind (*Nous*) is impassive and unmixed, since he makes it the principle of motion; for it could cause motion in this way *only by being itself unmoved*, and have control only by being unmixed (*Physics* VIII 5, 256b25-28).[8]

---

8   Sorabji repeatedly claims that Aristotle is worried about Anaxagorean doctrine and that the Northern Greek develops his own view of infinity to evade Anaxagoras's view that "everything is in everything," etc. Much as Aristotle dislikes the Anaxagorean view that everything is in everything, clearly

> ...Motion, then being eternal, the first mover, *if there is but one*, will be eternal also; *if there are more than one*, there will be a plurality of such eternal movers. We ought, however, to suppose that there is one rather than many, and a finite rather than an infinite number. *When the consequences of either assumption are the same*, we should always assume that things are finite rather than infinite in number (*Physics* VIII 6, 259a7-11).
>
> [Of his own generating principle, Aristotle adds:] ...the first mover causes a motion that is eternal and causes it during an infinite time. It is clear, therefore, that it is *indivisible and is without parts and without magnitude* (*Physics* VIII 10, 267b24-26) [my italics in all three passages].

Obviously, then, for Aristotle there could hypothetically be one eternal prime mover or multiple ones and, "if the consequences are the same," one is preferable. Also, Anaxagoras's Mind inspires Aristotle's notion of the "first mover," which usually, if not always, is ultimately identified with the Unmoved Mover of Lambda, given that the Unmoved Mover gets described as "thinking of thinking" or as the thought that has itself as its object (Lambda 9). Thinking is what a Mind does, and, perhaps shockingly, Aristotle's version is eternally like Narcissus. It thinks (only) of itself, not having eyes, a face and a celestial pond. However, leaving aside the issue for the moment of one versus many and of the absurd ramifications of how a purely self-centered Mind causes eternal motion in the physical universe, which I discuss in detail in the next section, the consequences of positing a first mover that is eternal, indivisible, without parts and without magnitude entail that the first mover has no matter or body, similar to the doctrine of Lambda. Moreover, the First Mover in *Physics* is also "Unmoved." Aristotle says that "that which is without magnitude cannot be in motion" (*Physics* VIII 10, 267a22-3). This similarity has helped per-

---

he is very sympathetic to Anaxagoras's concept of Mind at this stage in his own thought.

suade scholars that Aristotle had a consistent theory across treatises, and therefore across stages of his life, because the scholars ignore or downplay the doctrine of the eternal movers in *Metaphysics* IX 8 that only have the potential to change "from whence to whither."

Still, "across stages of his life" may only have been during his youth or middle age, and Aristotle could not have been so obtuse as to ignore the pressing questions: How could the Unmoved Mover of Lambda and the Prime Mover of VIII 10 cause motion when neither have matter or energy or any kind of physicality? That the Unmoved Mover of VIII 10 has no physicality is entailed by it having no parts and no magnitude. Even air or light (or fire) or the "whole heaven" has parts. Hence, the Prime Mover would not be any of those kinds of matter. Also, how could it be one, when oneness or a unit is something applicable to a man or a horse or a sentence (as an utterance or a written sequence of words), all of which have matter? To be "one" requires a boundary or magnitude, just as a single day requires a boundary (or boundaries). Even if these dilemmas could be handled, how is an alleged "entity" able to *cause* motion when it has no parts or magnitude? The claim appears absurd, in part for the reasons we saw pertaining to the Unmoved Mover of Lambda and for others when we examine Gerson's discussion of whether the Mover can satisfy any of the four causes (of motion). Consider, again, though, a related case about something with no magnitude for Aristotle that a critic might cite, which we examined before when the Northern Greek says at *Dramatics* 6.1450b24-26:

> We have laid down that tragedy is the representation of a complete (*teleias*) i.e. whole action which has some magnitude (*megethos*) (**for there can be a whole with no magnitude**). A whole is that which has a beginning, a middle and a conclusion [my bolding].

"For there can be a whole with no magnitude" is merely a figure of speech for Aristotle in this context,[9] elliptical for "...a whole with no

---

9   Cf. Scott, *Aristotle on Dramatic Musical Composition*, 2018, p. 394,

(perceptible) magnitude" insofar as "whole" is relevant to tragedy. It is impossible to have parts, especially a beginning, middle and end, and have no magnitude. Can we apply this passage, however, to the current situation, and to the Prime Mover without magnitude? It is possible that Aristotle in the *Dramatics*, in making the point about a whole with no magnitude, implicitly acknowledges the phenomenon discussed in the *Nicomachean Ethics*. There Aristotle states in arguing that pleasure and movement are different:

> We have discussed movement with precision in another work, but it seems that it is not complete at any and every time, but that the many movements are incomplete and different in kind, since the whence and whither give them their form. *But of pleasure the form is complete at any and every time.* Plainly, then, pleasure and movement must be different from each other, and pleasure must be one of the things that are whole and complete. This would seem to be the case, too, from the fact that it is not possible to move otherwise than in time, but it *is* possible to be pleased; **for that which takes place in a moment is a whole.**[10]

Thus, a supporter of the Prime Mover might claim that, similarly, the Mover can be whole even if it has no magnitude. If whole, and like pleasure, it can somehow cause motion. Yet this hardly seems possible. Pleasure is something corporeal animals experience. How could a Prime Mover (and similarly the Unmoved Mover) with no magnitude and no parts have, or be, pleasure or something like it (whether emotion, knowledge or some other psychological or intellectual state)? Another entity would be needed for the Prime Mover to be pleasure or an equivalent phenomenon like an emotion or thought. Besides, the assumption, indeed, the explicit statement, is that the pleasure is occurring "at any and every time." How can the Prime Mover be in

---

footnote 582.

10   *Nicomachean Ethics* X 4, 1174b2-8; the translator's italics, but my bolding. Transl. by W.D. Ross and revised by J.O. Urmson, in Barnes, *The Complete Works of Aristotle, op. cit.*

time, when time is a measure of motion and motion only applies to the physical universe? Even if a sensible answer could be given to all of this, how can the Prime Mover be, or be experiencing, something like pleasure, continually over years or over an infinity? As Aristotle had just said "the first mover causes a motion that is eternal *and causes it during an infinite time.*" Clearly, then, this "whole with no magnitude" is not lasting only at a single moment, and if it had duration, it would have magnitude.

Hedonists develop a hedonic calculus in which the longer the pleasure lasts, the better it is and the more pleasure one has, but none of this could apply to a Prime (or Unmoved) Mover that is whole *and without magnitude and that also has* **no** *other physical aspect*. This makes an analogy with pleasure or even thinking or continual contemplation hardly applicable. One might somehow be able to contemplate something in a moment without any change but it is impossible for one to continue contemplating without some change (if only because "continue" requires a change in time). Finally, something that does not have the physical attributes of a soul *qua psyche* and a mind could not contemplate. Aristotle the quintessential biologist surely knows this. Lambda can *say* that the Unmoved Mover thinks of itself, but these are words with no grounding in reality (analogous to a ridiculously fictional story). They are no better than Aristotle himself saying Anaxagoras's Unmixed Mind gave motion to the whole physical reality (but then rejecting the doctrine). Cicero, as we will see, (rightly) complained about the absurdity of Aristotle's theory; Brentano, *contra* Burnyeat, called it "prattle without all sense and reason"; and as we will also see, even the early Peripatetics rejected it.

To return to the topic of the Unmoved Mover not having either parts, magnitude or matter, while nevertheless causing motion: It is extremely puzzling how the Prime Mover of *Physics* (or the Unmoved Mover of Lambda) could cause eternal motion of a contingent universe, Aristotle's reason for positing the Mover. In Lambda, Aristotle gives more explanation. The Unmoved Mover causes motion of the planets because it is the object of thought or desire, which moves without itself being moved (*Metaphysics* XII 7, 1072a26-1072b14, especially b3). For example, a beloved who is sleeping and not moving causes the lover to move, who in seeing the beloved might move toward him or her (but who might move in other ways, to benefit her).

However, the analogy quickly breaks down for the Unmoved and Prime Mover, because the beloved and lover are both enmattered, and the beloved, the analog of the Unmoved Mover, is capable of being seen. Given that the Pure Actuality has no parts and thus no magnitude, like the Prime Mover of the *Physics*, how could it be apperceived in any way by a perceiver (say, a planet) or even intuited in order to cause any motion? Making the issue one of thought that causes another thought to want to be like it or to "seek" it or to be moved because of it, whatever that might mean, merely generates more arcane dilemmas. Thoughts for Aristotle, whether in images or words, also have discrete parts (and we saw how the simplest sentence involves at least a name/subject and verb). Those resulting dilemmas are mind-boggling, and the same dilemmas infect the Prime Mover of the *Physics* even if it is not identical somehow with the Unmoved Mover of Lambda that thinks always of itself.[11] It is no surprise that the dilemmas which have stumped thinkers for 1800 years would continue always to stump thinkers (as mentioned and as we see more when covering Gerson's history of the *Metaphysics,* I ignore the first 500 years because no one cared about the dilemmas until Alexander of Aphrodisias). The doctrine of the Prime (or Unmoved) Mover makes pure mockery out

---

11   If the two Movers are not identical, then since the *Metaphysics* was written "after the physics" (which, for any non-specialist reading this, is what the full Greek means, *tōn meta ta phusica*), presumably the Unmoved Mover of Lambda was at Aristotle's second stage of development, even if that was merely an extension, or modification, of the *Physics.* Given my account of what aspects of Lambda Aristotle dropped for the Not to Fear Proof, this all means that the most mature account in IX 8 was the third and final stage of his evolution over his forty-year professional life.

of empiricism, common sense and philosophy. One might as well believe in magic or supernatural religion. On reflection, it is too difficult to imagine that, in reaction to feedback from colleagues, the youthful Aristotle himself did not realize the absurd consequences of positing the Unmoved Mover of both the *Physics* and *Metaphysics* Lambda, of which more later, when discussing Theophrastus and Strato.

Once we notice the multiple prime movers in *Metaphysics* IX 8, we realize that Aristotle cannot be referring anymore in that text to the single eternal Mover of *Physics* VIII 7-10 or to the one and only Unmoved Mover of Lambda (which must therefore have been written earlier than IX 8, even if the standard corpus stemming from Andronicus in the 1st century BCE has it appearing later). What Aristotle says in *Metaphysics* IX 8 is preferable to the initially posited *single* eternal Mover in *Physics* VIII that has no parts or magnitude. Theta 8 is also preferable to the Pure Actuality of Lambda, as demonstrated. Aristotle's view regarding whether one or many is preferable must have therefore also changed after the *Physics*. Actually, his initial comparison was finite versus infinite, so even the outermost spheres, if they are limited in number, would be acceptable for him as a source of understanding.

In short, Aristotle realized that the conclusion of *Physics* VIII 10 is completely untenable. The "consequences of either assumption," which led to positing a single unmoved Mover with no matter whatsoever rather than multiple ones, and finite rather than infinite, are *not* the same, especially for an empiricist. Moreover, the two options—a single finite mover versus infinite movers—are not comprehensive, for there can be multiple but not infinite movers. Aristotle also must have realized that we cannot accept an Anaxagorean Mind or an equivalent Unmoved Mover that is "unmixed" (and that is Pure Actuality with no physicality), with no parts or magnitude, because of the absurdities in its connecting to a physical universe. For additionally forthcoming reasons, even less can one accept that such an entity also causes *circu-*

lar movement of the universe.¹² The Not to Fear Proof functions as a much better ground for the necessarily eternal universe.

Summary and the Platonic Influence

The Not to Fear Proof is more powerful and more sensible than the arguments in *De Caelo, Metaphysics* XII and *Physics*. Given the Proof, no need exists for Aristotle to depend on recorded or verbal history in order to justify the infinite past or the eternality of the universe. Again, without absolutely compelling grounds for the infinite past and for its ingenerability, no argument of *De Caelo* should persuade open-minded but skeptical thinkers that the universe is *necessarily* eternal. It still might be eternal contingently, as in Lambda. Obviously, if the Not to Fear Proof was held by Aristotle, no need exists for the strange doctrines of the Unmoved Mover *qua* Pure Actuality of Lambda or the Prime Mover (without parts) of the *Physics*. However, all of this still allows (a finite number of) "eternal prime movers" in the other ways that Aristotle often uses the terms—ways, though, that allow matter (and potentialities) in a restricted sense. Because the Not to Fear Proof in effect supports, or at least is consistent with, the arguments for ingenerability and for many, if not all, of the arguments

---

12   It does not help theoretically to inject Minds that themselves are also Pure Actualities into the bodies of men or planets that somehow then "grasp" or apperceive the Pure Actuality of the Unmoved Mover, such as Aristotle (or probably a later editor) suggests in *De Anima* III 5. The problems still exist: How can there be multiple Pure Actualities when they have no matter and thus no location or boundary, while at the same time claiming that the Pure Actualities have multiple identities? How do those other instances of Pure Actuality connect to the relevant bodies and brains? Descartes had the same, irresolvable problem of how the purely immaterial soul connects to the material body and was rash enough to posit a pineal gland in *The Passions of the Soul* (Articles 30-4), as if making the connection tiny or the gland a seat of branching nerves really solves the problem. One might as well say ghosts pass through walls and yet can grab a door handle and turn it because the handle is small. Surely the ghost's hand would go through the handle also.

about motion, Aristotle need not have renounced *De Caelo* and most of the *Physics*. In addition, I explained how little he had to change from Lambda to come to his fully mature position on the inherent necessity of the eternally moving universe.

Whether Aristotle renounced the Unmoved Mover because he realized the Not to Fear Proof, or whether the Proof resulted to fill the gap left by him dropping the Unmoved Mover, or whether Aristotle used both doctrines, one for the general public who might have needed "God" in their lives, and the other for those willing to consider objectively all views in the Lyceum is, I believe, impossible to determine with certainty, given the current evidence. I discuss this last point more toward the end of the book, but to finish this section, I present Plato's view of the soul as immortal in the *Phaedrus*, which shows issues that greatly overlap with the themes of this book. The view that Aristotle has in the *De Caelo*, in the *Physics* for the "First Mover (without magnitude)," and in Lambda for the Unmoved Mover has an origin in Plato's theory (even if Anaxagoras and Xenophanes were the earlier influences).[13] All of this helps show why the Unmoved Mover was early in Aristotle's career, for undoubtedly he would have been familiar with his mentor's dialogues, although another option, naturally, is that Plato was influenced by the views of his superb student.

---

13 How influential the *Phaedrus* is for Aristotle's work is shown in part by how its view of "scientific knowledge" helped determine the structure of Aristotle's *Dramatics* (also known as the *Poetics*) and by the emphasis on organic unity; cf. my *Aristotle on Dramatic Musical Composition*, pp. 141-2. That approach to scientific knowledge involves determining whether something is simple or complex. If simple, see how it affects other things and how it is affected by them (a point that Plato repeats at the beginning of the upcoming passage on the immortality of the soul). If complex, break the thing into the simple parts and follow the same procedure, recursively. Whether Plato or Aristotle or the general discussion in the Academy was responsible for the origin of this approach to understanding in general is something I leave for the future.

Take this passage. After Socrates discusses the benefits of god-sent madness, a phenomenon that he also says in the *Ion* is the cause of artistic inspiration for the rhapsode Ion:

> Now we first understand the truth about the nature of the soul, **divine or human,** by examining **what it does and what is done to it**. Here begins the proof: Every soul is immortal. That is because whatever is always in motion is immortal, while what moves, and is moved by, something else stops living when it stops moving. So **it is only what moves itself that never desists from motion,** *since it does not leave off being itself* [thus the grounding of eternal self-motion in the thing's own nature]. In fact, **this self-mover is also the source and spring of motion in everything else that moves**; and a source has no beginning. That is because anything that has a beginning comes from some source, but there is no source for this, since a source that got its start from something else would no longer be the source. **And since it cannot have a beginning, then necessarily it cannot be destroyed** [in agreement with Aristotle's *De Caelo*]. That is because if a source were destroyed it could never get started again from anything else and nothing else could get started from it—that is, if everything gets started from a source. This then is why a self-mover is a source of motion. And *that* is incapable of being destroyed or starting up; **otherwise all heaven and everything that has been started up would collapse, come to a stop, and never have cause to start moving again** [note the similarity to one of the conclusions of Theta 8 and of the Not to Fear Proof]. But since we have found that a self-mover is immortal, we should have no qualms about declaring that **this is the very essence and principle of a soul**, for every bodily object that is moved from outside has no soul, while a body whose motion comes from within, from itself, does have soul, that being the nature of a soul; and **if this is so—that whatever moves itself is essentially a soul—then it follows necessarily that soul**

should have neither birth nor death.

> That, then, is enough about the soul's immortality. Now here is what we must say about its structure...[14]

It is remarkable how this passage presages much of, or takes from, *De Caelo* 1 12 and the related issues in the *Physics* and *Metaphysics* that pertain to the themes of this book. My discussions in Parts 1 and 2 so far show that Solmsen was wrong in suggesting that Aristotle differed from Plato in one crucial respect when Solmsen says: "Unlike the Platonic world soul which is defined as always moving, Aristotle's prime mover is eternally unmoved." The prime mover(s) of Theta 8 are also *always* and *necessarily* moving, and indeed since nothing else moves them, they move in virtue of their own nature, exactly what Plato is propounding in the passage above.

Whether, though, The All or the outermost eternal prime movers each have a soul is a fascinating question. For Aristotle, a prime eternal mover may or may not be animate, even if a very special kind of animate thing. As he says: "...inanimate things...are always set in motion by something else from without; the animal, on the other hand, we say, moves itself."[15] Note the correspondence with the *Phaedrus*. When handling an objection that fire and earth (as manifested in the light and the heavy) might be said to move themselves, because they go by nature up and down, Aristotle denies that the two elements move themselves, saying that they could then stop or reverse their motion. He emphasizes "It is impossible to say that their motion is derived from themselves: this is a characteristic of life, and peculiar to living things."[16]

---

14   *Phaedrus,* 245c-e; transl. by A. Nehamas and P. Woodruff, in *Plato: Complete Works*, Ed. John Cooper and Assoc. Ed. D.S. Hutchinson (Indianapolis/Cambridge: Hackett Publishing Company) 1997; translators' italics; my bolding and bold-italics and comments in brackets.
15   *Physics* VIII 2, 252b20ff.
16   *Physics* VIII 4, 255a6-7.

Because, then, like fire, the prime movers cannot stop and reverse their motion of their own accord, they may instead constitute a fifth element, whose nature is just to move tirelessly in a circle (whereas the nature of fire is to go up, unless forced otherwise, and of earth to go down). In any event, whether they are truly alive and have a soul or are more similar to one of the four elements that have no soul, they move eternally.

I should add in closing that Plato is now giving a *seemingly* powerful argument for the immortality of *both* divine and human souls, applying perhaps Aristotelian concepts for his own benefit. He may well have recognized Aristotle's claims about eternal self-motion of the universe and, leaving aside the issues of the four elements having restricted natural motion without a soul (a doctrine that Aristotle may not have formulated at the time he formulated eternal self-motion of the planets), Plato may have applied Aristotelian insights to the human soul. His resulting doctrine appears to be a much more powerful argument for the immortality of the human soul than his earlier arguments for the immortality of the soul as found, e.g., in the *Phaedo* (such as the Doctrine of Recollection), even if Plato's newest account ultimately also fails. The reason is the same as before: Once a person dies, where and how does the soul survive? This is obviously a problem that Aristotle does not have, given his hylomorphic view of the soul (*psyche*) and the body, with the soul not surviving death.

Doctrinal Reasons the "Not to Fear" Proof Was Not Seen

Why the Not to Fear Proof has never been recognized until now is a tantalizing question. Obviously, given this book, the major reason pertains to the Principle of Plenitude, which is the crux of the Proof. Lear and Barnes, for example, thought that the Principle was not upheld by Aristotle, one superficially good reason being the counter-example of the cloak that dissolves before it is ever cut in the frequently discussed *On Interpretation* 9. All other scholars before Hintikka also seem to have missed Aristotle's advocacy of the Principle, whether or not for the same reasons. Certainly Leibniz and Lovejoy missed it, as we saw. Although Hintikka gives a solid rebuttal of the textual evidence that might be taken to support Lovejoy's position, the rebuttal was not first published until 1957 and then in book form in 1973.[1] However, we have seen that some scholars, for example, Barnes in his book review of Hintikka, still were not convinced subsequently by the rebuttal. Broadie was the exception or the best known of the few exceptions. Moreover, even though Hintikka and Broadie accepted that Aristotle held the Principle, they never considered the theological ramifications, one reason being for Broadie that, out of respect for the manuscripts, she attempted to protect the texts of Lambda at any and all costs. This would have made it extremely difficult for her to consider that Theta 8 was a replacement for the Unmoved Mover.

Another reason that the Not to Fear Proof has been missed is that Aristotle follows Plato with some of his premises or conclusions regarding the importance of eternality. Ironically, the importance of eternality seems to have convinced readers that the conclusion in *Metaphysics* IX 8 that the heavens would not stop was something Aristotle held, statically, his whole philosophical life, going back to his early days in

---

1   *Time and Necessity,* especially pp. 97-105.

the Academy. Thus, it was presumed that this chapter was written before, and somehow consistent, with Lambda and *its* universe being contingent. Certainly, Beere in his new interpretation of Theta takes that position, as we see shortly.

Yet another reason that scholars have wrongly assumed that Theta 8 is consistent with Lambda follows. All previous scholars to my knowledge after Roman times, when the *Metaphysics* was assembled (and assembled as a hodge-podge of texts, as many scholars believe), presumed that Aristotle in the *Physics* and *Metaphysics* identified matter with potentiality (and thus perishability) and that this was also a static doctrine held throughout his professional life.[2] I discuss in more detail shortly the history of the manuscripts until Roman times, as given by Gerson, but to stay focussed on Aristotle's doctrine being considered static: As Hintikka once reported, to declare that something material has no potential runs counter to just about everything in the *Physics* and the *Metaphysics* where matter is always identified with potential.[3] This suggests that the passage in Theta 8, in which Aristotle says that what is eternal has no potential, was easily considered by readers to refer to Pure Actuality, and, indeed, we will now see Burnyeat considering that somehow Theta 8 is applicable to the "God" of Lambda.

I merely mention one of Burnyeat statements for the moment but examine it and its fuller context more below, when addressing current

---

[2] A specialist in ancient Greek philosophy offered this in private communication, after merely reading the twelve statements of the Not to Fear Proof, and before reading any part of the book. I believe this will be a standard reaction for most or all specialists of Aristotle.

[3] This book has been in progress since 1994. I cannot find the reference for the words in my notes or in Hintikka's four obvious publications. I do not therefore put the words in quotations, although I would stand by them. Hintikka's professional output was so prodigious over 45 years that it might take me months to track down the exact publication and page number. If and when I ever find them, I will publish them on the "Updates" URL as given in the front matter.

exegesis by Makin of statements that are found in both the Not to Fear Proof and in Theta 8:

> It is as *final cause that* **God is the Prime Mover** *of everything*, starting with the most basic material elements (earth, air, fire and water) whose ceaseless interchange is their way of achieving constancy *in imitation of the eternal first cause* (*GC* II 10, 336b25-337a15; **Met. Θ 8, 1050b28-30**).[4]

The passage in Theta 8 that Burnyeat refers to here is the one that immediately follows one of the conclusions of the Not to Fear Proof, to wit, we need not have any fear that the heavens will ever stop. Burnyeat's citation is, as we see shortly, somehow supposed to help explain that conclusion. It is sufficient for the moment, though, to note that he treats the Prime Mover as "God" and associates It with Theta 8.

Other scholars just skim by the relevant passages in Theta 8 that include one conclusion of the Not to Fear Proof, being unsure how to treat the conclusion (and, again, I will examine soon Beere's treatment of Theta 8, showing that this still happens). They therefore do not grasp how Theta 8 is inconsistent with Lambda or they assume that any eternal prime mover also means, as it does for Burnyeat, the Unmoved Mover. However, again, Aristotle says:

> Nor does eternal movement, if there be such, exist potentially; and, if there is an eternal mover, it is not potentially in motion (except in respect of 'whence' and 'whither'; there is nothing to prevent its having matter for this).

Indubitably, Aristotle is speaking of eternal movement and an eternal mover being in motion with respect to "whence" and "whither," which cannot be relevant to the *Unmoved* Mover of Pure Actuality. Scholars simply have overlooked or downplayed that any eternal mover here in Theta is one or more of the outermost stars that always move and have (only) the potential for whence and whither but not the *substan-*

---

[4] Burnyeat, *Aristotle's Divine Intellect, op. cit.,* p. 42; my italics and boldfacing.

tial potential to stop or go out of existence. That is why, to reiterate, Aristotle can say that eternal movement, which in Lambda exists in association with the *contingent* universe, does *not* "exist potentially" in Theta 8. He must be implying that, in terms of *substance or of the essence* of this eternal mover, no potential applies. However, this claim does not prevent him from asserting immediately that *in terms of accidents* or non-substantial qualities the eternal mover has the ability to change place "in respect of 'whence' and 'whither'."

In short, the qualified matter of the eternal movers in the way described in IX 8 is actual and necessary, yet also potential in one, very specific way. No scholar has seen that the passage in IX 8 is Aristotle's mature thought on this topic and supplants all the similar doctrines in Lambda, yet we saw how little the Northern Greek had to change in that doctrine to arrive at the inherent necessity of the eternally moving universe. It took, though, an analysis of necessity, possibility and the Principle of Plenitude as Hintikka or Broadie gave for us to have the correct vantage point. Without that vantage point the better view of IX 8 as opposed to Lambda was simply obscured,—and I myself certainly did not see it for many years until I discovered the work of the two modern scholars.

How Other 20th-century Scholars Missed the Inconsistency of Theta 8 and Lambda

Another reason that the Not to Fear Proof has been missed is that passages of Theta 8 have been construed as simply restating, or supporting, arguments for the Unmoved Mover of Pure Actuality. The use of "eternal first cause(s)" that occur earlier in Theta 8, before the passage we just examined (in which an eternal mover has the non-essential potential to move from "here to there"), is thought to be somehow the Unmoved Mover of Pure Actuality or to be associated with the other *ungenerated* (and hence eternal) enmattered movers of Lambda 2 and 8 that somehow Aristotle accepted while advocating Pure Actuality. This requires some explanation.

We already saw, for instance, very briefly, and we will soon see in detail, that Burnyeat thought the passage right after the conclusion of the Not to Fear Proof was about God (*ho theos*) or the Unmoved Mover of Active Intellect. In addition, in the middle of the arguments of Theta 8 and while discussing whether actuality or potentiality is prior, Aristotle explains how from one perspective the first is prior and from another perspective the latter is prior, but that actuality is most crucial. Man begets man, and cultured the cultured. He adds further: "one actuality always precedes another in time right back to the actuality of *the eternal prime mover* [my italics; tr. Ross]" (*tou chronou aei prolambanei energeia heteras heōs tēs tou aei kinountos prōtōs*) (Theta 8, 1050b4-5).

For Ross, there appears to be only one eternal prime mover. Other scholars have presupposed, I gather (because I know of no discussion of the precise issue in this context), that this "eternal prime mover" is identical to the Unmoved Mover of *Physics* VIII 10 and *Metaphysics* XII 6-7 (especially 1072a24-1073a12). Alternatively they have presupposed that "the eternal prime mover" was like one from Lambda 2 and 8. Yet the first presupposition is a grave mistake. Aristotle is speaking of time and antecedent actualities or causes in *Metaphysics* IX 8, and the Unmoved Mover is presumably not an *antecedent* cause (to motion that itself goes infinitely to the past). Rather, it is a cause in Lambda based on necessity, a logical ground as it were, that always exists.

Similar to Lambda 2, passages like *Metaphysics* XII 8, 1073a24-1074a17 indicate that there are a plurality of Unmoved Movers, each being a substance and "separate" as substances are, even though Pure Actuality can have no potentiality and no matter. The passages also suggest that the plural Unmoved Movers are "in time." At 1074a11-16, their number is calculated to be 49 or 55, which results in a number of obvious contradictions (the Unmoved Mover is unique, and these unmoved movers must have matter). All of these issues are fraught with paradox and have been explored for years, indeed centuries, with no end in sight to a resolution. Suffice it to say that I can stay removed from all of these dilemmas given the focus of this book, but the crucial point for us here is that *the occurrence of such dilemmas in Lambda itself, where Aristotle unquestionably holds a doctrine of an Unmoved Mover of Pure Actuality, would make similar dilemmas in Theta 8 unsurprising* and, hence, no ground to question him holding Pure Actuality in Theta 8.

Let us be clearer about all of this. Consider Hugh Tredennick's translation for the passage in Theta 8, which is better I believe: "...one actuality presupposes another right back to that of the prime mover *in each case.*"[5] Thus, there may be more than one prime mover, and Aristotle leaves open whether each prime mover is eternal in and of itself. The term "prime mover" is ambiguous, representing whatever is considered to be the beginning of a causal sequence in each of the different circumstances. Analogously, the beginning of a drama (which Aristotle indicates has a beginning, middle and end) is not some static identical event for all dramas (meaning that the chorus of Thebes begging Oedipus from relief from a plague is not the beginning of each and every tragedy). Rather the beginning is an "arbitrary" if naturally appropriate starting point (so that *Antigone* begins with the heroine of the same name meeting secretly her sister Ismene outside the palace gates at night). Likewise, a "prime mover" may only be an epistemic or cognitive choice, relevant to any topic at hand even if within the context of time. In other words, we might pick as the "prime mover" an important demarcation point in one case but this

---

[5] Again, Theta 8, 1050b4-5; my italics. *Aristotle in 23 Volumes*, Vols. 17 & 18, translated by Hugh Tredennick (Cambridge, MA, Harvard University Press; London, William Heinemann Ltd.) 1933, 1989.

need not be the prime mover in other cases.

The various reasons why something might be considered a "beginning" is given by Aristotle in the *Metaphysics*, including "the point from which a thing is first comprehensible" (*Metaphysics* V 1, 1013a16). Thus, a "first cause" might simply mean that from which something (or some temporal sequence of causal events) is *comprehensible*. The phrase need not, and does not, always mean that an *absolute* efficient cause to everything in the universe or to some sequence of events occurs temporally. At any rate, given the infinite past, there cannot be a temporal first cause for the (whole) universe for Aristotle. The crucial point now is that anyone taking Tredennick's translation still might easily think that Theta 8 is consistent with the enmattered *plural* unmoved movers of Lamba 2 or 8.

Two other passages that have been similarly treated "innocently" (with respect to Lambda) by scholars follow. First, the Stagirite says, even in Ross's edition, that:

> For from the potential the actual is always produced by an actual thing, e.g. man by man, musician by musician; there is always *a (tinos)* first mover." (*aei gar ek tou dunamei ontos gignetai to Energeia on hupo Energeia ontos, hoion anthrōpos ex anthrōpou, mousikos hupo mousikou, aei kinountos tinos prōtou*).[6]

Tredennick, relying on the same Greek text, Ross's itself, translates similarly:

> for the actually existent is always generated from the potentially existent by something which is actually existent—e.g., man by man, cultured by cultured—there is always *some (tinos)* prime mover."[7]

---

6   *Metaphysics* IX 8, 1049b24-26; transl. W.D. Ross, *op. cit.*, 1924; my emphasis.

7   *op. cit.*, 1989; my italics.

A close reading of Theta indicates, then, that the prime movers are like the man and the musician. Aristotle suggests that there could be any number of prime movers (considered, presumably, as the starting points of any causal sequence under consideration), and these first movers are all separate substances. It is not the Unmoved Mover of Pure Actuality, therefore, that is being considered the "prime mover" in these cases, even though, as just suggested, scholars may presuppose that indirectly the Unmoved Mover of Lambda underlies any and all of these first movers. The scholars (including Ross) assume this just as they assume that the 49 or 55 unmoved movers of Lambda 8 also *imply* somehow Pure Actuality because, to stress, Aristotle presents this as his doctrine in Lambda 8.

Another reason for why the Unmoved Mover of Pure Actuality has been assumed by scholars to be lying under the surface in Theta 8 follows. The context of the chapter is that actuality is prior to potentiality in three ways: formula, time, and substance. In formula and substance, actuality is prior, but in time sometimes actuality is and sometimes potentiality. After covering all three cases, or as an addendum to the final set of arguments pertaining to why actuality is prior, Aristotle says:

> It [actuality] is also prior in a deeper sense; because that which is eternal is prior in substantiality to that which is perishable, *and nothing eternal is potential* (Theta 8, 1050b6-8; my italics).

Aristotle suggests that we can always find actuality to the past but only sometimes potential things (that are perishable). This is another reason why actuality, since it *always* exists, is prior to potentiality. Clearly, Aristotle is speaking of eternality with respect to substantiality (as he does in the passage in Lambda 6 that first introduces the Unmoved Mover of Pure Actuality). Here, in Theta 8, he emphasizes that nothing eternal is potential. Scholars reasonably suppose that

Doctrinal Reasons the Proof Was Not Seen

Pure Actuality is the reference here, because it is the only "thing" that has no potentiality (eternally), at least according to Lambda.

Contra Burnyeat's suggestion that "God" is being spoken of in Theta 8, the eternal things themselves in this chapter are substantial and separable, like "man" and "cultured" (who are themselves, though, finite). Thus, Pure Actuality cannot be meant in these passages of Theta 8 because Actuality cannot have, for instance, separability. Burnyeat might object and say that in Lambda the Unmoved Mover exists eternally and therefore in the past, too, but this highlights the problem alluded to: Pure Actuality cannot exist in time (which itself requires motion and physicality). In other words, saying that something exists eternally and yet is not in time is a contradiction in terms.

To summarize the aforementioned irony: Texts in Lambda 2 and 8 indicate that prime movers *are* separate and substantial and these passages at odds with the Unmoved Mover of Pure Actuality having no matter whatsoever. Consequently, even though tensions abound between Theta 8 and Lambda, it is because similar oddities already notoriously abound between the different chapters of Lambda that the ones from Theta 8 would not be so strident as to force scholars to consider Theta 8 a replacement for Lambda. We would need the very good reason that only something like the Not to Fear Proof with its Principle of Genuine Sortal Plenitude provides. We would need, in other words, the recognition that the universe is *necessarily eternal* according to Theta 8, which then generates an outright contradiction with the position from Lambda 6 that the universe is *contingently eternal*. However, even though someone like Makin clearly understands that the universe is necessary, it does not follow that he automatically perceives the tension with Lambda, as we see shortly. To rephrase all of this, the views of Theta 8 are compatible in most (but only most) ways with Lambda, which I am now arguing has led previous scholars to think that Aristotle merely "re-presents" the view of Lambda (including its oddities with 49 or 55 movers) in Theta 8.

Additional support for the view that the prime movers of Theta 8 are not identifiable with the Unmoved Mover of Pure Actuality (apart from their plurality) arises outside of Theta 8, in particular with Aristotle's use of "man" as the first cause or as the "prime mover" in an example from the *Physics,* which replicates the example that he gives (with "cultured") in Theta 8. The Northern Greek states:

> ...either the mover immediately precedes the last thing in the series, or there may be one or more intermediate links: e.g. the stick moves the stone and is moved by the hand, which again is moved by the man; in the man, however, we have reached a mover that is not so in virtue of being moved by something else. Now we say that the thing is moved by the last and by the first of the movers, but more strictly by the first, since the first moves the last, whereas the last does not move the first, and the first will move the thing without the last, but the last will not move it without the first: e.g. the stick will not move anything unless it is itself moved by the man (*Physics* VIII 5, 256a6-13).

Clearly, though, men are moved *always* by other things, including other men, animals (especially horses), and ships, so that the prime mover here must be following Aristotle's notion of prime as synonymous with "beginning" or "first": "the point from which a thing is first comprehensible." It is not necessarily "prime" in the sense of a temporal first, although it may be that too if a certain context is delimited. When we look at the grand scheme of events pertaining to the man with the stick, there have been many motions happening to, and affecting, him before he moves the stick (indeed he was born, learned to walk, and then grabbed the stick). Still, on Aristotle's view, one can arbitrarily, for comprehension, designate the man the prime mover. The same principles apply to why the (eternal) prime movers discussed throughout Theta 8 also can have matter *and a restricted, "accidental" potential.* They are considered prime movers from the standpoint also of comprehension, and perhaps even with respect to some point in time. Just as the "prime mover" man moves the stick which itself moves a rock, even though the man had been moving in many ways for years before grabbing the stick, so the prime movers move the lower heavens which themselves move the earth and its creatures and plants, even though the (prime) movers had themselves been moving for many years, indeed eons before moving any particular creature. A passage we saw before from *Meteorology* bears repeating in this context:

> The whole world surrounding the earth, the affections of which are our subject, is made up of these bodies [i.e., fire, air, water, and earth]. This world necessarily has a certain continuity with the upper motions; consequently all its power is derived from them. (For the originating principle of all motion must be deemed the first cause. Besides, that element is eternal...) So we must treat fire and earth and the elements like them as the material cause of the events in this world (meaning by material what is subject and is affected), **but must assign causality in the sense of the originating principle of motion to the power of the eternally moving bodies** (*Meteorology* 1.2, 339a19-32) [my emphases].

Recent Treatments of Theta 8

I finish this section on doctrinal reasons for scholars missing the Not to Fear Proof by examining how new perspectives on Theta 8 continue to show perplexity with Aristotle's conclusions of the Not to Fear Proof as given in Theta 8 or how the scholars simply ignore the inconsistency raised with Lambda's physical universe being contingent. Those perspectives are paradigmatically exemplified by two authors already cited: Stephen Makin in *Aristotle Metaphysics Book Theta* (2006) and Jonathan Beere in *Doing and Being: An Interpretation of Aristotle's* Metaphysics Theta (2009).

Let us start with Beere, who develops the thesis that Theta is a reaction to Plato's views, especially in the *Sophist*. This thesis in general is not my concern here, although I have reservations whether the motivation of Theta was *primarily* a reaction to Plato. Take first the similar case of the *Dramatics*: Aristotle presents his own systematic theory, at times very much influenced by Plato in terms of the meanings of terms and the importance, say, of good character in Chapter 15, but at other times opposed to Plato. The Northern Greek employs three means of mimesis rather than the form/content distinction of Plato's *Republic,* and in the *Politics* articulates an explicit defense of comedy against Plato's censorship, based on education, not on catharsis, a phenomenon that itself was important to Plato across many domains.[8] Nevertheless, one would hardly reasonably say now that the *Dramatics* as a whole is *primarily* a reaction to Plato, even if a few took that simplistic stance in the past.[9] The treatise is Aristotle's own theory, with Plato and others brought in *as appropriate.* Moreover, reacting when appropriate to Plato was much more fitting in dramatic theory than in metaphysics because very few previous Greek philosophers had written in detail about the theatrical arts, whereas they were extremely important for Plato, as evidenced by *Republic* III and *Laws* II, VII and VIII. In contrast, many had written about ontology, and Theta appears to be Aristotle's deep examination of the ontological issues that concern him, whether or not Plato is first and foremost in mind. Surely, certain chapters are motivated more by other previous thinkers than by Plato, e.g. the Megarians. Nevertheless, I grant to Beere that Aristotle at times purposefully shows both agreement and disagreement with his mentor and that some of Beere's comparisons with Plato are new and often very illuminating. Here are more details.

For Beere, Theta is (at least in large part) a response to Plato's compet-

---

[8]   *Sophist* 230b-d; *Laws* V 735bff; *Republic* II 385c & X 607a; *Phaedo* 69b-c; and *Symposium* 211e, where the form of Beauty is pure, *katharon*. Cf. *Aristotle on Dramatic Musical Composition,* pp. 382 and 484-89.

[9]   For other arguments for this claim, cf. Claudio William Veloso, *Pourquoi la Poétique d'Aristote? DIAGOGE,* with a Preface by Marwan Rashed (Paris: Vrin, 2018), espec. Chapter 1, pp. 33ff.

ing conceptions in the *Sophist* of Being as symbolized by the materialist Giants and the transcendental Gods (the Friends of the Forms). On Beere's reading, the Eleatic Visitor in Plato's work helps the Giants see that Being cannot be just physical bodies because wisdom and capacity in general also exist. Nevertheless, the Giants can hold these to be dependent on body. In addition, the Visitor helps the Friends see that, if Forms are completely static or inert, thinking cannot exist, because thinking requires a soul, and a soul implies life, which itself suggests change (all of which, I might add in passing, does not bode well for a doctrine that entails a "Mind" or "Unmoved Mover" thinking without being alive). The result is that, in Beere's own words:

> The Visitor thus seems to present what we might call a *two-state solution*: The Gods and Giants cease their battle, and each holds sway *on its own territory*. Alongside the earthly realm of perceptible, changeable body, is the heavenly realm of intelligible Forms, where Being mixes both with Change and with Rest. This is presumably the solution—not identified as such—to the problem with which the Visitor had confronted [the] Gods: the problem of how the unchanging Forms can live and think, given that living and thinking are doings, and hence changes. The solution consists in this: the Forms associate with Change, and this association enables them to think and to live, but they also associate with Rest (pp. 9-11; my italics).

Beere then indicates that Aristotle "advances a profoundly different conception of bodily being from the Giants" (p. 12). Aristotle "recognizes cases of doing that are not changes" (p. 12), such as thinking of a theorem or a geometer gazing on a diagram. Thus, being in activity or actuality (*energeia*) is more primary than being-in-capacity. It follows for Beere that:

> With the notion of *energeia*, Aristotle is able to introduce a new category of item, which played no role in the *Sophist*: eternal perceptible bodies, such as the heavenly bodies. These are bodies, but they are what they are **without**

being-in-capacity.... Rather, they are simply eternally actively what they are. Eternally active yet bodily entities fit neither the Giants' conception of bodies nor the Gods' conception of Forms... The Giants think of *being able* as the basic condition of bodily being. Against them, Aristotle claims that *being-in-energeia* is the basic condition of bodily being, just as it is for non-bodily being.

Thus the notion of *Energeia* allows Aristotle to achieve a **'one-state'** resolution to the Battle. Plato, through the Eleatic Visitor, advocates a conception of the totality of being on which...one part—the heavenly, intelligible, non-bodily part—has being in its own right, and another part—the earthly, perceptible, bodily part—has being in virtue of the other part. The difference between them is radical... But, for Aristotle, the primary way of being, namely being-in-*energeia*, is the same through the totality of being: for perishable bodies **as much as for imperceptible gods**, being-in-*energeia* has priority. The whole of Aristotle's cosmos is, to that extent, alike (p. 17; his italics but my bolding).

With some *caveats,* I can only praise Beere's awareness that for Aristotle "eternal perceptible bodies, such as the heavenly bodies are what they are without being-in-capacity.... Rather, they are simply eternally actively what they are." Moreover, his final conclusion, that Aristotle has a one-state reality, is persuasive. However, I am not completely convinced that *energeia* is what allows Aristotle "to introduce a new category of item, which played no role in the *Sophist*: eternal perceptible bodies, such as the heavenly bodies." Perhaps this is correct, but, as I already explained the issue, the better understandings of necessity and possibility and of substance and potentiality (including eternal accidents) give Aristotle the insights to see that the eternal bodies and their circular motion are inherently necessary. Nevertheless, I do not insist that *energeia* has no role in the related issues but that is a topic for another time. Puzzlingly, Beere does not add at the very end "imperishable bodies" (like the eternal spheres) to go along with perishable bodies and *imperceptible* gods (which arguably Aristotle in no way accepts, depending on what Beere means by "gods" here, and perhaps this is just a figure of speech for him for the imperceptible Unmoved Mover of Pure Actuality). Whatever the reason for Beere's omission, let us leave aside the question of whether Theta was primarily a reaction to the *Sophist* or was only motivated by the *Sophist* secondarily or tertiarily. Even a secondary or tertiary goal allows, or even requires, similar discussions at times. Thus, for our purposes, we might well accept Beere's account in general, with the upcoming caveats.

First, Beere says that the eternal perceptible bodies such as the heavenly bodies "are without being-in-capacity." This is ambiguous. Does he mean "without *any* being-in-capacity *whatsoever*" or does he mean "without *some* being-in-capacity"? Moreover, is he denying being-in-capacity with respect to (essential) substances or their accidents (in the second sense explained before) or both?

The answer is crucial in making sense of a passage that Beere finds baffling later, when he gets to the details of Theta 8, which of course has part of the Not to Fear Proof. Beere cites Aristotle's statement that (as he himself translates): "If there is something eternally moving, it is not moving in capacity, except from here to there" (1050b20-2). Beere, then, asks: "How should we understand this last, cryptic remark?" (p. 318). He goes on to explain what he thinks Aristotle might mean, indicating that he (Beere) hopes "to elaborate elsewhere on these thoughts" (p. 319).

I do not believe, however, that Beere can be correct in his initial assessment, and any further elaboration presumably would have to provide a new solution. The reason is that he explains that the motion could be from point A to point B *or vice-versa*. However, I have already started to explain why Aristotle would not allow a motion that is eternally in one direction to be capable of the opposite direction, at least for one star, even if *other* stars have different circular motions with respect to the earth as a reference *but on their own paths*. Just as fire cannot choose to stop or reverse its own direction (to move upwards) and must be forced by something else to move downwards, so a star's direction *with respect to the earth* (whether, e.g., clockwise or counter-clockwise) is part of its nature. The star cannot reverse itself. We have similar permanently "unique" aspects of things that are otherwise the same as other members of a class: My Microsoft Sculpt Ergonomic keyboard is wireless and communicates to the laptop through a "dongle" (a tiny wireless transceiver) that plugs into the USB port; similarly to the matched wireless mouse. If you lose the dongle or if it goes bad, the whole keyboard-mouse combination becomes worthless because of the way the system was designed and manufactured. Each keyboard combination is paired with one and only one dongle, with a unique identification number, like the absolutely unique MAC address of any computer.[10] Each star, then, for Aristotle has similarly its own "unique identification," its own direction and path in the universe, and it never changes. The *only* potential the star has is where it will be along *that* eternal circle at any given time. That is an "accidental" or non-substantial potential, but a potential or capability nevertheless (that as we saw exists eternally).

I will not explain the rationale for Microsoft designing their system in such a way that one cannot just replace a bad part, but, regarding the planets with their absolutely unique circular paths, one advantage for Aristotle surely is that the planets as a result would never collide and destroy each other, even if he never states this as such. If the planets moved on random paths, it would be possible that in an eternity they could collide. Since "what may be, will be" for eternal things for him, they *would* eventually collide, and presumably destroy each other. Yet that would contradict the Northern Greek's assumption (or reasoning)

---

10   When I lost a dongle, the company fortunately replaced *all* the components. It gave me a whole new set with the appropriate dongle for that set, provided I returned the original mouse and keyboard at my own expense.

that they are eternal. Hence, the circular paths must be unique for each planet and they will never cross paths.

As Beere correctly acknowledges, for Aristotle whatever is eternal has no capacity "without qualification" because then it would have the capacity for not existing, which contradicts the assumption that it is indeed eternal. Beere summarizes perfectly some of the important points:

> (5) And what could possibly not be is perishable, either simply, or in that very respect in which it is said to be possible not to be, either in place or in quantity or quality. **And perishable without qualification is perishable in substance.** (6) Therefore, nothing that is imperishable without qualification is in **capacity without qualification**. (7) But **nothing prevents its being-in-capacity in some respect**, for instance, in quality or location... [1050b6-19]."[11]

Beere, though, never examines further the passage immediately after this last quotation, which is one of the conclusions of the Not to Fear Proof, namely, that there is no fear the sun will stop. Yet the Greek *ara* and *dio* mark off steps of inference in this part of the whole chapter (from 1050b6-28), and the conclusion (that the sun moves forever) is one of Aristotle's major conclusions for the previous passages, including this one about an eternal mover that is "imperishable without qualification." It is baffling how Beere can just ignore it.

Similarly, Beere places no importance on the passage *right after* the conclusion that the sun, stars and the whole heaven are ever active. In this passage, Aristotle gives a further reason why the conclusion of this stage of his long argument is right:

> Nor do they [the eternally moving entities like the sun] tire[12] in this activity; for movement does not imply for

---

11   Beere, *op. cit.*, p. 317; my bolding.
12   Aristotle concerns himself with the tradition that Xenophanes may

them, *as it does for perishable things*, the potentiality for *opposites*, so that the continuity of the movement should be *laborious*; for it is that *kind of substance* which is *matter and potentiality*, not actuality, that causes this [type of laboriousness] (*Metaphysics* IX 8, 1050b24-8; my italics and comments in brackets).

Beere has missed the importance of the Not to Fear conclusion as found in Theta 8, and the import of this stage of the argumentation in Theta 8 (even if the conclusion comes within an analysis of how actuality is prior to potentiality in substance). The reason appears to be that he holds the view that Aristotle's Unmoved Mover, or God, *could* be at play and *could* destroy something eternally existing, even though Beere had just correctly acknowledged that eternal existents cannot have potential (for not existing). In his own words: "...nothing that is imperishable without qualification is in capacity without qualification." As he writes further:

> It seems that there could be something that exists forever, but of which it is true that **it could perish. God, for instance, might make something last forever, although it is within his power to destroy it or just to let it fall apart**. And this, in fact, is precisely the way in which Plato makes Timaeus describe the world. [Beere adds:] I am working on the assumption that God's being what God is just *is* God's thinking, much as my being what I am just *is* my living (p. 316; his italics but my bolding).[13]

I gather that the "God's thinking" that Beere mentions is the Unmoved Mover thinking of thought (or of itself thinking). Thus, Beere seems to accept that the universe for Aristotle is still contingent, as in Lambda,

---

have started. As we saw at the beginning of this book, Xenophanes claimed that "God" did not toil, of which more shortly.

13   Beere adds on his pp. 133 and 323-4 to this point, and has Aristotle switching senses of possibility in order to reply to Plato's God (on p. 323). However, given that Aristotle would not countenance an anthorpomorphic god that in anyway cares about the physical universe, we should not complicate the matters as Beere does.

Doctrinal Reasons the Proof Was Not Seen

and "could perish," making it similar to Plato's. Yet Aristotle is clear in many places, as I explained, for instance, in the section on eternal accidents. What is eternal cannot be destroyed, whether by a Platonic type God or by any other cause. One does great damage to Aristotle's thought, or certainly puts a dark cover over the texts, by analyzing his doctrines with concepts or frameworks from other systems. Aristotle in no way believes in an anthropomorphic god or a Platonic Demi-Urgos (divine craftsman) who creates and controls the universe (and who could stop eternal motion), *or who cares about the universe in any way*. Nor does the Unmoved Mover ever think about the physical universe, even if somehow, despite all of Aristotle's psychological doctrines to the contrary, it could think without a soul and mind. It is not even aware of the existence of a physical universe and, thus, could not put that universe out of existence.

I repeat this last point because too many readers do not recognize it, and I do not want any to miss it. The Unmoved Mover of Pure Actuality is utterly ignorant of anything other than its own thoughts. *It does not even know that a physical universe exists* and is always *utterly and completely selfish*, at least in the sense of being perfectly self-centered. So it would not, and could not, create a universe; nor would or could it choose ever to keep the universe in existence or to destroy it; nor would it know what human beings are. It has no ability to choose *anything*, in fact, for it has no ability or capability at all (and any choosing would require potentiality). Ironically, the Mover of Pure Actuality would not even have the power that measly human beings and lemmings have, to commit suicide or, in its own terms, to put itself out of existence. One should leave peculiarly Platonic-Christian doctrines out of Aristotelian exegesis.

In finishing my account of Beere's interpretation, I return to Plato and chronology. What I find rewarding about Beere's major thesis is that, for Plato in the *Sophist,* the soul and thinking requires life and change (and requires some Forms to participate in Change and Rest). By implication, I assume, an immortal soul involved in reincarnation as found in the early Platonic dialogues is very suspect insofar as the soul is between living bodies. Whether this seeming development in Plato's doctrine can be reconciled I leave to the specialists in Plato. For our purposes, it is enough to say that given how Plato discusses doctrines like the soul as an (eternal) unmoved mover in the *Phaedrus*, which I discussed earlier, it is obvious that many of the themes that we are examining here, including related dilemmas pertaining to a notion of an Unmoved Mover or an eternal mover that moves itself, were discussed in the Academy.[14] These topics and dilemmas are of the same kind, if not absolutely identical, as those of Pure Actuality that has neither matter nor potentiality and thus that cannot be alive, and yet that thinks of itself and that causes motion of the universe. Again, the relevant part of Plato's passage is:

> This then is why a self-mover is a source of motion. **And *that* is incapable of being destroyed or starting up; otherwise all heaven and everything that has been started up would collapse, come to a stop, and never have cause to start moving again.**

---

[14] As suggested in the quotations at the beginning of this book, the source of the Unmoved Mover can be traced back to Xenophanes, whose notion of god was something that with mere thought and no *toil* caused and moved the world. Alexander Mourelatos reminded me of Xenophanes's view in this context, so long ago had I forgotten what the Colophon had said. I repeat parts here: "without any toil he makes all things shake and quiver by the thought of his mind... [and] He remains ever in the same place, moving not at all..." Note the emphasis on the lack of exertion, which Aristotle considers important enough to mention when he says that the eternal (necessary) motion of the stars is done *without being laborious* (Theta 8, 1050b24-8). Surely this handles an expected, long-known and at least occasionally discussed consideration, of which more in a moment. Cf. Alexander Mourelatos, "Three Critiques of Anthropomorphism in Early Greek Philosophy," Gregory Vlastos Memorial Lecture, Queen's University, Ontario, October 2016, with the part on Xenophanes presented in his modern Greek translation at the University of Crete, October, 2017, forthcoming in *Ariadnê*, Proceedings of the School of Philosophy at the University of Crete.

Plato's conclusion that all the heavens would not come to a stop is exactly Aristotle's theme, of course, in one of the conclusions of the Not to Fear Proof and in the section of Theta 8 that Beere skips. Unsurprisingly, the details pertaining to how Aristotle and his mentor arrive at the same position of eternal movement are different, but that they are concerned with the same general issues seems indubitable.[15] Therefore, if I am correct in the major theses of this book, it did not take until Theophrastus or some other member of the Lyceum to question the absurdity of something with absolutely no matter, potentiality *or living nature* having the ability to "think of itself," when, again, in the *Sophist* thinking requires life and change. Rather, the general topic of an unmoved eternal mover and some of the resulting dilemmas were already set up by Plato, whether or not his perspicacious student from Stagira articulated problems and answers in discussion or whether, as may well have been the case, Aristotle himself was the "first cause" of Plato recognizing the dilemmas. This would all mean that at any time during or after the *Phaedrus* or *Sophist*, Aristotle began to change his view and to drop the doctrine of Pure Actuality. Also, Plato's treatise may have been a response to Aristotle's doctrine of the "thinking of Pure Actuality." This would continue to make Theta later than Lambda, in spite of the ordering of the extant agglomeration of books in the *Metaphysics*, but would make Theta much earlier than we might have expected otherwise.

Contrary to Beere, Makin does not import foreign concepts or frame-

---

15   Immediately after the passage in the *Phaedrus* in which Socrates discusses eternal self-motion and the heavens (not) coming to a stop (245b-e), he gives the analogy of the teams of charioteers and horses, symbolizing the immortal god (with the good horses) and mortals (with the bad horses). The good team easily arrives at the top of the rim of heaven, but the bad team suffers extreme toil (247b). Given the tradition from Xenophanes, it would not be far-fetched to think that Aristotle also had this passage of the *Phaedrus* in mind when he himself gives the exact same sequence in Theta 8: arguing that the heavens do not stop and then immediately after giving a reason why they (like the gods) do not toil.

works into his exegesis of Theta (such as a God that thinks *of*, or acts *on*, the physical universe or any part within it). He tries to clarify Theta as a whole "for readers who are not predisposed to be interested in Aristotle" (p. xxii). Given the perennial disputes about the structure and chronological relationships within the books of the *Metaphysics* and given the difficulty of the doctrines, and especially the lack of any clear organic unity, Makin's goal is admirable. He complements Beere's own aim to show the difference and commonality between Plato and Aristotle. As Makin notes in his introductory pages, actuality and potentiality are at the core of Theta, and he gives a close analysis of the chapters leading up to one of the conclusions of the Not to Fear Proof in Theta 8, a laudatory analysis that covers in much greater detail the summary I gave above, in which actuality is prior to potentiality in form, time, and substance.

Now comes the crucial analysis for our purposes. Makin writes:

> "[2] nothing eternal is potentially"... Claim [2] says that something which is eternally F should not be thought of as eternally manifesting a potentiality to be F. **On the contrary, something which is eternally F is actually F without being potentially F** (compare the compressed summary at *Int* 13, 23a22-6)... **This is a significant departure from the way in which the potentiality-actuality schema has been understood so far.** In Θ1-5 the focus was on change as originating from a capacity which of necessity is exercised in the right conditions... The hope in Θ6-7 was to see a substance as an actuality relative to the matter of which it is composed. **The model introduced by [2] is very different. An eternal change is *not* the exercise of an underlying capacity (potentiality).** A substance which is eternally (F) is *not* an actuality relative to any potentiality (to be F).[16]

Makin is perfectly accurate here, and his final point is in accord with

---

16   Makin, *op. cit.*, pp. 208-10; his own italics but my bolding.

Doctrinal Reasons the Proof Was Not Seen

Beere (and in my view a correct assessment of Aristotle's doctrine). Revealingly, and to his very great credit, Makin detects that the claim about nothing eternal being potential is a "significant departure" from what had been said before in Theta. In my terms, Θ1-5 is about possibility or potentiality as "immediately realizable" (the fifth notion of possibility in my list). Θ6-7 shows that the nature of something determines its potentialities and possibilities, following my third sense of possibility as "allowed by nature." Makin sees Θ8, though, and the doctrine of potentiality as being very different, and, in my view, it is because Aristotle employs the temporal notions of necessity, possibility/potentiality, and impossibility, and because the Northern Greek uses "possibility" (and potentiality) in the sense of contingency (that is *not* homonymous with necessity). If that is what Makin means by the "potentiality-actuality schema," I am completely in accord with him.

Makin also astutely recognizes a similar doctrine from *On Interpretation* 13 and hence realizes that the view of Theta 8 is not a complete anomaly for Aristotle. Makin's account shows how ambiguous actuality, potentiality, and possibility are for Aristotle and how the Northern Greek even in back to back chapters can change the meaning of the terms. Hence, I believe Makin gives, if unintentionally, another of the reasons why the Not to Fear Proof has not been seen before by others. Anyone who became attuned to the actuality-potentiality schema(s) in the earlier chapters would have either been perplexed or would have treated the current schema as an oddity or would have skipped over passages in Theta 8 (as Beere did to some extent), which of course has the conclusion of the Not to Fear Proof. In any event, they would have given it little consideration, similar to Beere not even pausing to discuss that conclusion.

Let us continue with Makin's account of the crux of the matter for our concerns. At the start of a section entitled "1050b22-8: A Cosmological Consequence," Makin states:

Aristotle's main argument concerning eternals and perishables is followed by three blocks of material. First he draws attention to a cosmological **consequence** of the preceding material (1050a22-8...). Second, there is a further comment on the relation between the eternal and the perishable (1050b28-34...)...

What is the line of thought in the present passage? Aristotle makes two points about an eternal change, such as the sun's motion in the heavens. **Each is supposed to follow from the main result of the preceding discussion, that something which is eternally (F) is not eternally actualizing a potentiality to be (F).**

First, there is no fear that the motion might stop (1050b22-4). This is the easier of the two points. The upshot of the preceding discussion is that the sun's eternal motion is not correlated with an underlying potential to move. Lines 1050b20-2 make it clear that the potentiality at issue is a potentiality *to move*. The sun does, while at one place, have an unactualized potentiality *to be at another place*. That aligns perfectly with Aristotle's main conclusion. **The sun is eternally moving, and has no potentiality to move** (1050b7-8); **but the sun is not eternally at any particular place, and so does have a potentiality to be at this place or that place** (1050b21-2). **Since the sun does not have a potentiality to move, which may be either actualized or quiescent** (1050b10-11...), there is a shift in the burden of explanation concerning the sun's motion. It is not necessary to explain why the potentiality should continue to be actualized rather than lapse into quiescence, because there is no such potentiality.

Second, **the sun does not get tired, and its eternal motion is not laborious** (1050b24-8). The task here is to see through the anthropomorphism [Subsequently Makin tries to explain the lack of tiredness by suggesting that tiredness can come from an outside influence or from being "non-natural"; because there is no outside influence on the sun and no unnatural movement, it does not tire].[17]

Let us start at the top and proceed through Makin's points. First, Makin confirms the claim I made when discussing Beere's account. The sun being ever active is a *consequence* of the preceding passages, and thus has the importance (within the context) that conclusions have for Aristotle. It makes no sense to discuss and explain premises and then ignore the conclusion or one of the intermediate conclusions. This shows again how in a book that is illuminating concerning why Aristotle differs (or not) from Plato, Beere simply ignores the statement that I have shown is an extremely important part of Aristotle's metaphysics. Second, how does Makin himself resolve the inconsistency in his two claims, as follows?

> The sun **does**, while at one place, **have an unactualized potentiality** *to be at another place...* It is not necessary to explain why the potentiality should continue to be actualized rather than lapse into quiescence, **because there is no such potentiality**.

In one breath Makin says that the sun has an (unactualized) potentiality and in the next breath "there is no such potentiality." How can this be? Makin might reply that the latter potentiality (which does not exist) refers to being at another place and the first potentiality refers to motion, and thus no inconsistency gets generated. However, since motion (and in particular locomotion, which is surely the kind of motion being discussed) is simply a change in location for Aristotle, there is no difference ultimately between saying the sun has a potentiality to change places (Makin's claim) and saying the sun has a potentiality to move. Rather, I contend, the better explanation is the one that takes into account two passages that Makin ignores in this precise setting, which I call now "Passage 1" and "Passage 2."

The first occurs right *before* the conclusion that the sun is always active. According to this passage, the eternal mover has the potential-

---

17   Makin, *op. cit.*, pp. 215-6; his italics but my bolding.

ity for motion from here to there *as an exception*. Again, the potentiality for motion is *only* in this respect.

> **Passage 1:** ...if there is an eternal mover [and for Aristotle there is], it is not **potentially in motion** *except in respect of 'whence' and 'whither'*; **there is nothing to prevent its having matter for this** (1050b20-22; my emphases and comment).

The second passage that has no seeming role in Makin's clarification for the issue at hand, when it should, occurs right *after* the conclusion that the eternally active celestial entities will never stop (even though Makin will discuss laboriousness):

> **Passage 2:** ...for movement does not imply for them [the celestial entities], as it does for perishable things, **the potentiality for opposites**, so that the continuity of the movement should be laborious; for **it is that kind of substance which is matter and potentiality, not actuality,** that causes this [laboriousness for the perishables] (1050b24-28; my bolding and comments).

As I have already explained in large part, Passage 1 indicates that an entity which is eternal (like the sun) can have matter, but it must be a special kind of matter that only has potential to move in a circular way and on an absolutely unique path, without having a potential "for opposites." "Opposites" must mean stopping (and then perhaps reversing course)[18] or disappearing, that is, for going out of existence. Consider analogously a fish or race cars *without a reverse gear* that have the potential to move "always" by their own accord going *forward* but *never backwards* (or not perfectly sideways, like a crab). As Aristotle confirms in Passages 1 and 2—and as is very fitting given the focus of this part of Theta 8 on why actuality is prior in substance to potentiality—eternal entities like the sun involve **substantial actuality** with the kind of matter that involves only "accidental" potentiality for motion in a very particular way (which can last eternally).

---

18   "Motion is in a sense the opposite both of a state of rest *and of the contrary motion*" (*Physics* VIII 7, 261b18-9; my italics).

Doctrinal Reasons the Proof Was Not Seen

As Passage 2 emphasizes, those eternal entities have a quality that the perishable things with *their* kind of "substantial matter" and "potentiality" do not have. The former can move forever "without getting tired" whereas the latter get tired (and even perish, whether or not from exhaustion). A cheetah by its nature can move very fast but obviously can get tired and expire (whether from starvation or other causes). Ironically in this context, it also gets extremely and dangerously over-heated very fast, just as a polar bear in summer in the heat has to be very careful about strenuous activity for the same reason. A human being and turtle move much slower, by their natures (and in more precise terms because of their musculature, lungs, etc.). However, because of the stars' or the sun's unique nature—its unique combination of special actuality and matter that involves only motion of a certain type—it moves forever. Of course, as mentioned before, Aristotle could not dissect the sun or the more remote stars to try to explain the mechanistic reasons why this might be so, whereas he could dissect a cheetah to try to explain what overall bodily structure allows the cheetah to far outpace a human and a turtle and what causes the dangerous over-heating.

Makin raises an interesting question and possible answer regarding the anthropomorphic remarks about the eternal movers not getting "tired," although I believe a better answer exists. His own explanation might be partially correct, but only partially. His claim that an outside force causes something to be tired or labored is indeed often true, given that outside forces can cause resistance. For example, when I walk against the resistance of a headwind, I tire more quickly than if the wind were at my back. As Makin says additionally, whether the motion is natural is also relevant. Yet even this consideration combined with outside forces is not sufficient as an explanation in the current case. I may desire to walk for the mere pleasure of viewing certain landscapes (and not, say, for health or because of an emergency) and thus no outside compulsion occurs. Moreover, let us say conditions are perfect and I even have a slight tailwind the whole time, plus the walking is obviously natural (as opposed to trying to slither like a snake). However, I will still get fatigued after a certain point, be it in 2, 5 or 300 miles. Why, then, would the naturalness of the movement in and of itself, without resistance, explain the *eternal* lack of fatigue on the part of the sun and stars? It does not. Rather, Aristotle advances himself the reason that the eternal movers do not tire, by saying it is only perishable things (like animals) that have the "potentiality for opposites."

Again, I contend that this must mean that *only* the perishable things can stop, get fatigued, or die. The eternal movers have only potentiality for movement of a certain sort, in accordance with their nature, and *they are inherently and essentially in terms of substance simply indefatigable.* Some (perhaps weak) evidence for this was noted already in *Generation and Corruption* and *De Caelo*, including the unvarying previous records of mankind. The use of anthropomorphism in Theta 8 probably acknowledges *and addresses* the philosophic tradition that began when Xenophanes began speaking of God, *without toil*, moving everything in the world with his mere thought.[19] I already suggested

---

19   Obviously, in myth the creators were anthropomorphic; what I recount is the history of "God" in the philosophic tradition starting with Thales. On this topic, in the final stages of this book, a fascinating article came to my attention at a conference, Robert Mayhew's "Aristotle on Helios' 'omniscience' in *Iliad* 3 and *Odyssey* 12: On *schol.* B* *Iliad* 3.277a (fol. 47r)" (unpublished as of May 2019). Mayhew writes:
> In *Iliad* 3, as part of his oath affirming that the Greeks will abide by the outcome of the duel between Menelaus and Paris, Agamemnon swears ... to Helios (the Sun), '*who oversees all things and overhears all things*' [my italics].

Mayhew then analyzes Aristotle's attempt to explain a paradox resulting from another passage, in which Helios needs a messenger. If Helios oversees all things, why would he need a messenger? The details of Mayhew's full answer, although persuasive, are not critical for the evaluation of the Not to Fear Proof. Nevertheless, Aristotle's concern helps show why he focusses on the *toil* of the eternal movers right after one of the conclusions of the Proof in Theta 8. Recall Fragments B24 and B26 from Xenophanes quoted at the beginning of this book: "All of him (God) sees, all thinks, all hears" and "Rath-

how Aristotle's sequence of argumentation mimics a similar point in the *Phaedrus,* and the Northern Greek probably also has in the back of his mind how Plato followed Xenophanes by positing a Demiurge, which of course also has anthropomorphic qualities. The youthful Aristotle himself, it hardly bears emphasizing, posits an Unmoved Mover of Pure Actuality that, in thinking of (itself) thinking, was paradigmatically anthropomorphic in one respect (and ironically more akin to Narcissus than the youthful Northern Greek initially realized or would care to admit). The emphasis on thinking is surely one reason for its attractiveness to medieval theologians and to others. As Mark Twain observes: "God created man in his image, and man returned the compliment." However, Theta 8 and the Not to Fear Proof reveals Aristotle renouncing all nonsense regarding anthropomorphic gods.

In short, Makin often gives incisive clarifications of the doctrines in Theta, without importing obvious foreign frameworks into his analysis, and the few quibbles I have on the points above should not be taken as representative of my reaction as a whole to his work.[20] Nev-

---

er, without any toil he makes all things shake and quiver by the thought of his mind." The most obvious explanation of Aristotle's concern for toil when discussing the eternal movement of the sun and stars in Theta 8 is that he not only cares about the technical philosophical proof but about addressing commonly-held views about deities, going back not just to Xenophanes, but, as Mayhew makes me realize, to Homer.

20   I have doubts, however, whether Makin's distinction between weak modalities and standard modalities, that goes along with his explanation of the difference between capacities and possibilities (especially pp. xxiv-xxv), is entirely Aristotelian. It might qualify as a "foreign framework." The issue is very complex and too lengthy to treat here in detail. Suffice it to say here that Makin ultimately claims "The moral Aristotle wishes to draw in the course of 1050b6-22 is that something's being temporarily or intermittently (F) involves an explanatory capacity (potentiality) to be (F), while something's being eternally (F) does not. Standard possibility [which for Makin means "necessity implies actuality which itself implies possibility"] is never explanatory" (p. 215). However, all of this flies in the face of the passages I discuss in this book showing that for Aristotle eternal truths and explanations are the best and that one should start with those eternal truths *and explanations*

ertheless, one relevant puzzle remains with his results, as alluded to earlier. He recognizes that possibility is contingency in Theta 8, and he also recognizes the various statements that nothing eternal is potential (where potential functions like possible). He indicates, too, that what is eternal is necessary (p. 211) and acknowledges Aristotle's conclusion that the sun and whole heaven "eternally move actually" (with only the non-substantial potentiality of changing place). It is a trivial step to deduce, then, that the whole heaven must be necessary. How, then, can Makin square the *necessity* of the whole heavens and of their eternal motion of Theta 8 with the doctrine of Lambda, in which the eternal physical universe is *contingent*? It is not clear and he never addresses the issue.[21]

(and thus with necessity). It seems to me that the contrary meaning of contingency can also be explanatory and Hintikka (and Broadie) established the four equivalences. In short, even though Makin brilliantly recognizes that the treatment in Theta 8 is a "significant departure" from the earlier chapters, he seems to resort to the meanings and implications of those chapters and thus takes less advantage of his profound insight than he could have.

21   Ironically, Makin astutely appeals to, in effect, Ockham's Razor (if I can remove it from any medieval, theological associations) when countering an anti-Aristotelian who argues against one of Aristotle's claims about potentialities failing to be actual at some point in eternal time:

> The trouble with this opponent is that her view concerning potentialities and capacities looks unmotivated. It is unclear what she gains by insisting on potentialities (capacities) which can *never* fail to be actualized. She goes beyond the position Aristotle argues for in Θ5: that capacities cannot fail to be exercised *in the right conditions*... However, the position is quite different if we attribute to A a capacity (potentiality) which is necessarily and eternally exercised (actualized). In that case the capacity serves no explanatory purpose. In particular, it does not explain why A is eternally (F). In order to explain that one would need to say *why* the capacity (potentiality) is eternally and necessarily exercised (actualized). If that is just a brute fact, then one may as well stick with the brute fact that A is eternally (F), and exclude the capacity (potentiality) from the picture altogether (p. 214).

On the same grounds, we should apply the Razor to the Unmoved Mover of

Doctrinal Reasons the Proof Was Not Seen

Pure Actuality. If, as in Theta 8, the whole universe, including its motion, is necessary (because eternal), what explanatory purpose, or need, is there anymore for Pure Actuality? Ockham should be happy that his Razor is being so gainfully employed.

Aristotle's "Not to Fear" Proof

Historical Reasons the Proof was not Seen

Whatever the doctrinal reasons have been for the Not to Fear Proof being unrecognized until now, the lack of publicity for it may have begun in Aristotle's own time and may have resulted from his desire to keep the Proof confined to the Lyceum and to esoteric texts, especially given the history of the Athenians persecuting philosophers who did not accept the gods of the state. The same might be said, of course, of *Physics* VIII 10, which clearly acknowledges a Prime Mover without parts and magnitude, but I contend that my position, with suitable caveats, is very plausible, given Gerson's illuminating account, which includes his own footnotes:[1]

> It would not be quite accurate to claim that Aristotle's *Metaphysics*, like Hume's *Treatise*, "fell dead-born from the press, without reaching such distinction as even to excite a murmur among the zealots." First, there was no press. Second, the *Metaphysics* would not have been published as a book had there been a press. And finally, the *Metaphysics* was not completely ignored by Aristotle's school. Still, if one peruses Fritz Wehrli's monumental *Die Schule des Aristoteles* and notes the few scattered and desultory references to ontological or theological topics, one cannot resist forming the impression that the *Metaphysics is pretty largely an academic failure*. Even Aristotle's formidable disciple and colleague Theophrastus, who himself actually composed a treatise on metaphysics, seems to write with a remarkably limited understanding of the work of his predecessor in this area.[2] Apart from a

---

1   Lloyd P. Gerson, "Plotinus and the rejection of Aristotelian Metaphysics," in Lawrence P. Schrenk (ed.), *Aristotle in Late Antiquity* (Washington D.C.: Catholic University Press) 1994, pp. 3-5; my italics throughout, with my translations of Gerson's untranslated Greek. Also at https://www.ontologymirror.com/theophrastus-metaphysics.htm

2   [Again, this is Gerson's own footnote, as are the following ones in this whole passage.] Theophrastus did not of course title his work *Metaphys-*

few references to book twelve, there is almost total silence regarding the central features of Aristotle's work as they are recognized today. There is nothing about the identification of first philosophy with wisdom and theology and a science of causes; nothing of the *aporiai* ["dilemmas"] facing the construction of such a science; nothing of the doctrine of *pros hen* ["related to one"] equivocity or of the conclusion that being in the primary sense is separate form. *Nor is there a word about the dialectical treatment of sensible substance in the central books of the Metaphysics, which has so exercised contemporary scholars.* The list of the disappearing doctrines could easily he expanded and reconfirmed by considering other philosophers both inside and outside the Lyceum. We must not be tempted to account for this extraordinary state of affairs by supposing that Aristotle's successors regarded his metaphysical doctrines as too sublime for comment, for both Theophrastus and Strato, the first and second heads of the Lyceum after Aristotle, *appear actually to have rejected the argument for the existence of an unmoved mover.*[3] *Strato's argument amounts to the claim that nature alone is sufficient to account for motion,* a claim

---

ics ta physika, but he does describe it as dealing with first principles (Theo., Met. 4a 1-2) and as distinct from physics (*ibid.*, 2-4) and mathematics (*ibid.*, 4b6-8). The first principles are apparently reducible to a unique first principle, i.e., god (*ibid.*, 4615). As Giovanni Reale, "The Historical Importance of the Metaphysics of Theophrastus in Comparison with the Metaphysics of Aristotle," appendix to *The Concept of First Philosophy and the Unity of the Metaphysics of Aristotle*, trans. John Catan (Albany: State University of New York Press, 1980), 364-91, shows, Theophrastus closely follows *Metaphysics* 12 in many respects. But apart from these and some less convincing parallels from *Metaphysics* 2, there is little awareness shown by Theophrastus of any connection between theology and a science of being *qua* being.

3   For Theophrastus's criticism, see his *Metaphysics* 563-10, and for Strato, see the testimony contained in Cicero, *Academica* 2.38. [GS: The references are Gerson's, whether or not correct. "563-10" makes no sense to me, given the standard numbering, part of which Gerson uses in Footnote 1 above. The section of Theophrastus's text that indicates nature alone is sufficient to account for motion is 10a6-17.]

that must have been intended to recall Aristotle's own admission that if separate substance does not exist, then there is no special science of substance apart from physics (cf. *Met.* 6.1.1026a27-29). Since Aristotle adds that the putative science of separate substance is first philosophy and the science of being *qua* being, Strato's denial of the need for the hypothesis of an unmoved mover is nothing short of a rejection of the entire enterprise of the *Metaphysics*. And this from within the Peripatos! If we look beyond the Lyceum to the tradition of Aristotelian commentaries, beginning with Alexander of Aphrodisias, we do indeed find something more like reverence for the words of the founder, but hardly any awareness at all of the problematic and crucial connection between the specific theological arguments in the *Metaphysics* and the science of being *qua* being. *Though the extant corpus of Aristotelian commentaries includes four works on the Metaphysics, there exists not a single commentary by one hand on the entire work as preserved and edited by Andronicus of Rhodes in the first century B.C. Alexander's commentary ends at book five and is completed by an anonymous continuator; Themistius has a commentary, or more accurately a paraphrase, of book twelve alone; Syrianus comments on books three, four, thirteen, and fourteen; Asclepius halts his commentary at book seven.* In the face of this modest harvest, one might well conceive the notion that the *Metaphysics* was doomed from the beginning to bear meager fruit.[4] The dominance of Stoicism throughout the Hellenistic period explains in part the near oblivion into which metaphysics in general and Aristotle's work in particular were cast.

---

4   See Gerard Verbeke's "Aristotle's Metaphysics Viewed by the Ancient Greek Commentators," in D. J. O'Meara, ed., *Studies in Aristotle* (Washington, D.C.: The Catholic University of America Press, 1981 114ff.) for a useful summary of some of the basic interpretations in the commentators. Verbeke concludes that there is a consistent interpretation among the commentaries that may be aptly termed "Neoplatonic." We should distinguish, however, a Neoplatonic interpretation of Aristotle from a Neoplatonic refutation of Aristotle, as is to be found in Plotinus.

A central principle of Stoic theoretical philosophy is the refusal—perhaps for methodological reasons as much as anything else—to countenance the existence of immaterial entities. Accordingly, physics becomes Stoic first philosophy, and theology becomes a branch of physics (cf. *Stoicorum Veterum Fragmenta* 2.42...). Within such a system there is little conceptual space for isolating being as a subject for investigation, and, especially, for raising Aristotelian *aporiai* regarding its nature. The evidence for this claim is to be found in the corpus of Stoic fragments, where a science of being *qua* being makes no appearance at all, not even as a dragon to be slain. *It is as if it had never existed.*[5] Considering that Stoics, and to a lesser extent Epicureans and Academic Skeptics, were the primary purveyors of theoretical philosophy throughout the Hellenistic period, *it is hardly surprising that the doctrines of the Metaphysics simply lay dormant.*[6]

---

5   Zeno, Chrysippus, and Antipater are all reported to have written books titled *Perí Ousías*. Of course, these Stoics all identify *ousía* with matter. The few scattered references to *tò on*, which identify it with body and make it a species of the genus *tò ti*, betray little more than a lingering memory of some Aristotelian terminology stripped of its argumentative context. The Stoic position was perhaps taken to follow immediately from the principle that immaterial entities cannot exist; hence, argument indicating the contrary can be safely ignored. F.H. Sandbach, *Aristotle and the Stoics* (Cambridge: Cambridge University Press, 1985), has argued the revisionary case that, for the Stoics, Aristotle was not rejected but largely unknown. But the lack of hard evidence, rightly insisted upon by Sandbach, is also explicable by the hypothesis that Aristotelian arguments, in metaphysics at least, were rendered irrelevant on the above principle.

6   [This is Gerson's last footnote.] Cf. Fritz Wehrli, *Die Schule des Aristoteles: Text and Komment Aristotle* (Basel/Stuttgart: Benno Schwabe & Co., 1959), 10:95-128, who suggests in a Ruckblick over the material he has collected that the disintegration of the Peripatetic school was owing to its undogmatic and aporetic character as compared to its Academic, Epicurean, and Stoic rivals. He also suggests that conflict in doctrine between the *Metaphysics* and the early dialogues of Aristotle might account for diffidence or confusion on the part of his disciples: "der Zerfall der Schule hatte seine tiefste Ursache im Werke des Meisters selbst" (*ibid.*, 96). Undoubtedly, there is much in what Wehrli has to say. One may also add the instability of the Peripatetic founda-

This concludes Gerson's penetrating and extremely illuminating history. Leaving aside now the various issues of "being *qua* being" and whether room still exists for any kind of metaphysics should an Unmoved Mover of Pure Actuality be abandoned (of course, an unmoved mover as a man hitting a ball with a stick, or the eternal movers of the upper cosmos, is a different issue), Gerson's account fits perfectly with my conclusion that Aristotle gave up his youthful theory of the Prime Mover of *Physics* VIII and the Unmoved Mover of *Metaphysics* XII once he realized the Not to Fear Proof. (Alternatively, the Proof resulted from the vacuum created by Aristotle realizing the absurdities of the Unmoved Mover.) As Gerson notes with an exclamation point, both Theophrastus and Strato appear to have rejected the argument for the existence of an Unmoved Mover and Strato's own argument amounts to the claim that nature alone is sufficient to account for motion, exactly the conclusion of the Not to Fear Proof.

If I am correct, Theophrastus and Strato did not, and did not have to, argue against Aristotle's Unmoved Mover of Pure Actuality simply because the mature Aristotle had already realized its problems and had renounced it within the Lyceum, if not already in the Academy, in favor of the view that "nature alone is sufficient to account for motion." Theophrastus' brief attention to, and rejection of, the Unmoved Mover is therefore easily explained. Even though Aristotle only held the doctrine when youthful, it was a tantalizing doctrine, in spite of its author's age, and some members of the Academy or Lyceum or others might have been still influenced by it. Moreover, it followed in the tradition of Xenophanes and Anaxagoras and so was worth at least mentioning from a historical standpoint. That the doctrine was tantalizing originally, even if later rejected by not only Aristotle but Theophrastus and Strato, is proven by how many generations of not-very-young and experienced scholars have accepted it from the commentator Alexander and his "anonymous continuator" onwards! Alexander, like

---

tion owing to political reasons.

Gerson, grants the Unmoved Mover credence seemingly because the Great Master himself, Aristotle, proposed it. Somehow, they think, Aristotle must have had compelling reason for positing and maintaining Pure Actuality over his whole life. However, we must recall that Alexander lived and wrote 500 years after Aristotle, and was therefore working with a patchwork of manuscripts that came to be called the *Metaphysics,* with no easy or meaningful chronological relation usually determinable between them *and with no previous commentary*!

I hasten to add, though, that Gerson would not necessarily accept the Not to Fear Proof. Twenty-two years after publishing the article just cited, he continues to believe in the importance of the Unmoved Mover:

> Physics would be first philosophy if the Unmoved Mover did not exist *just because there would be no supersensible substance*. But this does not mean that physics would be the science of being *qua* being; rather, it means that there could be no such science. The primary science or primary philosophy would, in that case, be *the science of the changeable qua changeable or the science of all that which has a principle of motion and standstill in itself.* In other words, what I think Aristotle is clearly saying is that the science of theology and the science of being *qua* being, as he conceives of it, are identical and the demise of the one means the demise of the other. I should add here that the rejection of what seems to be a reasonable hypothesis, namely, that it is at least possible **[i] that the Unmoved Mover does not exist, has no traction for Aristotle.** This is so because **[ii]** *if the Unmoved Mover exists, it exists necessarily, and* **[iii]** *the denial of the existence of a necessary existent is a contradiction.* **[iv]** *It is to suppose that it is possible that the necessary is not necessary.*[7]

---

7   Lloyd Gerson, "The Central Hypothesis of Aristotle," paper given at the *World Congress 2400 Year Aristotle Conference,* University of Aristotle, Thessaloniki, June, 2016, p. 4; my emphases throughout, and my numbering

Gerson, though, is too hasty with these remarks.[8] I examine the numbered statements individually, in order.

[i] ... that the Unmoved Mover does not exist, has no traction for Aristotle.
On the contrary, this book shows that the Unmoved Mover not existing has overwhelming traction for Aristotle. His giving up the Unmoved Mover for the conclusions in Theta 8 may be almost as certain as anything else in the corpus given the arguments above, and those to come. Moreover, ironically Gerson himself provides extremely powerful arguments against [i] with his own history of the reception of the Unmoved Mover and of the *Metaphysics* and with his own (upcoming) account of how the Unmoved Mover cannot cause motion in the physical universe. That is, he articulates persuasively why none of Aristotle's four causes apply in this context, refuting Burnyeat's claim that God as the Unmoved Mover is the *final cause* of the eternal motion of the contingent universe.

[ii] ...if the Unmoved Mover exists, it exists necessarily.
We can grant the hypothesis as a *hypothesis*. *If* Pure Actuality exists and has no potentiality, then *by mere definition* it would be necessary. However, there is no evidence of any kind whatsoever that the protasis is true. Aristotle *positing* the Pure Actuality is no evidence *per se*,

---

in square brackets.

8   For fullest disclosure, I should note that as a Ph.D. student I was a Reader for Gerson's undergraduate Plato course at the University of Toronto. It is with slightly heavy heart, then, that I contest his views, but as Aristotle once said, truth is more important than friendship. Perhaps, however, Gerson will take a little satisfaction (even though he might consider this diabolical) in knowing that I use his history and his upcoming explanation of how the four Aristotelian causes are irrelevant to the Unmoved Mover causing eternal motion as additional ammunition to demonstrate that Aristotle renounced the Mover. At the least, this all obviates any future effort to make sense of what is arguably an impossible-to-understand doctrine. Even Gerson himself, then, can concentrate on more fruitful projects.

even though it has persuaded some people because of the Northern Greek's power as a thinker, but the positing is no better than Anaxagoras positing that a Mind *started* the motion in the physical universe. Also, as we have seen Aristotle say a number of times, the thinking is an accident and no proof that something really exists, and definitions in and of themselves are not claims of existence. One has to add the verb "is" or the like and make a categorical claim about the thing being defined existing. I can define a Divine Unicorn and say "If the Divine Unicorn exists, it exists necessarily"; it does not follow that it exists. It is far from sufficient, then, to state that the Unmoved Mover is Pure Actuality and that, by definition, it is necessary and that this in and of itself guarantees, or is evidence for, its existence. One has to give some actual proof that it exists.

Perhaps Gerson provides a reason for the protasis, namely, for the *existence* of the Unmoved Mover, with his third claim: "*the denial of the **existence** of a necessary **existent** is a contradiction.*" This *assumes*, however, the same thing that Gerson is trying to *prove*, namely, that the Unmoved Mover exists and is necessary (or is a "necessary *existent*"), as we can see now by addressing that third claim.

[iii] ...the denial of the existence of a necessary existent is a contradiction.

First, if I deny the existence of something that is truly a necessary existent, like the universe, then the denial is only an utterly false statement. It shows me perhaps to be out of my mind and in need of psychiatric treatment before I deny also that the cliff in front of me exists as I start walking toward it. Moreover, if I deny the existence of something that is only an *alleged* necessary existent, like the Divine Unicorn, that is even safer and not even a false utterance. "I deny that the necessarily existent purple octopus the size of a planet exists in our solar system." Surely this is neither a contradiction nor a false utterance. As is very well known, Aristotle distinguishes between a claim being false and being a contradiction. A contradiction is to say of x that it is and is not *at the same time and in the same respect.* In this setting, it would be "The Unmoved Mover *qua* necessary existent exists and does not exist at the same time and same respect."

No one on my side, such as Brentano or Jaeger, makes such a (contradictory) claim. We only deny that the Unmoved Mover (*qua* necessary existent or Pure Actuality) exists. This disputes the *truth* of Gerson's claim about the Unmoved Mover. Similarly, Aristotle says that the past is necessary and this is true if "necessary" means "cannot be otherwise" and if time is uni-directional. Someone might contest the claim that the past is necessary, but then it is an issue of truth that depends on the meaning of the terms in that categorical sentence. The one contesting the claim is not uttering a contradiction *per se*.

Why the claim that "the necessary Unmoved Mover exists" is false stems from the absurdity of the nature of the Unmoved Mover. Nothing could be Pure Actuality in the way (the youthful) Aristotle claims. This is an empirical matter in part and also a matter of the meaning of the terms, especially whether something with no physicality whatsoever could interact with the physical universe (including souls and minds of individuals, which require bodies). No reasonable person would try to defend such a claim once the person understands some of the ramifications. More evidence is given by the reaction of Theophrastus, Strato and later schools of philosophy, as Gerson himself perspicuously recounts. Surely, Theophrastus, the other Peripatetics and, for instance, the Stoics were not so cowed by Aristotle that they dared not contest his views, especially after he died. They argued about anything and everything important if they did not agree with it.

Finally, the most powerful evidence is abundantly clear in Theta 8: The universe is necessarily eternal, in and of itself, and thus *not* contingent, as Aristotle claimed in Lambda. Gerson does not even recognize this, much less show how Aristotle can then still hold that the universe is *contingently* eternal. If Gerson rejects these arguments of

Theta 8, then we can easily turn his own words—"**the denial of the existence of a necessary existent is a contradiction**"—against himself. Theta 8 shows that the universe in necessary in and of itself, without the Unmoved Mover. If Gerson denies the "existence of a necessary existent," namely, the eternal physical universe, then he utters a contradiction.

[iv] It is to suppose that it is possible that the necessary is not necessary.
Because Brentano, Jaeger and myself (among others) only deny, for some of the reasons just given, the existence of Pure Actuality or of eternal divine unicorns or the like (which because they are allegedly eternal must be therefore necessary for Aristotle in the ontological sense of necessary), we in no way need to presuppose that the necessary is not necessary. Gerson attributes the proverbial straw man to us. Now, if he says that I myself claim that (it is possible that) the necessary eternality of the universe of Theta 8 is *not* necessary, that would indeed be a problem. However, the problem would be him misrepresenting my claims. Not only Hintikka but Makin recognize that Aristotle in this chapter identifies necessity with omnitemporality, which *excludes* possibility (*qua* contingency).

Gerson's remarks about whether first philosophy or metaphysics exists for Aristotle if the Unmoved Mover does not exist is irrelevant to the conclusions of this book but deserve a few words. First, if the Unmoved Mover did not exist, there could be another focus for "first philosophy" apart from the two that he lists. "First philosophy" might be the science of all those substances (or the totality of these substances, "The All") that have a principle of motion in themselves and yet have no ability to stand still (in contrast to Gerson's second option, where the substance, like perishables, stand still). As we saw in IX 8, the eternal sun, stars and whole heaven have the potential for change only with respect to place and time, even though Aristotle calls them necessary and omnitemporal and **even though from the perspective of**

essential substance they have no potential. Perishable things, by contrast, we saw have the potential for not moving or changing direction or going out of existence or for all three. In other words, "first philosophy" might deal with eternally moving things (with matter) insofar as they are eternal and have no potential with respect to non-existence or to stopping, even though they have potential and matter for change (only) of "whence and whither." That is, even though some of these issues are discussed in the *Physics,* it may be that part of that treatise should really be a treatise on restricted topics or marked off as "first."

As we saw before vis-à-vis Plato, for Aristotle the eternal things are the first and best objects of knowledge, which is an excellent reason for calling the theory about them "first." Yet, these would not be the only topics in "first philosophy." These types of substances, and related issues, such as whether Forms and mathematical objects that in the ontological sense are not (separable) substances like men and trees, also exist eternally, and if not, why not, are the kind of topics that could make up metaphysics, or "first philosophy," if the Unmoved Mover does not exist. Arguably, discussions of the Forms and the status of mathematical objects are not part of physics (cf. *Metaphysics* XIII-XIV). Recall the previous discussion of mathematics done within optics or geometry; one is more practical and one more theoretical, as if "separate from nature." Thus, even if we decide that some topics pertaining to eternal movers should fall under physics, at least the issues of Forms and the like, those things "separate from nature," might comprise a "first philosophy." At any rate, this issue is completely independent of the important concerns of this book, and so I leave it for the future. Those who want a detailed introduction to the whole topic might well supplement Gerson's views with Patzig (1979).[9]

---

9   G. Patzig, "Theology and Ontology in Aristotle's *Metaphysics*," in Barnes, ed., 1979, *op. cit.*, 33-49.

Let us now turn to Gerson's admirable account of how none of the four causes helps us understand the means by which the Unmoved Mover of Pure Actuality causes eternal motion in a contingent universe.[10] To repeat, this account ironically provides more evidence against his own attempt to save the God of Pure Actuality.

In summary, Gerson says that the Unmoved Mover cannot be the formal cause because in effect it would be the definition of the universe, which would mean everything is "thinking," clearly absurd. The Actuality cannot be the material cause because it is utterly without matter. It cannot be the efficient cause, in part because to be the equivalent of the sculptor, who is the efficient cause of the statue, the Mover would necessarily have physical capabilities and would physically cause changes in the shape of the universe. Yet the Mover cannot have any physical aspect whatsoever and therefore cannot do *anything* to the universe, including triggering any motion. Moreover, for Aristotle the universe is infinite temporally, and no first *temporal* cause exists. As we saw earlier, with the man *qua* unmoved mover who holds the stick that hits a rock, "prime" or "first" is meant by Aristotle in terms of comprehension but it is not enough in this context that we are comprehending the issue. Our comprehension would not generate the planets' motions and the man and stick are indubitably in physical time. Lastly, *pace* Burnyeat, the Unmoved Mover cannot be the final cause. As Gerson concludes:

> Final causality is a poor explanation for the being of anything. Indeed, Aristotle elsewhere seems to assume this, for when he speaks of the explanation for the being of something (*aition tou einai*) he normally offers a formal cause, though in one place he offers an efficient cause of coming to be... See *An. Post.* B 2, 90a9; *De An.* B 2, 415b12; *Meta.* D 8, 1017b15; H 2, 1043a3, b13. At *EN* I 2, 1165a23, the parents are an efficient cause of the coming

---

10 Gerson, *op. cit.*, 2016.

to be of the child.[11]

Let me supplement Gerson's astute remarks. If running is for the sake of health, with health being the final cause, in what way would the Unmoved Mover or "thinking of (itself) thinking" be the final cause of the *eternal motion* of the universe? We ourselves see other runners who are fit and so strive to be like them, because we think fitness is good, which causes us to run, i.e. to move. However, why would planets and the stunningly problematic individual Active Intellects (as ascribed to individual minds in the infamous *De Anima* III 5) *move or want to move* as a result of apperceiving the Grand Active Intellect of the Unmoved Mover of Pure Actuality, assuming that magically the individual Active Intellects can apperceive something else that has no matter or distinguishable characteristic of any kind whatsoever? (And how would any of them know that they are apperceiving the same Pure Actuality as any other individual?) If anything, the planets and individual Active Intellects would want to be *like* the Unmoved Mover, and *hence their goal would be to think of thinking also*, the analog of me wishing to run when I see, and wish to emulate, a fit runner who runs for health. The planets, therefore, would not care about moving. They would desire to be selfishly contemplating for all eternity, not moving. In fact, the moving in no way helps the contemplation and sometimes hinders it, as our own experiences confirm.

I discussed already Aristotle's own comment on how an unmoved object (the beloved) can cause movement, but, again, this is impossible in the context of the Unmoved Mover and the planets because no physical analog holds that is comparable to the beloved who is physically seen. Likewise impossible is that Pure Actuality has the animate requirements of a mind to think, a consideration that we saw above must have been debated after the *Phaedrus* and *Sophist* appeared, if not before. Even intuited ideas or mental phenomena have a physical aspect in the mind, if only as an internal representation, as is obvious

---

11   Gerson, 2016, pp. 1-2.

from the other, more grounded chapters of *De Anima* and as is commonly known for Aristotle, the great biologist and psychologist. The incongruous view of *De Anima* III 5, that mind is immortal and eternal, can be seen even more now to be impossible for the mature Aristotle. If the mind is "unmixed," as the text there says, and thus purely immaterial (in line with *Physics* and Aristotle's approval of Anaxagoras's *Nous*), we have the same problem as the beloved causing a type of physical action when the beloved has no physical aspect *whatsoever*. The conclusions in this book, therefore, strongly support those who argue that III 5 also was renounced by Aristotle or was wrongly interpolated. Again, he could not have been such an imbecile as to ignore the absurdities of Pure Actuality, even if the absurdities had been first articulated by colleagues or competitors in the Academy. The integrity of the rest of Aristotle's sensible and consistent texts (given his typical frame of reference and his unquestionable empiricism) must take precedence. My contention, then, following Jaeger and many others, is that the theory of the Unmoved Mover of Pure Actuality causing motion of the eternal universe would not have withstood criticism from Theophrastus and others in the Lyceum or in the Academy for even a week, much less a month or year.

I discuss Theophrastus more in a moment, but let us return to the issue of how Pure Actuality could cause motion of a contingent universe as a final cause, analogous to us imitating a fit runner with health as the final cause of our own running. Even though I applauded Burnyeat's recognition that "there is nothing new under (or above) the sun," I cannot agree with his other claims that also pertain to Theta 8. We saw part of the view before and I examine it more fully now. Burnyeat writes:

> If Aristotle substitutes the first principle and best thing in his universe for the first principle and best thing in Plato's universe and leaves the analogy otherwise untouched, the result will be the theory that Alexander, the best and most purely Aristotelian of the ancient commentators, found in

> *De Anima* III 5; the theory that Brentano dismissed as "prattle without all sense and reason." The Active Intellect is God.
>
> At this point it is appropriate to recall that in the Aristotelian universe **all nature imitates the deity**. *It is as final cause that God is the Prime Mover of everything*, starting with the most basic material elements (earth, air, fire and water) whose ceaseless interchange is *their way of achieving constancy in imitation of the eternal first cause* (*GC* II 10, 336b25-337a15; *Met.* Θ 8, 1050b28-30).[12]

Leaving aside the reasons that Gerson already articulates for how the Unmoved Mover *cannot* be the final cause of motion, I emphasize in other ways how Burnyeat's (and Alexander's) view is completely unwarranted. I start by augmenting my aforementioned brief reason for why emulation would not cause motion on the part of any "mini"-Active Intellect (like an outer star) or "micro"-Active Intellect (like a human soul).

The only activity that the Unmoved Mover does is think of itself thinking, which itself is preposterous because thinking requires a mind. For the Mover to have a mind would require *some* kind of matter or capability. However, for the sake of argument, let us ignore this problem. To imitate the Unmoved Mover, the parts of the universe would or should be thinking of themselves thinking. That this is absurd is shown first by the passage in *GC* (*Generation and Corruption*), which Burnyeat cites. Aristotle speaks there of the four elements imitating circular motion (by being transformed continually because of the circular motion of the outer heavens). Yet, the elements cannot think; nor does the Unmoved Mover move in any way, circular or not. Thus, that passage in no way supports Burnyeat's view that all nature imitates the Deity (in the way I would imitate a runner, for health),

---

12 Burnyeat, *Aristotle's Divine Intellect, op. cit.*, p. 42; my italics and boldfacing.

making the Unmoved Mover the final cause of motion. At the best, the passage supports the four elements imitating *other* physical, eternal things (the outermost planets). Indeed the only part of nature that I can imagine imitating "thinking of (itself) thinking" to some extent is little children or selfish creatures like Narcissus in general thinking only of themselves (thinking), which takes me to the next point.

Perhaps philosophers and other theorists think of (themselves) thinking but usually even they are thinking of issues or problems or meanings of words, and not just of "thinking" itself (or of themselves thinking). Moreover, the "thought" that the Pure Actuality has must be like a passive contemplation, were something that has no potentiality actually able to think. The thought or passive contemplation must be without parts, and hence without multiple images or words, because any type of complex thought would require change or differentiation (whether of images or words), both of which are ruled out by Pure Actuality having absolutely no potential or matter whatsoever. The Actuality has no capability to distinguish anything separate, like a noun or a verb (and even for Plato thinking would require a plurality of Forms). To imitate the Pure Actuality, the philosopher or anything else in the universe with a localized, micro-Pure Actuality would have to be like a yogi who hums one mantra "Om," whereas the philosopher would reduce it to one sound "o" or "m," because again, there can be no differentiation in Pure Actuality. Similarly to the yogi, who is ostensibly trying to free himself from the distractions of the sensible world, the philosopher would try to imitate Pure Actuality for all eternity (as far as he or she is able). That is, since Pure Actuality does the thinking of thinking for eternity, the imitating philosopher would not eat or drink but would just continue to think "O" or would only eat and drink enough quickly to allow him to think "O" more. I hardly expect philosophers, however, even at the religious institutions, to drop their lifestyles and pursue such a path.

Aristotle's mention of "God" (*ho theos*) at *GC* 336b32, to which Burnyeat refers, also in no way could mean the Unmoved Mover, because of the anthropomorphic event of creation ascribed to it. Burnyeat falls into the same trap that ensnared Beere (and countless previous commentators). Either the passage in *GC* about "God" is rhetorical, to accommodate religious-minded readers in ancient Greece and the theological tradition starting with Xenophanes, or was interpolated, because it plays no role there in the explanation of how the eternal rotation causes generation and destruction, the theme of the chapter and of *GC*. The passage could be athetized and the chapter would be more sensible. Moreover, it blatantly contradicts Lambda's view of the Unmoved Mover never focusing on, *or even knowing about*, the physical universe.

Similarly, the passage from Theta 8 that Burnyeat cites cannot be reasonably read as suggesting that the Unmoved Mover is being imitated. What Aristotle says is the following, immediately after the statement that the entire heaven will never stop:

> Imperishable things [i.e., the sun and stars] are imitated by those that are involved in change, for example, earth and fire. For these also are ever active; for they have their movement (*kinēsis*) of themselves and in themselves (*kath' auta...kai en autois*).[13]

---

13   1050b27-31; transl. W.D. Ross, *The Complete Works of Aristotle*, ed. Barnes, *op. cit*; my comment. Makin notes that "they have their movement of themselves and in themselves" is difficult and he discusses W.D. Ross's interpretation along with his own reading, which involves the movement having a source within the earth and fire. The (source of the) movement is "of themselves," which means not in any source outside of themselves (like another element or another non-element), and "in themselves," which means they themselves move. Fire by its nature wants to move (itself) up; earth down. Aristotle has said, though, as we have seen, that "It is impossible to say that their [the elements'] motion is derived from themselves: this is a characteristic of life, and peculiar to living things" (*Physics* VIII 4, 255a6-7). How is it, then, that the source is "of themselves," with that different from "in themselves"? It is plausible that the movement is "in themselves," presupposing the *caveat* noted before, that the outer heavens are the *primary* cause of all

Burnyeat might gleefully remark that some things which cannot think, earth and fire, are said here to be imitating. Yet, clearly this is just a figure of speech, and Burnyeat's view that this passage helps him justify a God remains unwarranted. Not only does Aristotle mention now two of the same four elements as in *Generation and Corruption* to make a similar point but it is not the Unmoved Mover here that is being imitated (especially because the imitation is of *motion*). Rather, it is the plural "imperishable things" that have matter, such as the sun and stars, that are being imitated. Moreover, if that is not enough, the imitating earth and fire hardly have micro-Active Intellects and thus the passage here in no way helps explain how a planet would move (eternally) because of a (selfish) Pure Actuality that is a final cause.

Burnyeat's notion of the Unmoved Mover as the final cause of the eternally moving universe and as what is being imitated is completely backwards. If anything, the Unmoved Mover as the final cause would mean the universe would attempt to be *at rest*, merely thinking of thinking. Anyone who like Burnyeat, and *contra* Gerson, believes that the Unmoved Mover is the final cause, "that for the sake of which," needs to show why movement (and *circular* movement at that) rather than rest and thinking would result. The Mover is not circular in shape, nor is it like a beloved who leads the lover in a circle like a dog-owner leading a prize dog in a competition. Thus, the planets would not move in a rotary fashion for either reason, be it circular shape or circular motion on the part of the Mover. Even leaving aside those considerations, why would the planets not engage in rectilinear motion if they are "attracted" somehow to the Mover, instead going for it, wherever they think it is? If I am attracted to my beloved I do not start moving in a circle. I move towards her. Aristotle never even broaches this consideration when examining why the only kind of (single) eternal motion

---

movement. The issue seems to be how the elements could also be the source of their own movement. Perhaps *kai* is "that is," and so only one aspect of motion being in the elements is noted. Another option perhaps is that Aristotle is (elliptically) only excluding the source being from other elements.

is rotary (*Physics* VI 10, 241b19-20 and *Physics* VIII 8). Rather, the kind of consideration he explores is, for instance, the ways in which something moves something else in one of only four possible ways: pulling, pushing, carrying, and twirling (*Physics* VII 2, 243a15-8). He cares not a jot about whether a mini-Pure Actuality somehow apperceives a grand-Pure Actuality and, for whatever strange reason, moves *in a circular way* as a result. Gerson himself has given a powerful, if brief, argument why we should not expect anyone at any point, even in another 1800 years, to explain any of this.

These are merely some of the absurdities of the Unmoved Mover being either the final cause for eternal motion or the "entity" being imitated. Thus, suffice it to say here that I must concur with Gerson on the issue of the final cause and with Brentano. The doctrine of Pure Actuality is indeed "prattle without all sense and reason." Not only is the equation of God with the Active Intellect unbelievably naïve but the view that the Unmoved Mover of Pure Actuality has the ability to somehow interact with, and be recognized by, creatures (or stars with matter that may or may not have souls) and to cause their eternal motion would count as one of the greatest philosophical hoaxes ever perpetrated, if not the greatest, were it intentional. Even if the individual material entities have the ability to contemplate, the result still is insufferably paradoxical. The Active Intellect would have to be in each individual (above and beyond the *separate* Grand Intellect, the Unmoved Mover *per se*). Yet, to emphasize, something with no matter or potency of any type whatsoever cannot be located in different individuals or be located anywhere, for location would require physically restraining boundaries. Pure Actuality cannot exist in multiple forms or bodies, given Aristotle's strictures, although "unmoved movers" described in the other manner, like the man with the stick, or the planets causing motion to the lower regions of the cosmos, is a different story.

A better analysis of the two passages that Burnyeat appeals to, from *GC* and from Theta 8, is given by Makin, who says that: "**In certain**

respects perishable things *imitate* the continuous activity exhibited by eternal things..."[14] Clearly, Makin does not believe that the imitation is manifested in all respects (like thinking or locomoting in a circle), and he incisively explains the passage with respect to how in *GC* the corresponding passage on imitation means the elements transform themselves eternally because of the outer spheres. He gives also the better underlying import of the whole passage at hand in Theta 8, with respect to imitation, saying:

> ... the perishable and eternal realms are not brutely independent. *The way in which certain potentialities are actualized* in the realm of perishable things *reproduces (mirrors, imitates) the eternal realm. And that secures a degree of unity between the two realms. Perishable and eternal things, however different, nevertheless constitute a single universe* [for Aristotle].[15]

There is no implication here that the elements have the desire to imitate thinking of thinking. The conclusion of a single reality for everything for Aristotle is one that we saw Beere also commending for Theta, although his reasons are complementary to Makin's and, as we saw, are related to Aristotle's implicit reaction to the *Sophist* and to Plato's thought in general. I completely concur in this respect with both scholars and simply add that this all means, from the perspective of this book, that the whole heavens, including the sun and stars and the natural elements and objects within them, including earth, animals and plants, are the entirety of fundamental existence for Aristotle. No God exists outside of this "All," although whether this makes Aristotle a rank materialist is a completely separate question that would take its own book or series of books to begin to answer (and I for one do

---

14   pp. 217-8; his italics but my bolding.

15   p. 218; my italics and comment in brackets. Cf. Veloso, who gives independent reasons why Makin and I are correct on fire and earth "imitating," *op. cit.,* 2018, espec. pp. 322-3. See there also his Part II, Ch. 2, where he gives the general arguments against Pierre Aubenque for why elements in the world cannot (*contra* Aubenque) be imitating or trying to imitate a deity, especially an Unmoved Mover.

not believe it does, depending on how one defines "rank materialist").

Nevertheless, even though Burnyeat misconstrues the phenomenon of imitation in the current context, his motivation because of the tradition is to be expected. Commentators, with some reason but unfortunately sometimes at any and all costs, try to preserve the legitimacy of texts rather than the sensibility of the thought behind them. Burnyeat's misconstrual is also illuminating for my purposes in another way. If Pure Actuality is God, and therefore important, then presumably we and the universe would want to imitate it. It would be very logical, then, that Aristotle wishes to speak of imitating the Unmoved Mover of Pure Actuality when he discusses parts of the physical world imitating eternal subjects. Yet absolutely no mention of the Unmoved Mover of Pure Actuality explicitly occurs in the passages at hand, where we would expect them. Burnyeat expected it, but, again, only because he follows the tradition stemming from Alexander of Aphrodisias that Lambda is the mature view of Aristotle and only because both of them try to drive a square peg through a round hole. It would be better, though, to consider that Aristotle threw away the square peg, or put it back in his woodpile, and instead inserted gently the round peg that symbolizes eternal circular movement of the (inherently) necessary universe.

Theophrastus and Later Ancient Thinkers

Aristotle's acceptance of the Not to Fear Proof helps, if but a little, resolve some of the debate about the relationship between Theophrastus' *Metaphysics,* with its very cursory acknowledgment (and rejection) of, an Unmoved Mover, and Aristotle's own treatise (or agglomeration of treatises now called *Metaphysics*). I should first acknowledge, however, that my conclusions do not address in any great depth the debate over:

- whether Theophrastus rejected teleology in favor of a mechanistic view of the universe (the outer sphere causing motion and change in the rest of the lower cosmos);[16]
- whether Theophrastus' own work was, as Marlein van Raalte proposes, his "notes for his first course on metaphysics shortly after taking over the leadership of the Peripatetic school (that is, shortly before or after Aristotle's death)...somewhere between 323 and 320 B.C.,"... [which van Raalte acknowledges is a] "rather speculative proposition";[17] and correspondingly
- whether Theophrastus wrote his work early or late (because he may have written it early and then, given its aporetic character of presenting *aporiai* with a thesis and antithesis, used it as a foil for or against Aristotle's own views after he took over the leadership, just as we often present the views of those with whom we disagree or just as we often present historical views

---

16   Cf. John Ellis, "The Aporematic Character of Theophrastus' *Metaphysics,*" in *Theophrastean Studies: On Natural Science, Physics and Metaphysics, Ethics, Religion, and Rhetoric,* Studies in Classical Humanities, Vol. III, eds. William W. Fortenbaugh and Robert W. Sharples (New Brunswick [USA] and Oxford [UK]: Transaction Books) 1988, pp. 216-23, espec. pp. 216-7 and pp. 220ff.

17   Marlein van Raalte, "The Idea of the Cosmos as an Organic Whole in Theophrastus' *Metaphysics,*" in *Theophrastean Studies,* eds. Fortenbaugh and Sharples, *op. cit.,* pp. 189-215, p. 198.

without intending to champion them one way or the other).[18]

What my arguments help decide is why Theophrastus perfunctorily and disapprovingly treats of the doctrine of the Unmoved Mover that apparently comes from Lambda.[19] Ironically, the disapproval has caused some to claim that Lambda was very late in Aristotle's life and was his most mature view, because it was assumed that any criticism of the Master and the Mover would only have occurred after Theophrastus took over as head of the Lyceum. This would be a reason to reject that Aristotle held the Not to Fear Proof late in life, disproving the Jaegerian position that Aristotle's theories evolved to be more empiricist. For the following grounds, though, a much earlier rejection by Theophrastus of the Mover can still be very plausibly maintained.

First, relatively recent scholarship by Daniel Devereux shows that Theophrastus probably wrote his text early in his twenty-year association with Aristotle, based on a few reasons, one being that identical doctrines of the kinds of unity (numerical, specific, generic, and analogical) are found in Aristotle's earlier works *and* in Theophrastus' work. However, "focal point" unity, a later doctrine of Aristotle, is completely missing from Theophrastus' treatise.[20] Second, because of the aporetic nature of Theophrastus' work, it is sometimes very hard to tell whether Theophrastus advocates himself a certain position or not. Nevertheless, as another Theophrastean specialist, John Ellis, states, all scholars now seem to agree that Theophrastus at least questioned the conception and soundness of the Unmoved Mover, and

---

18 Later, I touch, but only touch, upon this topic more, reporting some of the views that reflect Theophrastus' work (originally known seemingly as *On First Principles*) coming early in Theophrastus' association with Aristotle, and even before the middle books of Aristotle's *Metaphysics,* which are often agreed to have been written *after* Lambda.

19 Cf. Daniel T. Devereux, "The Relationship between Theophrastus' *Metaphysics* and Aristotle's *Metaphysics* Lambda," in *Theophrastean Studies,* eds. Fortenbaugh and Sharples, *op. cit.,* pp. 167-88, esp. pp. 168-9.

20 Cf. Devereux, *op. cit.,* pp. 182-4. The passage in Theophrastus is 9a5.

Ellis provides examples of the other recent scholars who have focused on the issue, along with some of the texts. One citation suffices here:

> In his commentary on Theophrastus' *Metaphysics*, Giovanni Reale...notes a point made by another commentator, that at [Theophrastus' *Metaphysics*] 10a9-21, Theophrastus is clearly opposing Aristotle's proof of the immobile mover. *There Theophrastus suggests that the movement of the heavens may simply be a part of their essence, and indeed "a sort of life of the universe."* The movement of the heavens may sufficiently be explained by that very fact, just as the life in animals needs no more explanation than that it is part of their essence... [and then Ellis elegantly summarizes after explicating Theophrastus' line of dialectical arguments:] ... *the movement of the heavens...need not be explained by introducing the notion of the unmoved mover, but may simply be analogous to the case of life in animals* and plants. Just as the latter would not be what they are without life, so the heavens would not be what they are without their rotary motion (pp. 217-8; my italics).

For my purposes, it does not matter whether Theophrastus himself believed in the particular dialectical passage that the whole heaven (that is, the whole universe) carries "its own reason for existing with it," to use Leibniz's phrase from above. It is enough that Theophrastus articulates the position, for this is exactly in effect a conclusion of the Not to Fear Proof and exactly the reason why Aristotle as he matured need not keep the Unmoved Mover with all of its absurdities.

This also allows us to resolve a puzzle that Devereux had, namely:

> If Theophrastus formulated his criticisms of key doctrines in Lambda as early as we have suggested, it is odd that Aristotle seems to take no account of them in his later works. For instance, one might have expected him either to acknowledge the force of Theophrastus' objections to his account of how the unmoved movers cause the movement of the celestial bodies, or to try to show why the ob-

jections fail (p. 184, *op. cit.*).

However, we need not expect Aristotle to have broadcast loudly the somewhat embarrassing acknowledgement that he was wrong in his earlier work and that he has changed parts of it. Rather, Aristotle quietly dropped the Unmoved Mover of Pure Actuality, while keeping "unmoved movers" like the outer heavens and while keeping the other doctrines that I explained, when I showed how little he dropped from Lambda to arrive at the Not to Fear conclusion of Theta 8 and the inherent necessity of eternal motion. Thus, whether Theophrastus or someone else gave the very easy and powerful objections to the absurd doctrine that a Pure Actuality triggers motion in the physical universe, Aristotle evolved to the mature doctrine of the Not to Fear Proof in Theta 8. Aristotle did not think the "Theophrastean" objections failed. Rather Theta 8 shows he agrees with, and learned from, them. (I suggest the objections were from Theophrastus but naturally they could have come from many other colleagues or Aristotle could have realized the absurdities himself, especially when considering the similar doctrines in the *Phaedrus* that I discussed earlier.[21])

We can also establish how prescient Ellis's further account is, given Gerson's history of the lack of debate on the Unmoved Mover into Stoic times and beyond, and recall that Themistius only paraphrased Lambda, as if it had a special status in our collected treatises called the *Metaphysics*, whatever that status would have been. In my view, Themistius' narrow focus helps show that Lambda was separate from Theta or from the other middle books of the *Metaphysics*. As Ellis

---

21 Additional, detailed support for Devereux's thesis that Theophrastus' work was early in his life and association with Aristotle, and indeed that Lambda was from around the same time, but that the central books of Aristotle's *Metaphysics* were later, come from Dimitri Gutas, *Theophrastus on First Principles (Known As His Metaphysics)*, (Leiden: Brill) 2010, espec. pp. 4-6. Gutas (inadvertently) provides powerful evidence for my own thesis, albeit without recognizing the discrepancy between Theta's necessary universe and Lambda's contingent one.

adds:

> Van Raalte... believes that not only did Theophrastus question the principle of teleology and the conception of an immobile mover in his *Metaphysics* (*on which point all seem to agree*), but he in fact also abandoned them [teleology and the immobile mover] in favor of a different world view altogether. And since the particular world view he favors turns out to have striking similarities with that of the Stoics, Theophrastus' position would...be of historical interest. *For if she [van Raalte] is right, the work of Theophrastus would enhance our understanding of the way in which it was possible for Greek philosophy to make the transition from an Aristotelian to a Stoic world view* (p. 216; my italics & bracketed comments).

Van Raalte and Ellis arrive at the right result but for the wrong reason. If the Not to Fear Proof was Aristotle's view, then indeed he and not Theophrastus was ultimately responsible for the Stoics' own "world view" in this regard (and Theophrastus and Strato simply continued Aristotle's mature theory). Optionally, Theophrastus' early *On First Principles aka Metaphysics* may have been the first work to advocate the nature of the universe being necessary in and of itself, or friendly criticism by Theophrastus or by other Peripatetics caused Aristotle to drop the Unmoved Mover and devise his most mature solution. In short, either Aristotle or both he and Theophrastus or any of the other Peripatetics may have inspired the Principle (of Genuine Sortal) Plenitude and the resulting Not to Fear Proof in its entirety. In that case, the credit for the inherent eternal necessity of the universe would better be shared by a number of thinkers in the Lyceum, even if done during any Academic tenure.

The temporary disappearance shortly after Aristotle's death of most, or all, of his personal library until Roman times (with only a few dozen manuscripts apparently having multiple copies available to the early Peripatetics and to other schools, like the first Stoics and Epicureans) also did not help matters in making exoteric what had probably been esoteric, that is, written for the staff and students of the Lyceum.[22] Recall part of the history: Following Xenophanes, Anaxagoras himself, a supposedly materialist philosopher, had advocated a Mind (*Nous*) that on reflection also appears to be a "god" (like the Prime Mover in the *Physics,* as we saw, and as the Unmoved Mover is construed to be in *Metaphysics* XII 7). However, this did not stop Anaxagoras from being exiled by the Athenians; just the opposite. In many or all ways his theology, which involved the claim that the sun was a fiery rock rather than a god (a status only reserved for him for *Nous*), provoked his death sentence and subsequent exile. It was not enough to be a believer in Athens; one had to believe in the *state* gods. In spite of Aristotle's frequent disagreements with Anaxagoras, the Unmoved Mover was very similar to *Nous*, as we saw with the passages from the *Physics,* one difference being that Anaxagoras, like Xenophanes, has *Nous* focus on, move, and put order into the undifferentiated "all," whereas the Unmoved Mover is absolutely self-centered and thinks only of itself thinking, paying no attention to matter or moving things of any kind. Nevertheless, both "entities" for Anaxagoras and Aristo-

---

22   I touch on the ancient views of Posidonius, Strabo and Plutarch, along with Jonathan Barnes's recent examination of the issues pertaining to the corruption and re-ordering of texts, in *Aristotle on Dramatic Musical Composition,* 2018, pp. 408-9. In my recent *A Primer on Aristotle's DRAMATICS (also known as the POETICS)* (New York: ExistencePS Press) February 2019, I include a whole appendix (#2) to explore much more rigorously the account of Aristotle's library, demonstrating that Posidonius, Strabo and Plutarch indeed are believable. The ancients describe how Aristotle's library was hidden underground in Scepsis, corrupted, re-assembled and edited, sometimes badly, for sale in Athens and then the Roman marketplace. Scholars like Eduard Zeller, Gerald Else and Daniel de Montmollin have argued that the *Dramatics* is an assemblage of different texts, although others like Richard Janko and Stephen Halliwell still argue that the chapters are an organic unity. However, I believe my Appendix 2 forever destroys the latter option. This book demonstrates that the collection of texts known as the *Metaphysics* is similarly an assemblage from different periods in Aristotle's life, as supported by Gerson's history above.

tle are "Minds" and in a sense both "gods."[23] Obviously, in his youth or middle age, Aristotle in *Physics* VIII and Lambda believed that this Anaxagorean-type *Nous*, the Unmoved Mover of Pure Actuality that thinks of itself forever, solved some dilemmas (notwithstanding the differences between the two kinds of *Nous*).

Surely, for some Athenians these doctrines would have posed a threat

---

23 Simplicius reports Anaxagoras saying:
...Mind...is the finest of all things and the purest, *it has all knowledge about everything* and the greatest power; and Mind controls all things, both the greater and the smaller, that have life. Mind controlled also the whole rotation, so that it began to rotate in the beginning. And it began to rotate first from a small area, but it now rotates over a wider and will rotate over a wider area still. And the things that are mingled and separated and divided off, all are known by Mind. And all things that were to be—those that were and those that are now and those that shall be—Mind arranged them all... [my italics] (Fr. 12, *in Phys.*, as given by G.S. Kirk, J.E. Raven and M. Schofield, *The Presocratic Philosophers*, 2nd ed., Cambridge: Cambridge University Press, 1957 first publ., 1983 2nd ed., p. 363).
In conference papers that I presented in the 1990's, which will probably stay in that form because of more pressing books even though I still hold the conclusions, I argued that Anaxagoras was not the type of pure materialist that he became famous for, as shown in the passage above attributing all knowledge to Mind. Rather, I argued that Anaxagoras believed in a god (*Nous*) and that by keeping it separate from the primeval "all," Anaxagoras could satisfy the five Parmenidean conditions of being (which include the requirement that there be no differentiation in reality), at least at the beginning of the "modern" universe. Anaxagoras then provides an account that (rightly or wrongly) permits that undifferentiated mass to become the world as we know it. Were I ever to return to this topic, I would call him not only one of the firsts (along with Xenophanes) to advocate Intelligent Design but the predecessor (with respect to how science can connect to religion) to Francis S. Collins, the scientist who heads, or headed, the National Institutes of Health and who has written a book *The Language of God*, 2006, arguing (if very unconvincingly and in some ways shamefully) for the truth of Jesus Christ as god.

to their own gods, just as philosophical ethics pose a threat nowadays to the morality of the Bible or of other religious tracts like the Koran and to their adherents. Even Cicero continued to chastise Aristotle for his (early) theology, not realizing Aristotle had dropped it in favor of the Not to Fear Proof:

> Aristotle, in the third book of his work *On Philosophy*, creates much confusion through dissenting from his master Plato. For now he ascribes all divinity to mind... And when he himself demands that God be without a body, he deprives him of all sense-perception, *and even of foresight*.[24]

Cicero strangely ignores the account of Lambda, as if he had no awareness that Aristotle both wrote the treatise and advocated a Pure Actuality that, like in *On Philosophy*, has no body. F.H. Sandbach has argued that for the Stoics Aristotle was not rejected but largely unknown, which would explain Cicero's ignorance of the Unmoved Mover *per se*.[25] *On Philosophy* was an exoteric text.

Cicero articulates another problem of an Unmoved Mover of Pure Actuality not having physicality, above and beyond the Unmoved Mover not being visible to function as unmoved beloveds who move lovers. Without foresight, what good what such a god do for Athenians wanting help from superior powers, especially if they burn (probably expensive) offerings to deities for that help? A god without foresight would have no ability to help us defeat our enemies. Moreover, a pure mind without body, and one with no focus on anything other than itself thinking, would have as much concern for humanity as it would for sands on the beach. This might be another reason Lambda was kept esoteric. However, even if Aristotle allowed the work to go

---

[24] Cicero, *On the Nature of the Gods*, I. 13. 33, my italics; as given in W.D. Ross, *The Works of Aristotle*, Vol. XII, *Select Fragments* (Oxford: Clarendon Press) 1952, p. 97.

[25] F.H. Sandbach, *Aristotle and the Stoics* (Cambridge: Cambridge University Press) 1985.

public—which might have happened because *On Philosophy* is reputed to be for the general public and it also presents a notion of god that Cicero suggests would be different from typical Athenian ones—Cicero thereby supports my view that the Unmoved Mover of Pure Actuality is from early in Aristotle's career. The reason is that *Physics* II 2 (194a36) and *De Anima* I (404b19) refer to *On Philosophy*, which was therefore written (at least in part) before those two tracts. Anton-Hermann Chroust in a detailed examination of the surviving fragments and references dates *On Philosophy* to the period 357-46 BCE, which means Aristotle would have written it between the 27th and 38th years of his life (or starting with his tenth year in the Academy).[26] That coincides with the similar doctrine in Lambda of a god without a body being early or maybe even middle-aged. My conclusions in this book still are completely plausible.

After Alexander the Great died in 323 BCE, Aristotle moved away from Athens for the second time, saying supposedly that he would not let the Athenians sin twice against philosophy. With Alexander gone and the Macedonians no longer easily subjugating Athens, the Northern Greek was well aware that the Athenians might prosecute him. (Aristotle himself passed away a year later.) Carlo Natali suggests that Aristotle was "linking his case to that of Socrates,"[27] although surely the Athenian "sin" against Anaxagoras could not have been too far from the Northern Greek's memory either. There had been other philosophers prosecuted in the generations before Aristotle on sim-

---

26   Anton-Hermann Chroust, "The Probable Date of the *On Philosophy*," in *Aristotle: New Light on His Life and On Some of His Lost Works, Volume 2* (London and New York: Routledge) 2016 (first published in 1973), pp. 145-158, espec. pp. 156-8. Chroust says additionally: "If pressed for a more concise date...the present author would maintain that the *On Philosophy* was written (and 'published') between the fall of 349 and the spring of 348 B.C." (p. 158).

27   Carlo Natali, *Aristotle: His Life and School*, ed. by D.S. Hutchinson (Princeton: Princeton University Press) 2013, p. 63.

ilar charges of impiety[28] (just as some are prosecuted and executed in Middle Eastern countries for blasphemy even now). In any event, whether it was because of the worry that the Stagirite might be jailed for presenting "Hermias [of Atarneus, Aristotle's friend] as a deity, by praising him with the epigram and the *Hymn to Hermias* that was sung in his honor, as to a god,"[29] or for any of the other, ancient recorded reasons, Natali states that "Almost all ancient authors report that Aristotle left Athens to avoid being condemned to death *for impiety.*"[30]

Aristotle, then, may well have been very sensitive throughout his scholarly life about jeopardizing his position as a metic[31] and about broadcasting unnecessarily proofs that contradicted Athenian theology, even if citizens of Athens themselves could be braver and speak more freely (but still not too irreverently, as was shown by the case of Anaxagoras, who even had the ear and apparent support of Pericles before the court ruled against him). This suggests that some, although admittedly not all, of the seemingly exoteric tracts like *On Philosophy* may have been intended not for the general public *per se* but for a *restricted* public who might be willing to listen to different views about theology and reality without charging their author with impiety. In any event, even those like Theophrastus who knew that Aristotle had given up the God of Pure Actuality would presumably have been discreet. They would have been reluctant to advertise that the replacement of the Unmoved Mover was a proof that showed nature to be eternally necessary in and of itself, *with no gods in the anthropomorphic sense whatsoever.* Otherwise, Theophrastus would be throwing

---

28 Cf. Natali, *op. cit.*, p. 61.

29 Natali, *op. cit.*, p. 61.

30 Natali, *op. cit.*, p. 61; my italics.

31 For non-specialists, a metic is a foreign resident of Athens, who, e.g., was not allowed normally to own land in Athens and who did not have the full rights of citizens. Think similarly (although not exactly) of a green-card holder in the United States.

his friend and mentor into the fire that religious fanatics in ancient Athens always seemed to have going, similar to the one that modern American evangelicals always have stoked.

A more sophisticated perspective on these matters is given by Arthur Melzer:

> ...there are two entirely distinct ways in which a writer may contrive to speak differently to different audiences: either by giving each audience its own separate set of works (although, over the long run, it is nearly impossible to maintain this separation) or by conveying, within the same work, one teaching on the surface and the other beneath it—multilevel writing. Teachings can be separated either by work or by level. In exploring Aristotle's manner of communication, we need to ask about both techniques, as well as the—not unlikely—possibility that he combines the two (given the inherent difficulties of the first technique).
>
> In what follows, I will argue for the latter possibility, that Aristotle puts forward two distinct teachings, separated by both level and work. The testimonial evidence from the ancient commentators, we will see, is virtually unanimous and uncontradicted in depicting Aristotle as a multilevel writer. It is divided, however, on the question of whether Aristotle assigned distinct teachings to the two sets of works. Yet that question can be answered in the affirmative, I will argue, by consulting the evidence of the texts themselves...
>
> One thing making it difficult to answer these questions is that we do not possess any of the exoteric works, but know of them only by report. On the other hand, we are aided by the existence of a huge ancient and medieval literature of commentary on Aristotle. Just the ancient Greek commentaries run to over fifteen thousand pages. Yet two problems threaten to undermine their usefulness. They disagree regarding at least one of our ques-

tions. And, as modern scholars emphasize, most of them were influenced by neo-Pythagoreanism, Neoplatonism, and other mystical tendencies in the later empire period, which may have significantly biased their views on these questions. We need to consult this voluminous evidence, then—but with caution.

The first clear statement on these issues that has come down to us is found in Plutarch (46-120 AD) and seconded, several decades later, by Aulus Gellius (c. 125-after 180 AD)—both of whom are relying, as the latter indicates, on Andronicus of Rhodes (c. 60 BC), a philosopher and the authoritative ancient editor of Aristotle's works. Plutarch claims that the second, less popular category of Aristotle's writing concerns the "secret [*aporrata*, not to be spoken] and deeper things, which men call by the special term acroamatic and epoptic and do not expose for the many to share."...He continues that when Alexander the Great, Aristotle's former pupil, heard that his teacher had decided to publish some of the acroamatic discourses, he wrote to him in protest. Aristotle then replied in the following letter, which is featured in Andronicus's edition of his writings, and which Plutarch carefully describes and Gellius quotes in full:

> Aristotle to King Alexander, prosperity. You have written me about the acroatic discourses, thinking that they should be guarded in secrecy. Know, then, that they have been both published and not published. For they are intelligible only to those who have heard us.

The authenticity of this letter is doubtful. But regardless of who wrote it (During conjectures that it was Andronicus himself), it may well present an informed account of the character of Aristotle's writings. What we do know is that a thinker and historian of the stature of Plutarch finds the *content* of the letter accurate in light of his own personal reading of Aristotle. For, as he goes on to explain:

> To say the truth, his books on metaphysics are written

in a style which makes them useless for ordinary teaching, and instructive only, in the way of memoranda, for those who have been already conversant in that sort of learning.

These statements directly address—if only partially —our two questions. Regarding the first, Plutarch and Gellius (and probably Andronicus, their source) clearly embrace the view that **the distinction between Aristotle's exoteric and acroamatic writings is not simply reducible to elementary vs. advanced, as our scholars claim**. It obviously involves something esoteric: a firm desire to conceal from most people certain of his deepest views (by excluding these views from the exoteric works), while also revealing them to others (by including them in his distinct, acroamatic works).

But Plutarch et al. also clearly affirm that Aristotle employs the second, multilevel form of esotericism as well —in answer to our second question. **While the "secret and deeper things" are contained only in the separate, acroamatic writings, even there they are not presented openly but secreted behind a veil of artful obscurity. The acroamatic works are both "published and not published": they are multilevel writings that speak to some people and not to others.**[32]

All of the above strikes me as part of the reason why the Aristotelian "proofs" for the eternality of the universe without an anthropomorphic god of any sort were not published for the general public, even if the content itself was somehow available to them, and that in and of itself is extremely debatable. The god of the third book of *On Philosophy* that Cicero refers to, and criticizes, perhaps still was anthropomorphic enough to pass muster, at least when Aristotle initially formulated it.

---

32   Arthur M. Melzer, *Philosophy Between the Lines: The Lost History of Esoteric Writings* (Chicago; London: University of Chicago Press) 2014, pp. 34-6; his italics but my bolding. I appreciate Peter Saint-Andre directing me to this book.

Historical Reasons the Proof was Not Seen

Maybe Aristotle could argue that his type of god merely extends the Athenian gods. Still, whether it was not until Aristotle reflected some time after *On Philosophy* that he renounced "thinking without an enmattered mind," Melzer suggests that different audiences received different doctrines. Melzer's account must make us question whether the metaphysical doctrines would have been understood well enough to be grounds for impiety. Trained specialists themselves have difficulty understanding Aristotle's use of modals and his doctrines in Lambda and Theta, as we have seen throughout this book. All of this, therefore, helps explain why anything like the Not to Fear Proof would be unknown, or if known, not even understood, outside of the Lyceum.

The history I have described is merely one possible explanation that reflects Theophrastus and Strato taking over at least the conclusion of Aristotle's Not to Fear Proof, or partially inspiring it, if Theophrastus deserves credit for first recognizing that nature is inherently eternally in motion. I say "partially" because Aristotle had to take an additional step, identifying necessity with eternality, to conclude that the eternal motion was *necessary* and not contingent. Hence, I am not committed to the previous account (of Aristotle's concern with Athenian religious forces) as being the *only* plausible reason that the Not to Fear Proof was kept esoteric,—nor will I dwell on it anymore in this book, fascinating or important as it may be in the history of philosophy. Suffice it to say that the Proof shows unanimity with Theophrastus and Strato and explains why the other schools of philosophy also had no reason to target Aristotle's Pure Actuality in debate. They knew the master had already disowned the child, or they simply did not know about this particular doctrine, as mentioned before when discussing Cicero. However, the primary reason is that the Peripatetics themselves never cared about it, a different consideration from making sufficient copies to allow other schools to become familiar with certain manuscripts.

Nor will I enter here into the many complicated issues pertaining to the texts of the *Metaphysics*, as summarized by Gerson, whether they were all intended by Aristotle to be part of one whole, organic work or whether the current order is Aristotle's true order (which I cannot believe for a moment) or whether they are a combination of related texts, coming from different periods of Aristotle's life (my own view and that of many others).³³ Gerson's summary above strikes me as very apt and sufficient in this context, and I leave it to other experts in the Stoics or in other post-Peripatetic and Roman philosophy to adjudicate the details, if that is even possible given the dearth of evidence.

The paleographical matters themselves, too, pertaining to the various books of the *Metaphysics,* could generate, and have generated large tomes. All of these issues—historical, political, exegetical and paleographical—would eventually be helpful in providing the absolutely convincing case to, e.g., specialists in medieval theology that Aristo-

---

33   I have already referred to Patzig, *op. cit.* Consider in addition the following:

> ...the treatise... on metaphysics... are only fragments, and there is no reason for assigning the latter to some other author because it is not noticed in Hermippus and Andronicus, especially as Nicolaus (Damascenus) had already mentioned it (see the scholia at the end of the book). But throughout[,] the text of these fragments and extracts is so corrupt that the well-known story of the fate of the books of Aristotle and Theophrastus... might very well admit of application to them (*A Dictionary of Greek and Roman biography and mythology*, William Smith, Editor, as found on the Perseus Project, 2/9/17:
>   http://www.perseus.tufts.edu/hopper/text?doc=Perseus%3Atext%3A1999.04.0104%3Aentry%3Dtheophrastus-bio-1).

The "well-known story" must be the history by Strabo *et al.* To reiterate, the Aristotelian manuscripts do not constitute an inviolate Bible, and one cannot assume, simplistically and mechanically, that all the texts are part of Aristotle's one and only one static theory that he held at his death. Jaeger was essentially right, if not on every precise point, and one must exert the philosophical effort to show how any one doctrine is better, and more mature, than another. Some scholars, especially those who like tidy packages of doctrines and the option that the texts we have are all in authentic order, may not like it, but call it "job protection."

tle not only accepted the Not to Fear Proof but that it supplanted the "proofs" of the Unmoved Mover of *Metaphysics* XII and the Prime Mover of *Physics* VIII 10. However, examining the relation of the various "proofs" and the chronology of the various themes in Aristotle's corpus must be postponed for another day. Logically, as I once mentioned, Aristotle could have dropped his empiricism in late age and could have finished his life believing in the Unmoved Mover, although I take it this is more mere conceptual possibility than genuine possibility, given the rest of Aristotle's work and even just the Peripatetic tradition itself afterwards. Here, I have concentrated primarily on the philosophical matters *per se*, and have tried to show that the Not to Fear Proof is right on the surface in his extant texts, for example, in the *Metaphysics*, *Physics*, *De Caelo* and, maybe surprisingly to some, the *Dramatics*, with the premises being indubitable and well-known doctrines for him. The clue to my findings is his temporal grounding of necessity and possibility, along with his acceptance of versions of the Principle of Plenitude, which Hintikka first explained for me and which Broadie in her own way confirmed.

Conclusion

One should not think that all scholars before Hintikka (like Leibniz and Lovejoy) missing that Aristotle held the Principle of Plenitude is any evidence that Aristotle did not embrace it. Without question, the Northern Greek says clearly and with no need for qualification that *for infinite things, what may be will be*. Thus, the history only shows, as it were, how bad the previous scholars' eye-sight was. Hintikka and Broadie deserve the highest praise for defending the Principle and trying to handle the only difficulties that really apply: How and when the Principle applies to finite things or events. By clarifying the presuppositions that must be implied concerning finitudes, which Hintikka and Broadie debated, and by showing that by treating individuals (Broadie's concern) as *implicitly* members of kinds (Hintikka's solution), I believe I have demonstrated that they were both right in certain ways.

By distinguishing, moreover, between the different senses of the modals, especially possibility *qua* contingency and necessity *qua* omnitemporality, and between the formulations of the Principle, and by taking the Principle of Genuine Sortal Plenitude to be the most comprehensive and effective version, I have also been able to explain what the scope of the Principle really is and how broadly it was intended by Aristotle. This version is impervious to the objections of scholars like van Rijen, Barnes and Lear, all of whom mostly or wholly rejected Hintikka, even if they, and especially van Rijen, explained correctly that Hintikka may have gone too far in trying to apply one version of the Principle and one sense of "possibility" to all areas of Aristotle's thought. This book has revealed the modals to be very rich terms, with different meanings, and we cannot expect a univocal meaning to make sense of the different arguments in the various disciplines: logic, metaphysics, science, epistemology and dramatic theory, the last of which has a number of insightful passages about possibility that previous scholars working in this area simply ignored.

These pages also confirm the view of some previous scholars, namely, that the books of the *Metaphysics* as we have them are out of order. Lambda was surely written before Theta. However, to obviate the anticipated reaction that with my solution I am basically throwing Aristotelian scholarship into disarray—because if we cannot trust the way the manuscripts have come down to us, what can we trust?—I add the following.

In no way do I advocate arranging texts in any willy-nilly way. Rather, we should proceed in a manner that protects as much as the corpus as possible *and* that prioritizes the kind of reasonable thought Aristotle could have produced. If a text is absurd, then we must question it.

Historical Reasons the Proof was Not Seen

Wherever good sense and a legitimate meaning of the Greek words lead us in the corpus, we should at least consider the results. We can subsequently re-order the texts accordingly, even if it means in this context maintaining that some late chapters in the notoriously chaotic *Metaphysics* are earlier (Jaeger's wise position). We must protect Aristotle's mature thought as much as can be established because our choice is sometimes between making him an idiot (for example, being unaware of the types of absurdities that infect the Unmoved Mover of Pure Actuality) or making him prudently drop the doctrine as he reflected more about it (which then explains why Theophrastus and Strato and later schools like the Stoics never argued against him on that particular point and why the relevant manuscripts had no commentary for 500 years). In my view, his consistently expressed thought and reputation are more important than dead words on manuscripts that cannot talk, *if the thought and reputation are in conflict with some of the words*. We should show more respect to Aristotle as a thinker than to manuscripts that are full of mysteries, not because their doctrines are necessarily mysterious, but because the manuscripts were and are too often assumed to have come from the hand of the thinker himself, when they really have been established by others' rearrangements, assumptions, corrections and interpolations.

Given the foundational work of Hintikka and Broadie, the Principle of (Genuine Sortal) Plenitude and all the other statements of the Not to Fear Proof are clearly Aristotle's doctrines. If some scholars choose to protect the haphazard arrangement of texts that now exist as being Aristotle's own ordering and mature thought, they can continue with the same trend that has been ongoing since Alexander of Aphrodisias. That is, they can continue to try to make the hypotenuse of a triangle equal to one of the sides, and they can go on forever trying to demonstrate an impossibility, namely, how a Pure Actuality of no physicality whatsoever can cause eternal motion. Fortunately, to continue the theme from the *Dramatics* on believability, since some scholars have already accepted Brentano's and Jaeger's views, we can easily believe, and expect, that other (kinds of) scholars will also accept the new version of Aristotle's mature thought developed in this book.

Given the tradition of scholars accepting absurdities for so long and trying to explain how Aristotle himself might have accepted them, it is fair for me to finish with a few absurdities of my own that are, however, easily comprehensible.

It is a pity that Alexander of Aphrodisias could not have traded places with Hintikka, at least for a few years of their lives. Also, I detect Jaeger and Brentano now sleeping much more contentedly in their resting places, vindicated by this book, although I sadly also detect Flew tossing and turning somewhat regretfully in his own, wishing he had not succumbed at the end of his life to Aristotle's "God." Finally, to return to the other author who helped start this book, Comte-Sponville, who himself spoke of absurdity in claiming that "contingency is an abyss in which reason loses its bearings" and who asks why we do not just accept absurd truths (instead of believing in a more absurd God): Contingency is simply one of the meanings of possible, "to be or not to be," something that happens for Aristotle in this context at least once in an eternity, in contrast to necessity, which always happens, and impossibility, which never happens. Thus, the French scholar can reclaim his bearings and no longer "vacillate or hesitate" when he confronts the "cosmological proof" for the existence of God. With the extra free time, if he likes making clothes for himself or his loved ones, he can even cut some fabric as a bit of tribute to *On Interpretation* 9 (and I emphasize the "if" because he is probably too busy writing).

Bibliography

Aristotle:

The Complete Works of Aristotle, vols. 1 & 2. 1984. Ed. Jonathan Barnes. Princeton: Princeton University Press, including the following:
- ---. *Generation and Corruption*. Transl. by H.H. Joachim.
- ---. *Physics*. Transl. by R.P. Hardie and R.K. Gaye.
- ---. *Prior Analytics*. Transl. by A.J. Jenkinson.
- ---. *Rhetoric*. Transl. by W. Rhys Roberts.
- ---. *Topics*. Transl. by W.A. Pickard-Cambridge.
- ---. *On Interpretation*. Transl. J.L. Ackrill.

Aristotle. 1989. *Aristotle in Twenty-Three Volumes, Vol. VI, On the Heavens*. Tr. W.K.C. Guthrie. Cambridge: Harvard University Press. 1986 (first printed 1939). Vols. 17 & 18, translated by Hugh Tredennick. Cambridge, MA: Harvard University Press; London: William Heinemann Ltd. 1989 (first printed 1933).

W.D. Ross. 1952. *The Works of Aristotle*, Vol. XII, *Select Fragments*. Oxford: Clarendon Press.

Metaphysics. 1924. Ed. W.D. Ross. Oxford: Clarendon Press.

Metaphysics. 1933. Translated by Hugh Tredennick. Cambridge, MA: Harvard University Press and London: William Heinemann Ltd.

Poetics. 1987. Transl. by Richard Janko. Indianapolis: Hackett Publishing Company.

Bäck, Allan. 1992. "Sailing through the Sea Battle," *Ancient Philosophy* 12, 133-51.

---. 1995. "Aristotelian Necessities," *History and Philosophy of Logic* 16, 89-106.

Barnes, Jonathan. 2011. "The principle of plenitude," *Method and Metaphysics: Essays in Ancient Philosophy I*, ed. by Maddalena Bonelli. Oxford: Clarendon Press, 364-70. Originally printed in *Journal of Hellenic Studies* 97, 1977, 97-133.
---. 1979. *Articles on Aristotle 3. Metaphysics*. Ed. by Jonathan Barnes, Malcolm Schofield, and Richard Sorabji. London: Gerald Duckworth & Co.

Beere, Jonathan. 2009. *Doing and Being: An Interpretation of Aristotle's* Metaphysics Theta, Oxford: Oxford University Press.

Brentano, Franz. 1975. *On the Several Senses of Being in Aristotle*, ed. and transl. by Rolf George. Berkeley: University of California Press.

Broadie, Sarah. 1994. "What Does Aristotle's Prime Mover Do?" Paper presented to the Society of Ancient Greek Philosophy, Boston, Massachusetts, December 28, 1994, available at http://orb.binghamton.edu/sagp/239/
with an alternative version published in French in *Revue Philosophique* 2, 1993, 375-411. (See "Waterlow" for publications under her maiden name.)

Burnyeat, Myles F. 2008. *Aristotle's Divine Intellect*, Milwaukee: Marquette University Press.

Chroust, Anton-Hermann. 2016. "The Probable Date of the *On Philosophy*," in *Aristotle: New Light on His Life and On Some of His Lost Works, Volume 2*. London and New York: Routledge. 145-158. First published in 1973.
---. 1973. "The 'Great Deluge' in Aristotle's *On Philosophy*,"

Bibliography

L'Antiquité Classique, 42-1, 113-22.

Cicero, *On the Nature of the Gods*, as given in W.D. Ross, *The Works of Aristotle*, Vol. XII, *op. cit.*

Comte-Sponville, André. 2006. *The Little Book of Atheist Spirituality*. New York: Penguin Books. Transl. by Nancy Huston, 2007.

Dancy, R.M. 1980. "Aristotle and the Priority of Actuality," in *Reforging the Great Chain of Being: Studies in the History of Modal Theories*, ed. SimoKnuuttila, 73-115. Dordrecht: D. Reidel.

Devereux, Daniel T. "The Relationship between Theophrastus' *Metaphysics* and Aristotle's *Metaphysics* Lambda," *Theophrastean Studies,* eds. William W. Fortenbaugh and Robert W. Sharples, cited below, 167-188.

Ellis, John. "The Aporematic Character of Theophrastus' *Metaphysics*," in *Theophrastean Studies*, in *Theophrastean Studies*, eds. William W. Fortenbaugh and Robert W. Sharples, cited below, 216-223.

Fortenbaugh, William W., and Robert W. Sharples, editors. 1988. *Theophrastean Studies: On Natural Science, Physics and Metaphysics, Ethics, Religion, and Rhetoric*, Studies in Classical Humanities, Vol. III. New Brunswick, USA, and Oxford, UK: Transaction Books.

Gerson, Lloyd P. 1994. "Plotinus and the rejection of Aristotelian Metaphysics," in Lawrence P. Schrenk (ed.), *Aristotle in Late Antiquity*. Washington: Catholic University Press. 3-21.
---. 2016. "The Central Hypothesis of Aristotle," paper given at the *2400 Year Aristotle Conference*, University of Aristotle, Thessaloniki.

Graham, Daniel W. 2010. *The Texts of Early Greek Philosophy*, Part 1, Cambridge: Cambridge University Press.

Grimes, William. "Antony Flew, Philosopher and Ex-Atheist, Dies at 87," *New York Times*, 4/17/10, p. B10.

Gutas, Dimitri. 2010. *Theophrastus on First Principles (Known As His Metaphysics)*, (Leiden: Brill).

Hintikka, Jaakko. 1973. *Time and Necessity: Studies in Aristotle's Theory of Modality*. Oxford: Clarendon Press.
---. 1979. "Necessity, Universality, and Time in Aristotle," in *Articles on Aristotle 3. Metaphysics*. Ed. by Jonathan Barnes et al (op. cit.), 108-24.
---. 1979. "Aristotelian Infinity," in *Articles on Aristotle 3*, ed. by Jonathan Barnes et al (op. cit.), 125-39.

Hume, David. 1974. *An Enquiry Concerning Human Understanding*; reprinted in *The Empiricists: Locke, Berkeley and Hume*. Garden City, NY: Anchor Press.

Irwin, Terence and Gail Fine. 1995. *Aristotle: Selections*, Translated with Introduction, Notes, and Glossary by T. Irwin and G. Fine. Indianapolis/Cambridge: Hackett Publishing Company, Inc.

Jaeger, Werner. 1948. *Aristotle: Fundamentals of the History of his Development*, transl. Richard Robinson, 2nd ed. Oxford: Oxford University Press. Originally published as *Aristoteles: Grundlegungeiner Geschichte seiner Entwicklung*. Berlin: Ostern. 1923.

Johnson, Monte Ransome. Forthcoming 2019. "Aristotle on *Cosmos* and *Cosmoi*," in *Cosmos in the Ancient World*, ed. P.S. Horky.

Cambridge: Cambridge University Press. 74-107.

Judson, Lindsay. "Eternity and Necessity in *de Caelo* I. 12," *Oxford Studies in Ancient Philosophy*, 1983, Vol. 1, 217-55.

Kirk, G.S., J.E. Raven and M. Schofield. 1987. *The Presocratic Philosophers*, 2nd ed. Cambridge: Cambridge University Press. 1957 first publ., 1983 second ed.

Lear, Jonathan. 1980. "Aristotelian Infinity," *Proceedings of the Aristotelian Society*, Vol. 80 (1): 187-210. Also at: https://doi.org/10.1093/aristotelian/80.1.187 (published September 8, 2015).

Lovejoy, Arthur. 1936. *The Great Chain of Being*. Cambridge, MA: Harvard University Press.

Makin, Stephen. 2006. *Aristotle Metaphysics Book Theta*, translated with an Introduction and Commentary. Oxford: Clarendon Press.

Natali, Carlo. 2013. *Aristotle: His Life and School*, ed. by D.S. Hutchinson. Princeton: Princeton University Press.

Mayhew, Robert. As yet unpublished. "Aristotle on Helios' 'omniscience' in Iliad 3 and Odyssey 12: On schol. B* Iliad 3.277a (fol. 47r)." Paper given at the Society for Ancient Greek Philosophy, Cristopher Newport University, October, 2018.

Melzer, Arthur M. 2014. *Philosophy Between the Lines: The Lost History of Esoteric Writings*. Chicago; London: University of Chicago Press.

Mourelatos, Alexander P.D. 2016. "Three Critiques of Anthropomorphism in Early Greek Philosophy," Gregory Vlastos Memorial Lecture, Queen's University, Ontario.

---. 2017. "Xenophanes" (from "Three Critiques"), presented in modern Greek translation at the University of Crete, forthcoming in *Ariadnê*, Proceedings of the School of Philosophy at the University of Crete.

Owen, G.E.L. 1974. "Plato and Parmenides on the Timeless Present," in *The Pre-Socratics: A Collection of Critical Essays*, ed. by Alexander P.D. Mourelatos. Garden City, NY: Anchor Press/Doubleday; orig. published in *Monist* 50, 1966, 317-40.

Patzig, G. 1979. "Theology and Ontology in Aristotle's *Metaphysics*," in Barnes, ed., 1979, *op. cit.*, 33-49.

Patterson, Richard. 1995. *Aristotle's Modal Logic: Essence and Entailment in the* Organon. Cambridge: Cambridge University Press.

Philo, *de aeternitate mundi* III 10-11. Fragment 18 (from Rose's 3rd edition of the *Fragmenta*, Teubner, 1886) as found in *The Complete Works of Aristotle*, ed. Barnes, *op. cit.*

Plato. 1997. *Plato: Complete Works*, ed. John Cooper and Assoc. Ed. D.S. Hutchinson. Indianapolis/Cambridge: Hackett Publishing Company.

---. 1993. *Philebus*, transl. by Dorothea Frede. Indianapolis: Hackett Publishing Co.

Sandbach, F.H. 1985. *Aristotle and the Stoics*. Cambridge: Cambridge University Press.

Scott, Gregory L. 2018. *Aristotle on Dramatic Musical Composition: The Real Role of Literature, Catharsis, Music and Dance in*

Bibliography

the POETICS. New York: ExistencePS Press, 2nd edition; originally published 2016, CreateSpace/Amazon.
---. 2019. *A Primer on Aristotle's DRAMATICS (also known as the POETICS)* (New York: ExistencePS Press) .

Sedley, David. 2000. "The Ideal of Godlikeness," in *Plato 2: Ethics, Politics, Religion and the Soul*, ed. by Gail Fine. Oxford: Oxford University Press, 309-28.

Smith, William, editor. *A Dictionary of Greek and Roman biography and mythology*, as found in the Perseus Project, February 9, 2017: http://www.perseus.tufts.edu/hopper/text?doc=Perseus%3Atext%3A1999.04.0104%3Aentry%3Dtheophrastus-bio-1)

Solmsen, Friedrich. 1960. *Aristotle's System of the Physical World: A Comparison with his Predecessors,* Cornell Studies in Classical Philology, Vol. XXXIII. Ithaca: Cornell University Press.

Sorabji, Richard. 1986. *Time, Creation and the Continuum.* Ithaca: Cornell University Press (first printing 1983).
---. 1980. *Necessity, Cause and Blame,* London: Duckworth.

Spellman, Lynne. 1986. "Critical Notices. Passage and Possibility: A Study of Aristotle's Modal Concepts by Sarah Waterlow." *Philosophy and Phenomenological Research*, Vol. 46, No. 4. 688-692.

Tarski, Alfred. 1944. "The Semantic Conception of Truth," *Philosophy and Phenomenological Research* 4, 341-376.

Thorburn, John E. 2005. *The Facts on File Companion to Classical Drama.* Infobase Publishing / Facts on File, Inc.; New York.

van Raalte, Marlein. "The Idea of the Cosmos as an Organic Whole in Theophrastus' *Metaphysics*," in *Theophrastean Studies,* eds. William W. Fortenbaugh and Robert W. Sharples, cited above, 189-215.

van Rijen, Jeroen. 1989. *Aspects of Aristotle's Logic of Modalities.* Dordrecht/Boston/London: Kluwer Academic Publishers.

Vasiliou, Iakovos. 2013. "Theoretical *Nous* and its Objects in Aristotle," in *Proceedings of the Boston Area Colloquium in Ancient Philosophy*, Vol. XXVIII, 2013, ed. by Gary Gurtler and William Wians. Leiden/Boston: Brill. 161-80.

Veloso, Claudio William. 2018. *Pourquoi la Poétique d'Aristote? DIAGOGE*, with a Preface by Marwan Rashed. Paris: Vrin.

Waterlow (Broadie), Sarah. 1982. *Passage and Possibility: A Study of Aristotle's Modal Concepts.* Oxford: Clarendon Press. (See "Broadie" for her other publications.)

Zabel, Gary. Undated draft. "Excursus: A Short History of Infinity before Spinoza." From Chapter 3 of *All Things in Common: Spinoza and the Collegiant Letters.* Published online (10/15/16) at: https://www.academia.edu/19971501/Excursus_A_Short_History_of_Infinity_Before_Spinoza

Index

Ancient texts are indexed under the following *Index Locorum*. Modern texts are listed usually first under general title, followed separately in some cases by title then chapter.

Symbols

∞ 25, 26, 45, 51
(T) 72
(T)-(T***) 16

A

A´ 124, 126, 131, 132, 133, 135
absolute infinity 62
absolutely necessary being 184
absolute necessity 17
absurd theoretical baggage 228
academic failure 279
Academic Skeptics 282
accident 93, 197, 137
accidental particular 121
accidental particulars 76
Ackrill 50
acroamatic 311
active 14
Active Intellect 251, 293, 297
Active Intellects 291
actual existence 28
actual infinity 29, 45, 52
actuality 1, 117, 202, 254, 272
actuality is prior 104
actualized possibilities 113
actually infinite number 36
actually occurring 28
actual nows 133, 134, 149
adapted semantic model 121
addition 47
admissible 208

advanced beings 170
aesthetics 110
affection 21
affirmations 216
after the *Physics* 240
Agamemnon 274
Agathon 97
air 156
aition tou einai 290
Alexander 283, 292
Alexander of Aphrodisias 281
Alexander the Great 308, 311
Al-Khwarizmi 48
Allegory of the Cave 177
allowable given the laws of nature 85
alterations 157
always 10, 175
always in time 207
ambiguous 142
American evangelicals 310
analogical 229, 301
analogy with pleasure 239
analytic 128
Anaxagoras 12, 35, 235, 239, 243, 305, 306
ancient treasure 227
Andronicus 314
Andronicus of Rhodes 281, 311
animals 157, 159
animals other than man 159
anonymous continuator 283
Anscombe 106
anthropomorphic god 265, 312
anthropomorphic remarks 273
Antheus 97
Antigone 252
Antipater 282
antithesis 300
ants 159
aphthartos 188

Index

apodeictic 109
apodeictic generalizations 204, 212
apodeictic logic 206
apodeictic sentences 113
apodeictic syllogistic moods 108
aporetic character 300
aporetic nature 301
aporiai 280, 282, 300
aporrata 311
a posteriori 183
a priori proof 183
Aquinas 93
Aristotelian exegesis 265
Aristotelian manuscripts 314
Aristotelian *Metaphysics* 123, 125
Aristotelian modal asymmetry 127
Aristotelian modality 127
"Aristotelian Necessities" 18
Aristotelian necessity 106
Aristotelian necessity statements 117
Aristotle on Dramatic Musical Composition 19
Aristotle's modal concepts 106
Aristotle's notion of truth 208
Aristotle's successors 13
Aristotle's System of the Physical World 13
Armani 161
art 158
artifact 152
artifacts in general 154
artificial 161
artificial construction of kinds 135
artificial natural kind 160
artificial products 158
artificial sub-kind 168
Asclepius 281
assertoric 17, 18, 104, 109
assertoric and apodeictic generalizations 204, 213
assertoric and apodeictic logic 206
assertoric forms of validity 210

assertoric logic 212
assertoric versus apodeictic generalizations 215
atheistic philosophy 184
Athenian religious forces 313
Athenians 305
Athenians persecuting 279
Athenians raiding Sardis 227
Athenian theology 309
atomic elements 215
attributes 157
authentic order 314
Averroes 33

B
B´ 126
Babylonians 224
Bäck 18, 27, 49, 50, 105
Ball 170
bArbArA 109, 211
Barbara NAN 110
Barnes 68, 183, 186, 201, 247, 316
basic syllogism 104
Beere 11, 197, 224, 257
beginning 44, 256
beginning number 37
Being as symbolized by the materialist Giants 259
Being as symbolized by the transcendental Gods 259
being in activity 259
being in all the categories 137
being-in-capacity 259
being-in-*energeia* 260
being *qua* being 284
believability 84, 99
believable 84
believer 305
Berkeley 170
Bible 314
Big Bang 36, 173
Big Bang *ex nihilo* 173

Index

billiard ball 94
biological father 162
bivalence 50
bivalent propositional calculus 49
blasphemy 309
bodily being 259
Bonaventure 41
Borges 30
Brahmagupta 48
brain 12
brane 173
brane theory 36
Brentano 51, 87, 102, 130, 293, 297, 318
bright argument 186
Broadie 15, 124, 127, 128, 133, 136, 175, 223, 315
brute fact 276
Burnyeat 11, 167, 248, 290, 292, 296

C

Cantorian mathematics 46, 47
capacity 29
cataclysms 226
categorical sentences 114, 207
catharsis 258
causal continuity 141
causal sequence 252
caused change 127
celestial bodies 179
central books of the *Metaphysics* 280
chance 63, 200
change 21, 127
Change 259
change-capacity 118
change in states of things 127
chicken-like kind 141
chorus of Thebes 252
Christian apologist 40
Christianity 3
Christian Trinity 40

Chroust 227, 308
Chrysippus 282
Cicero 12, 168, 239, 307, 312
circularity 104
classical Aristotelian conception of truth 130
classical mathematics 49
cloak 71
cloaks 157
closed or coherent doctrine 114
clothing 161
coat 121
coherent 48
collection of substances 230
Collins 306
combination of concepts of the thinking mind 102
comedy 258
commonsensical assumptions 163
communicating 207
competing paradigms 114, 122
complete 237
complete nothingness 172
compliment 275
comprehensive survey 227
computer simulation 170
Comte-Sponville 2, 183, 318
conceivability 83, 93, 96, 99
conceivable 19
conceivable possibility *qua* fiction 200
conceivalists 99
conceiving 96
conceptual frameworks 76
conditionals 49
Conservation of Mass and Energy 179
consistent 48
contemplation 291
contingency 2, 3, 19, 86, 105, 112, 123, 164, 172, 183, 188, 213
contingent 143
contingent eternal motion 224
contingent eternal universe 197

Index

contingently eternal 224
contingent universe 1, 250
continuity 142
contradictory 15
contrary motion 272
conventional 207
conversions 212
copula 205
cosmogonical theories 36, 172
cosmoi 4
cosmological consequence 270
cosmological proof 183
cosmos 4, 135
crab 272
culture 111
cultured 255
cuttable 75

D

dance 161
Dancy 115
Darwin 12
dated future contingent 129
Dawkins 2
day 38
de dicto necessity 17, 215
de dicto properties 205
deductions 210, 212
deep confusion 133
definite in a way 64
definition 199
definition of possibility 81
definition of tragedy 199
deliberation 159
Demi-Urgos 265
de Montmollin 305
de re claims 206
de re necessity 17, 151
de re possibility 151

Descartes 19, 92, 242
determinate 64
determinism 16, 67, 125, 127, 142
deterministic doctrine 120
deus ex machina 99
Devereux 301, 302, 303
dialectical treatment of sensible substance 280
different senses of the modals 316
dilemmas 280
Diophantus 48
discontinuity 142
discoveries 99
discovering the truths 227
distinctive matter 229
distributively 139
diversity 232
divine 226, 244
divine and human souls 246
divine craftsman 265
divine intellect 167
"divine" super-computers 170
Doctrinal Reasons 247
doctrine of flux 200
Doctrine of Recollection 246
dogs 232
doing 259
Doing and Being 11
domains of discourse 107
drunken-eight 25, 37, 43-9, 53-7
dunamis 86
dunata 84, 98
dunaton 82, 208
duration 27
During 311
dynamei on 102
dynamis 103
dynaton 102

Index

E
earlier thinkers 227
earth 156, 157
earthly realm of perceptible, changeable body 259
efficient cause 227
efficient cause of coming to be 290
egg-like kind 141
Egyptians 224
Eleatic Visitor 259
ellipsis 44
elliptical statement about sea battles 120
Ellis 300, 301
Else 305
empirical world 185
endecheston 82
endechomenon 208
energeia 253, 259
entire approach to modality 133
entire enterprise of the *Metaphysics* 281
entropy 172
epic 99
Epicureans 195, 282
epistēmē 201
epistemological domain 206
epistemology 220
epoptic 311
equivalences 186, 218
equivalent 175
equivocal 68
esoteric 304
esoteric texts 279
essence 199
essential conditions 199
eternal 105, 201
eternal accident 189
eternal accidents 195, 225
eternal enmattered mover 235
eternal first cause 250
eternal heavenly bodies 203

eternal kind 136
eternal kinds 154
eternal lack of fatigue 274
eternally circumscribed circular path 232
eternally-existing spheres 200
eternal movement 249
eternal mover 249
eternal movers 236
eternal objects 228
eternal perceptible bodies 259
eternal-perishable 118
eternal phenomena 203
eternal prime mover 251
eternal prime movers 242
eternal self-motion 246
eternal species 76
eternal things 68, 202
eternal things are prior 104
eternal unmovable substance 1, 229
eternal unmovable substances 230
eternity 166, 175
Euclidean geometry 49
events 149
exceptions 170
exclusive disjunction 61
exist potentially 250
exoteric 304, 310, 312
extendible finitude 54

F
fear 14
fictional 18
fictional creation 157
fictional literature 49
fictional possibility 83
fifth element 246
final cause 249, 291, 293, 297
final cause of the eternal motion 285
Fine 103

Index

finite 24
finite duration 119
finite space 23
finite straight line 25
finitist 54
finitudes 46, 64
fire 156, 157
First Antinomy 41
first cause 156
first comprehensible 253
first falsehood 184
first mover 235
First Mover 243
first of the movers 256
first philosophy 221, 288-9
first principles 217
five numbered points 108
Flew 2, 318
flux 200
"focal point" unity 229, 301
forefathers 226
foreign frameworks 275
foresight 307
formal cause 290
formal logic 4, 17
form/content distinction 258
Forms 155, 185, 201, 259, 289
formula 254
formulations of the Principle 316
founder of modal logic 204
four elemental bodies 156
four equivalences 202, 219
four senses of unity 229
Friends of the Forms 259
fulfillment 172
full particularity 136, 138
fully infinite 60
functions 157
functions and attributes of substances 157

future and past truth 127
future contingent 129
future contingents 51, 128
future contingent statements 142

G
Games 29
Gellius 311
general causes 140
generated 137
generated universe 63
generic 229, 301
generically 141
generic capacities 74
generic causes 140
generic effects 140
generic identity 140
genuine 14, 71, 78, 80, 99
genuine-ness 116
genuineness 97
genuine possibilities 75
genuine possibility 14, 71, 95
geometry 289
Gerson 279, 284, 285, 296, 313
god 9
God 1, 2, 3, 184, 249, 251, 264, 275, 293, 294, 307
God of Aristotle 3
gods 226
god-sent madness 244
golden mountains 96
Gonzalez 197
good character 258
Graham 9
Gregory Vlastos Collection 224
Grimes 2
Gutas 303

H
Halliwell 305

Index

Hamlet 157
Han Dynasty 48
Harris 2
Harry Ransom Center 224
health 291
heaven 10, 14
heaven as a whole 157
heavenly bodies 202
heavenly realm of intelligible Forms 259
hedonic calculus 239
Helios 274
Hellenistic period 282
Henry of Harclay 34
Heraclitus 200
Hermias 309
Hermippus 314
higher-level kinds 135
Hintikka 15-6, 67, 106, 112, 124, 127, 133, 136, 186, 201, 219, 228, 315
historical records 225
historical views 300
Hitchens 2
hōistai pōs 64
Holy Grail 110
homonymous 85, 100, 269
homonymously 85
hōrismenon 64
ho theos 251, 294
house 158
human history 242
human invention 152
human product 168
human soul 246
human species 154
Hume 19, 92, 99
Hume's case of the billiard balls 83
Hutchinson 10, 308
hylomorphic 246
Hymn to Hermias 309
hypothetical necessity 17, 122, 142

I

idealist 170
Iliad 3 274
image 275
imitated 111
imitating circular motion 293
imitating "thinking of thinking" 294
imitation 111, 249
imitation of the eternal first cause 249
immaterial entities 282
immediately realizable 89, 115, 150
immediate realizability 172
immobile mover 304
immortal 244, 292
immortality 246
impassive 235
imperceptible gods 260
imperishability 175
impersonate 111
impiety 309
impossibility 15
impossible 4, 15, 98, 99, 180
inclusive disjunction 61
indeterminacy 50
individual Active Intellects 291
individual causes 140
individual (of a kind) 137
individual of a kind 74
individuals 315
individuals of a kind 138
indivisible 236
induction 174
infinite 23, 32
infinite circular motion 223
infinite divisibility of magnitudes 190
infinite dogs 43
infinite in number 25
infinite in one direction 57
infinite in only one direction 32

infinite mathematical series 25
infinite men 43
infinite number 25, 43
infinite physical object 30
infinite regress 232
infinite time 67
infinity 23, 175
infinity of numbers and of time 190
infinity of time 166
inflexion of a verb 207
ingenerability 175
inherent diversity 232
inorganic 161
inorganic matter 173
inquiry 159
instant 28
intelligence 159
Intelligent Design 306
internal representation 291
Irwin 103
"is"-claims 119
Islam 3
Ismene 252

J
Jaeger 1, 3, 124, 314, 318
Janko 305
Java programming language 170
Johnson 4, 10, 135, 155
Judson 134
juvenile indiscretions 167

K
Kant 41, 190, 93
kata metaphoran 103
kath' auta...kai en autois 295
kind of possibility 142-4, 151
kinds 125
kinds of events 71, 149

kinds of individuals 71, 152
kinds of possibilities 126
kinēsis 295
King Laius 163
kinountos 253
kinountos tinos prōtou 253
knowledge in the full sense 201
Koran 307
kosmos 155

L

laborious 266, 270, 272
language 207
Law of Non-Contradiction 220
laws of logic 70
laws of nature 80, 161
Lear 41, 190, 247, 316
learning 217
Leibniz 19, 83, 92, 183, 247, 315
living nature 267
living substances 156
locomotion 21
logical analysis 189
logical and natural possibility 204
logical treatises 206
logic of modal operators 114
Lovejoy 69, 106, 247
lover 240
lower cosmos 179
lower *kosmos* 155
luck 63
Lyceum 11, 13, 226, 279
lynchpin 131

M

Macedonians 308
magnitude 21, 60, 236, 237
Makin 11, 87, 249, 255, 257, 268, 295, 297
mammals 232

Index

man 209, 255
mapping the sound 207
material adequacy 130
material cause 257
material cause of the events 257
materialist 298
materialist philosopher 305
mathematical equality 175
mathematical objects 289
mathematics 289
matter 2, 231, 234, 272, 282
matter of fact 94
maxima 223
maximal finite number 51
maximum capacity 91
Mayhew 274
measure of motion 14
mechanistic view of the universe 300
medieval theologians 275
Megarians 258
megethos 60, 237
Melzer 310
member of a kind 137, 162
member of a kind *per se* 121
members of a natural kind 155
members of kinds 315
Menelaus 274
mental constructs 27
mental impression 44
me on 103
mere conceivability 84, 99, 185
mere contingency 150
merely conceivable 77
"mere" necessary conditions 199
metaphysical-theological domain 206
Method and Metaphysics 186
metic 309
middle age 237
Middle Eastern countries 309

middle term 215
mimēsis 110
Mind 12, 235, 306
mind actualizes the form 96
mind of God 170
Minds 242
Miyake 161
modal 18
modalities 17
modality 128, 133
modal logic 67, 101, 112, 121, 125, 204, 209, 211, 214
modally qualified sentences 114
modal operators 143
modal possibility 121
modals 313
modal terms 215
modern mathematicians 37
modern principles 212
monkey on a typewriter 72
monstrous cacophony 38
motion 21, 23, 234
movement 21, 238
movement of themselves and in themselves 295
movements 157
moving in a circle 295
multilevel writing 310
Musk 170
must be 208
"must be"-claims 119

N

Narcissus 236, 275
Natali 308
natural 155, 157
natural and artificial kinds 158
natural history 80
natural kinds 152, 155, 161
natural laws 170
natural material conditions 162

Index

natural mental phenomenon 157
natural necessity 86, 96
natural philosophers 14
natural possibility 96
natural products 158
nature 158
Nature 200
nature of a soul 244
nature of the soul 244
near oblivion 281
necessary 4, 14-5, 105, 180, 208
necessary characteristics 199
necessary propositions 50
necessary things 203
necessary truth 128
necessity 112, 127, 142, 202
Necessity, Cause, and Blame 17
necessity of temporally definite, true sentences 114
necessity operator 113
necessity *qua* actuality 217
"Necessity, Universality, and Time in Aristotle" 16
negation 208
negations 216
negative numbers 48
Neoplatonic 281
Neoplatonism 311
neo-Pythagoreanism 311
nervous system 12
Nicolaus 314
nominalist 141
non-existence 200
non-existent particulars 79
non-fulfillment 172
non-natural 270
non-necessary 15
non-omnitemporality 117
non-substantial potential 262
Normore 41
No Stopping sign 78, 149

nothingness 14
not necessary 15
not possible 208
Not to Fear Proof 125, 128, 183
Nous 12, 235, 305, 306
Nouveaux essais sur l'entendement humain, II, xxx, Sec 4 83
now 58
number 48
numerical 229, 301
numerical identity 140

O

object of scientific knowledge 202
object of thought 240
Ockham's Razor 276
Odyssey 12 274
Oedipus 162, 252
omnipotent 39
omniscience 274
omniscient 39
omnitemporal 105, 180
omnitemporality 117, 118, 142, 181
one core notion of possibility 125
one-directional infinity 62
one heaven 230
oneness 229
one of a kind 135, 152
one-sided infinities 60
'one-state' resolution 260
ontological formulations 113
ontological level 113
"ontological" necessity 17
ontological possibility 121
ontology 122, 214
opinions 228
optics 289
ordered body movement 161
organic 155, 161
organic kind 173

organic substance 141
organic substances 124
organic unity 305
originating principle 156
originating principle of motion 257
ouranus 135
ousía 282
out of time 207
outside force 273
over-arching sense of possibility 107
Owen 83

P
paganism 34
painting 38
paradigms 115
Paris 274
Parmenides 19, 83, 233
part 53
partial possibilities 114
partial possibility 132, 150
particular causes 140
particular effects 140
particular individual 137, 138
particularity 129
particular object 126
particulars 216
Passage and Possibility 15
past 52
past truth 127
patchwork of manuscripts 284
patricide 162
Patterson 101, 102, 109, 112, 116, 212
Pericles 309
Peripatetics 195
Peripatetic school 282
Peripatos 281
perishable 87
perishable substances 232

perishable things 202, 272
Persian war 227
Philo 9
Philoponus 23, 33, 34, 36, 59
Philosopher's Stone 67
philosophical hoaxes 297
pineal gland 242
pisteuomen 98
pithanon 84
place 21
plane 26
Plato 33, 203, 220, 243, 258
Platonic-Christian doctrines 265
Platonic Form 155
Platonic Forms 104
Platonic world soul 245
Plato's censorship 258
Plato's influence 104
play 68, 111
pleasure 238
Plotinus 281
Plutarch 311
point 38
point in time 28
pollachōs legetai to endechesthai 101
possibility 15, 18, 19, 67, 77, 82, 99, 100, 112, 127, 142, 150
possibility in accord with probability and necessity 80
possibility operator 112
possibility *qua* believability 85
possibility *qua* contingency 87, 225
possibility *qua* (distinct) conceivability 92
possible 4, 15, 98, 101, 103, 180
possible event 82
possible in accordance with probability or necessity 84, 86, 99
possible *qua* contingent 89
possible things 82
potency 103
potential 101, 102
potential infinities 45

Index

potentiality 1, 29, 86, 117, 202, 231, 254, 272
potentiality-actuality schema 268
potentiality for essential opposites 232
potentiality for opposites 272, 274
potentiality of infinite mathematical divisions 29
potentially infinite series of points 52
potentially in motion 272
powers of mathematics 103
prattle 239, 297
predicate 205
present tense 208
present-tensed verbs 215
primary world of reality 185
prime eternal mover 245
prime mover 256
Prime Mover 237, 240, 249
prime movers 3
prime movers of IX 8 255
primitivity of the necessity operator 105
principle of a soul 244
Principle of Genuine Plenitude 78
Principle of Genuine Sortal Plenitude 13-4, 14, 67, 121-3, 125, 131, 164, 186, 221, 316
principle of motion 200
Principle of Plenitude 14, 67, 69, 108, 112, 116, 175, 186, 315
Principle of Sortal Plenitude 75, 79, 114, 116
principle of sufficient reason 183
principles of production 159
principles of reproduction 159
prior 202
prior in substance 202
priority 103
priority in substance 117
process 38
propositional modality 18
pros hen ["related to one"] equivocity 280
protasis 223
psyche 239, 246
Pure Actuality 1, 3, 11, 167, 228

purely fictional 97
pure nothingness 14
Pythagoras 129
Pythagorean theorem 84

Q
qualities 21
quantitative comparisons 46
quantitative properties 49
quantity 25
Quattuornonagintanongentillion 47

R
rank materialist 298
ratio 177
rational creatures 161
ratios 35, 44, 46, 64
reach 121
real 80, 99
Reale 280, 302
reality 309
realizability at some time 98
realizability in time 162
realizable conceivability 97
real-life cases 214
real possibilities 31
"real" possibility 99
reductio ad absurdum 35
relevant maximum capacity 91
relics of ancient treasure 228
religion 306
religious fanatics 309
reproduction 159
Rest 259
reverse gear 272
rhuthmos 160
Riemannian geometry 48
Roman philosophy 314
Roman times 248

Index

Ross 101
Russell 93

S
Sandbach 282
science 220, 306
science of accidents 76
science of being *qua* being 280-4
science of causes 280
science of separate substance 281
science of theology 284
scientific knowledge 201, 217
scientific law 121
scope 149
scope of "possibility" 73
sea battle 50, 120, 127, 128, 142
sea battles in general 120
second-order 18
Sedley 167
self-centered 265, 305
self-centered Mind 236
self-driving cars 170
semantic 113
semantic counterpart 114
semantic level 112
semantics 121, 213
separability 255
separate 38
separate field of logic 208
separate from nature 289
separate Grand Intellect 297
separate intelligence 167
separateness 27
Shakespeare 86
signs 78
simplest version of the Principle of Plenitude 71
Simplicius 35, 306
singularity 36
situation itself 127

six "major" senses of possibility 101
six senses (of possibility) 82-92
Skeptics 282
sleeping 94
Sleeping Beauty 150
smartphone 168
Smith 314
Socrates 42, 46, 244
Socratic *elenchus* 33
solid object 26
Solmsen 13, 245
Sorabji 16, 23, 32, 34, 59, 110, 119, 175
(sort of genuine) possibility 67
sortal 14, 80
sortal accounts 141
sortal form of the Principle of Plenitude 75
sortal presuppositions 75
sortals 152
soul 243, 244
soundness 18
special science of substance 281
species 124, 141
specific 229, 301
specifically 141
Spellman 69
spiders 159
Stagira 10
stars 10, 14
state gods 305
statistical interpretation of modal operators 106, 113
statistical model 122
"statistical" necessity 18
statistical possibility 19
Steady State 36, 173
stick moves the stone 256
Stoic first philosophy 282
Stoic fragments 282
Stoicism 281
Stoics 195, 282, 313, 314

Index

Stoic theoretical philosophy 282
stops living 244
stops moving 244
story-telling 83
Strato 11, 13, 304, 313
strings of information 170
sub-atomic particle 174
substance 1, 28, 82, 254, 272
substance-matter 118
substances 23, 157
substantial change 202
substantial potential 249
substantial potentiality 232
sui generis 152
sun 10, 14, 271
supernatural 99
supernatural god 183
supernatural religious thinking 200
supersensible substance 284
supposing-true-at-another-time 133
sustaining cause 3
syllogism 215
syllogistic validity 214
symphony 38
synthetic 128
Syrianus 281
systematic use of modals 110
system of logic 214

T

ta aidia 188
ta aphtharta 188
Tarski 130
tautological description 82
teaching 217
teleias 60, 237
teleology 300, 304
temporal associations 215
temporal definition of Aristotelian modalities 117

temporal first cause 253
temporal implications 221
temporal infinity 30, 175
temporality 208
temporally unrestricted generalization 204
temporal modal conception 68
temporal, ontological aspect 88
temporal qualification 207
temporal restrictions 150
temporal sequence 38
tenseless statements 121
terminus technicus 106
terms 82
The All 10, 13, 36, 35, 135, 226, 10
The Book of Sand 30
The Great Chain of Being 69
The Language of God 306
The Little Book of Atheist Spirituality 2
Themistius 281, 303
theological arguments in the *Metaphysics* 281
theological coloring 106, 124
theological *Metaphysics* 67
theological ramifications 115
theology 282, 284, 305, 307, 309
Theophrastus 11, 13, 220, 226, 228, 279, 300, 304
theory of the infinite 190
the sake of an end 158
thesis 300
things 23
think 12
thinking 96
thinking of a theorem 259
Third Man Argument 185
third truth-value 50
three-dimensional object 217
three-dimensional solid 26
three kinds of substance 229
three logical systems 212
three means of mimesis 258

Index

three-sided geometrical figure 199
three-valued logic 50
tidy packages of doctrines 314
time 14, 27, 254
Time and Necessity 15
timeless 70, 207
tinos 253
tired 270
to be or not to be 86
to endechomenon 82
tò éndechómenon 87
toil 266
tōn meta ta phusica 240
tò on 282
to pan 10, 36, 225
total possibilities 114
total possibility 115
tò ti 282
tragedy 99
transfinite numbers 47
traversing the infinite 39
trecentillion 46, 54
triangle 199
true knowledge 220
truest of all kinds of knowledge 104
true unrestricted generalizations 204
truth 107, 121, 125, 128, 133, 142, 207, 214
truth of a proposition 127
truth-values of *logoi* 127
T-schema 130
turning point 34
Twain 275
two-state solution 259

U

unactualized potentiality 270
unchanging Forms 259
uncut cloak 72
undated propositions 131

undifferentiated "all" 305
ungenerated 137
ungenerated universe 63
ungodliness 9
unicorns 96
unidirectional 127
uni-direction of time 134
unique identification 262
unit 48
unity 301, 220, 229
universal 215
univocal 68
univocal meaning 316
univocal sense 111
unmixed 235
Unmixed Mind 239
Unmoved Mover 1, 3, 10-1, 13, 115, 124, 219
Unmoved Mover of Active Intellect 251
Unmoved Mover of *Physics* VIII 10 251
Unmoved Mover of Pure Actuality 10, 14, 131
unmoved movers 3
unnatural 159, 169
unnatural act 159
unnatural solutions 99
upper cosmos 155
upper *kosmos* 155
upper motions 156, 257

V
valid forms 18
validity 18, 109, 214
van Raalte 300, 304
van Rijen 68, 105-6, 108, 134, 212, 316
Vasiliou 167
Veloso 258, 298
verb 207
Verbeke 281
Vlastos 224

Index

W
water 156
Wehrli 282
what cannot be otherwise 180
what "is or happens" 149
whence 231, 249, 272
white 209
whither 231, 249, 272
whole 237
whole of time 176
whole rotation 306
whole world 156
will of God 224
world champion miler 200

X
Xenophanes 9, 243, 266, 295, 305

Y
youth 237

Z
Zeller 305
Zeno 224, 282
Zeno's famous paradox 52
Zeno's paradox 45, 58
zero 47
zero dimension 26

Aristotle's "Not to Fear" Proof

Index Locorum

Passages are usually listed in the form they are used by an author. Thus, e.g., for *On Interpretation*, check also *De Interpretatione* and for *On the Heaven(s)* check also *De Caelo*. References simply to a book or book chapter will come before references to specific passages in a chapter. Passages for synonyms for a chapter, e.g., (*Metaphysics*) IX instead of (*Metaphysics*) Theta, are listed separately (but in the same section).

A
Academica 2.38   280
An. Post. B 2, 90a9   290
An. Pr. I 13, 32b4ff   73, 79, 120

D
de aeternitate mundi III 10-11; Fragment 18   9
De Anima I, 404b19   308
De Anima B 2, 415b12   290
De Anima III 4-5,   167
De Anima III 5,   242, 291, 292, 293
De Caelo   10, 12, 65, 128
De Caelo I 12,   119, 175
De Caelo A 12,   187
De Caelo I 3,   223
De Caelo I 6, 274a8   177
De Caelo I 9,   10
De Caelo I 9, 279a27   175
De Caelo I 10, 280a24-28   174
De Caelo I 10, 280a29-31   223
De Caelo I 11, 28b12-20   91
De Caelo I 11, 280b12-14   92
De Caelo I 12,   57, 64, 108, 126, 134-7
De Caelo I 12, 281a26   91
De Caelo I 12, 281a28-282a5   219
De Caelo I 12, 283a6-8   156
De Caelo I 12, 283a10   32, 57

De Caelo I 12, 283a31-283b5 198
De Caelo I 12, 283b1-2 61
De Caelo I 12, 283b12-13 29, 172
De Caelo I 12, 283b13 59
De Caelo II 1, 283b27-31 57, 225
De Caelo II 6, 289a11-12 135, 230
De Caelo III 1, 298a26-b1 157
De Interpretatione 102
De Interpretatione 9, 19a12ff 113
(The *Dramatics* is also known as the *Poetics*:)
Dramatics 19, 60, 80, 109, 184, 199, 237, 258, 305
Dramatics 4, 1448b4-6; b21-22 160
Dramatics 6, 1450b24-26 237
Dramatics 9, 84, 99
Dramatics 9, 1451b17-8 162
Dramatics 25, 1460b11 83
Dramatics 25, 1460b30-61a2 85

E
EN I 2, 1165a23 290
Eth Nic, VI 3, 1139b18-23 202

G
GC 336b32 294
GC II 10, 336b25-337a15 249, 293
Generation and Corruption 293
Generation and Corruption I 2, 316a30-34 26
Generation and Corruption, 336a18-20 21
Generation and Corruption 337b35-a2 187
Generation and Corruption II 11, 338b12ff 162

I
Int. 9, 19a9-18 119
Int. 13, 23a22-6 268

L
Lambda 1, 11, 139, 167, 181, 224, 228-235, 316

Index Locorum

Lambda 2,   234
Lambda 8,   1073a23-1073b1   254
Lambda 6,   3
Laws II 665a   161

M

Mechanics 24, 855b35-856a1   95
Mechanics 31 & 33, 858a3ff   95
Metaphysics   240
Metaphysics II 2, 994b27   177
Metaphysics IV 4,   70
Metaphysics IV 4, 1007a16   25
Metaphysics IV 7, 1011b25   51
Metaphysics V 5,   105
Metaphysics V 8,   230
Metaphysics D 8, 1017b15   290
Metaphysics V 12, 1019b23   103
Metaphysics V 1, 1013a16   253
Metaphysics V 5, 1015a20-1015b16   15, 191
Metaphysics V 5, 1015a20-1015b16   180
Metaphysics V 5, 1015a34-34   105
Metaphysics V 5, 1015b9-12   17, 203
Metaphysics V 5, 1015b15-16   17, 203
Metaphysics V 8, 1017b12   230
Metaphysics V 8, 1017b19   74
Metaphysics V 25, 1023b12-13   53
Metaphysics V 30, 1025a14-17   198
Metaphysics V 30, 1025a30-34   198
Metaphysics V, 1017b22   74
Metaphysics 6 1, 1026a27-29   281
Metaphysics VI 2, 1026b2-3   76
Metaphysics E, 1026b27-37   187
Metaphysics VII 7, 1032a26   74
Metaphysics VII 7, 1032b30   174
Metaphysics H 2, 1043a3, b13   290
Metaphysics Theta 7,   90
Metaphysics Theta 7, 1049a1-3; a14-15   90
Metaphysics Theta 8,   10-2, 17-9, 21, 51, 100, 102, 104, 115, 316

Metaphysics Theta 8, 1049b10-50a3   167
Metaphysics Theta 8, 1049b24-26   253
Metaphysics Theta 8, 1050b4-5   251, 252
Metaphysics Theta 8, 1050b6-24   188
Metaphysics Theta 8, 1050b6-8   254
Metaphysics Theta 8, 1050b24-8   266
Metaphysics Theta 1050b7-8   270
Metaphysics Theta 1050b10-11   270
Metaphysics Theta 1050b20-22   272
Metaphysics Theta 1050b21-2   270
Metaphysics Theta 8, 105022-8   270
Metaphysics Theta 8, 1050b24-8   270
Metaphysics Theta 8, 1050b24-28   272
Metaphysics Theta 8, 1050b27-31   295
Metaphysics Theta 8, 1050b28-34   270
Metaphysics Theta 8, 1050b28-30   249, 293
Metaphysics Theta 10,   51
Metaphysics Theta 10, 1051b6-17   207
Metaphysics IX 3, 1047a12-14   108
Metaphysics IX 4, 1047b3-6   69, 187
Metaphysics IX 6, 1048b10-17   27
Metaphysics IX 8, 1049b28-29   74
Metaphysics IX 8, 1049b24-26   253
Metaphysics IX 8, 1050a34   23
Metaphysics IX 8, 1050b7   172
Metaphysics IX 8, 1050b18-19   202
Metaphysics IX 8, 1050b19-24   9
Metaphysics IX 8, 1050b22-24   179
Metaphysics IX 8, 1050b24-8   264
Metaphysics IX 9, 1051a22-34   25
Metaphysics XI 7, 1063a13-16   104, 202
Metaphysics Lambda 8,   228
Metaphysics XII 6,   1, 2
Metaphysics XII 6-7,   228
Metaphysics XII 6-7, 1072a24-1073a12   251
Metaphysics XII 6, 1071b3ff   2
Metaphysics XII 7, 1072a26-1072b14   240
Metaphysics XII 8, 1073a24-1074a17   251
Metaphysics XII 8, 1074b1-b12   227

Index Locorum

Metaphysics XIII 1-3,   27, 49, 289
Metaphysics XIV   289
Metaphysics XIV 1-4,   49, 289
Meteorology   231, 233
Meteorology I 2, 339a19-32   156, 257

N
Nicomachean Ethics VI 3,   159
Nicomachean Ethics X 4, 1174b2-8   238

O
On First Principles   304
On Generation and Corruption, 337a22-4   27
On Interpretation   16
On Interpretation 2 & 4,   207
On Interpretation 3, 16b6   207
On Interpretation 4, 17a3-6   207
On Interpretation 5, 17a7-9   207
On Interpretation 7,   165
On Interpretation 7, 17a38-17b1   215
On Interpretation 9,   15, 49, 50, 71, 108, 127, 128, 129, 131, 133, 142, 206, 318
On Interpretation 9, 18b38-39   207
On Interpretation 9, 19a9-19   142, 319
On Interpretation 9, 19a33   207
On Interpretation 10,   216
On Interpretation 10-11,   215
On Interpretation 12-3,   49
On Interpretation 12, 21a34-37   216
On Interpretation 12, 22a10-12   15, 49
On Interpretation 13,   269
On Interpretation 13, 23a19-23   217
On Philosophy   307, 308, 312
On the Heavens I 6, 274a8   34
On the Heavens I 7, 275a13   34
On the Nature of the Gods I. 13. 33   307, 321

P
Parts of Animals   18

Parts of Animals I 1   17
Parts of Animals I 1, 639b24-640a11   17
Perí Ousías   282
Phaedo   246
Phaedrus 267,   243, 245
Phaedrus 245c-e   245
Physics   12, 65, 159
Physics II 1, 192b29-30   159
Physics II 1, 193a4   70
Physics II 2 ,   26
Physics II 2, 194a36   308
Physics II 3, 195b25   140
Physics II 8, 199a19-24   159
Physics III 1, 200b12   200
Physics III 1, 200b32   23
Physics III 4,   191
Physics III 4, 203b30   69, 119, 219
Physics III 5,   24
Physics III 5, 205b29-30   53
Physics III 5, 206a2-4   25
Physics III 6,   175
Physics III 6, 206a9ff   32
Physics III 6, 206a10   172
Physics III 6, 206a21-26   28
Physics III 6, 206a22-23   52
Physics III 6, 206a26-7   24
Physics III 6, 206a33   32
Physics III 6, 206b34-207a14   23
Physics III 7,   24
Physics III 7, 207b7   48
Physics III 7, 207b21-7   24
Physics III 7, 207b25   21
Physics III 7, 207b2831   25
Physics III 8, 208a20   32
Physics IV 12, 220a27   48
Physics IV 12, 220b32   27
Physics VI 10, 241b19-20   296
Physics VII 2, 243a15-8   297
Physics VIII 1 251a10-11; a21-23   23

Index Locorum

Physics VIII 1, 251b11-28   21
Physics VIII 1, 251b18-19   33
Physics VIII 1, 251b29-252a6   172
Physics VIII 1, 252a12-13   177
Physics VIII 2, 252b20ff   245
Physics VIII 4, 255a6-7   245, 295
Physics VIII 4, 255a33-b4   90
Physics VIII 5, 256a6-13   256
Physics VIII 5, 256b13   21
Physics VIII 5, 256b25-28   235
Physics VIII 6, 259a7-11   236
Physics VIII 7, 261a27-28   21
Physics VIII 7, 261b18-9   272
Physics VIII 8,   42, 297
Physics VIII 8, 263a4ff   45
Physics VIII 8, 263a13-15   39, 41
Physics VIII 10,   251, 279
Physics VIII 10, 267a22-3   236
Physics VIII 10, 267b24-26   236
Poetics   19 (and see *Dramatics* for other instances)
Politics   258
Politics VII 10, 1329b25-35   227
Posterior Analytics   82
Posterior Analytics I 4-6,   108
Posterior Analytics I 6, 74b   74
Posterior Analytics II 11, 94a35ff   227
Prior Analytics   17, 206, 212
Prior Analytics A.3, 25a37-b14   101
Prior Analytics A.8-11   109
Prior Analytics 1 9-10,   70
Prior Analytics 1 13,   92
Prior Analytics 1 13, 32a18-20   82, 87
Prior Analytics I 2, 25a1-2   210
Prior Analytics I 8,   103
Prior Analytics I 8, 29b29-35   210
Prior Analytics I 13,   73, 212
Prior Analytics I 13, 32a20   85
Prior Analytics I 13, 32b2   210
Prior Analytics I 46, 51b27-28   50

S

Sophist   257, 259, 267, 291
Stoicorum Veterum Fragmenta 2.42   282

T

Theophrastus *Metaphysics*   300
Theophrastus *Metaphysics* 4a 1-2   280
Theophrastus *Metaphysics* 563-10   280
Timaeus   223, 264
Timaeus 23e   224
Topics IV 1, 120b35   197
Topics VI 6, 145b27ff   107
Topics VII 3, 153a15   199
Topics VII 4,   152
Topics VII 4, 154a18-9   141

ABOUT THE AUTHOR

Gregory Scott finished his doctoral dissertation, *Unearthing Aristotle's Dramatics: Why There is No Theory of Literature in the Poetics*, under Francis Sparshott at the University of Toronto, while also studying there under one of the esteemed 20th-century scholars of the *Poetics*, Daniel de Montmollin. Other mentors included Joseph Owens (Aristotle's *Metaphysics*) and Brad Inwood (Pre-Socratics).

He then taught for four years as a full-time philosopher at universities in the U.S. and Canada. Afterwards, he engaged in a post-doctoral fellowship under Sarah Broadie at Princeton University (Philosophy) while simultaneously directing the doctoral program in dance education at New York University (NYU).

Scott has published on Aristotle's theory of drama in Cambridge and Oxford University presses and on the philosophy of dance in scholarly journals such as *Dance Research Journal*. His "Twists and Turns: Modern Misconceptions of Peripatetic Dance Theory" appeared in *Dance Research*, Edinburgh University Press, 2005, and in 2016 he published *Aristotle's Favorite Tragedy: Oedipus or Cresphontes?* and *Aristotle on Dramatic Musical Composition: The Real Role of Literature, Catharsis, Music and Dance in the POETICS*. The 2nd edition of both books were made available in 2018. In early 2019, his *A Primer on Aristotle's DRAMATICS (also known as the POETICS)* appeared.

He has taught *The Meaning of Life* and *The Art and Theory of Dance* intermittently from 1995 in Humanities at NYU (SPS) and is currently working on two books: *The Meanings of Life* and *The Philosophy of Western Theatrical Dance*.

Scott can be reached at gs30@nyu.edu or gls62@columbia.edu.

www.ingramcontent.com/pod-product-compliance
Lightning Source LLC
Chambersburg PA
CBHW070526010526
44118CB00012B/1070